WE MATTER

ATHLETES AND ACTIVISM

ETAN THOMAS

EDGE
OF SPORTS

We Matter: Athletes and Activism is the fourth title in Dave Zirin's **Edge of Sports** imprint. Addressing issues across many different sports at both the professional and nonprofessional/collegiate level, Edge of Sports aims to provide an even deeper articulation about the daily collision between sports and politics, giving cutting-edge writers the opportunity to fully explore their areas of expertise in book form.

Published by Akashic Books
©2018 Etan Thomas

Hardcover ISBN: 978-1-61775-594-1
Paperback ISBN: 978-1-61775-591-0
Library of Congress Control Number: 2017936007

Edge of Sports
c/o Akashic Books
Brooklyn, New York, USA
Ballydehob, Co. Cork, Ireland
Twitter: @AkashicBooks
Facebook: AkashicBooks
E-mail: info@akashicbooks.com
Website: www.akashicbooks.com

TABLE OF CONTENTS

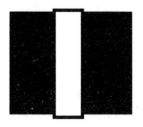

Introduction

Over the past decade, we have witnessed an unprecedented number of athletes across all sports using their positions, their platforms, their celebrity, and the power of their voices for change. Athletes have a unique ability to influence fashion, pop culture, and politics with their actions. It is refreshing to see many acting on their convictions. Muhammad Ali once said, "I don't have to be who you want me to be. I'm free to be who I want."

Athletes of today are following in the footsteps of pioneers before them, which is why it was such an honor to be able to interview figures such as Kareem Abdul-Jabbar, Bill Russell, Dr. John Carlos, Oscar Robertson, Dr. Harry Edwards, Mahmoud Abdul-Rauf, and Craig Hodges for this book. Their wisdom and courage laid the groundwork for athletes of today to be able to speak freely on various issues that affect us as a society.

Today, there is a new resurgence of this athlete-activist we love and hold in such high regard. They are courageous, high profile, have access to millions with a push of a button thanks to social media, and they are ready and willing to risk fame, fortune, and endorsements, and endure criticism, to stand up for what they believe in. It was a great pleasure to have been able to sit down with modern-day activists such as Carmelo Anthony, Dwyane Wade, Swin Cash, Michael Bennett, Eric Reid, Laila Ali, Russell Westbrook, Tamika Catchings, and many others.

Today's athlete-activists have delved into politics, current events, presidential elections, Black Lives Matter, women's rights, murders at the hands of the police, mass incarceration, and the list goes on and on. In this book, I have interviewed over fifty different athletes, members of the media, and the families of the victims of police shootings for many reasons: to highlight and discuss this new wave of athlete activism; to dispel the myth that current athletes are not connected and affected by what goes on not only within the confines of their own communities, but across society as a whole; to give credit and pay homage to the athletes of yesteryear who have paved the way for the Colin Kaepernicks and LeBron James's of the world to be as vocal as they are today; and to encourage athletes of the future to continue to use their voices to bring about change. Unfortunately, there will undoubtedly be many more murders at the hands of the police, acts of police brutality, and other injustices for athletes to speak out about. Which is why it is important to create an atmosphere where their effectiveness and opinions do in fact matter. In this book, you will hear firsthand accounts from family members of victims of police violence as they express how appreciative they are for the athletes who have spoken out and have brought awareness to the deaths of their loved ones. You will also hear personal accounts from athletes as to what made them decide to use their voices in particular cases.

When I first started putting together this book, and was thinking of different people who I wanted to interview, I imagined it would be on a much smaller scale. I honestly didn't think that so many prominent athletes, many of whom I have idolized my entire life, would be so eager to sit down and allow me to interview them, and would give such in-depth interviews. I have had Dr. John Carlos's picture on my wall since high school. I read Kareem's book and watched videos of him playing in elementary school. I studied Mahmoud Abdul-Rauf in high school. I remember doing a research paper on Bill Russell that my teacher thought was so good, she had me present it to the high school when I was still in middle school. I was equally surprised that so many accomplished media personalities and authors would so quickly agree to be a part of this project. They couldn't wait to delve into these topics, and the amount of time they took to answer each question and properly explore the subject really amazed me. They weren't giving surface one-sentence answers; they were thinking about these matters carefully and thoroughly.

What also surprised me was the number of current athletes, many of whom were in the middle of their seasons, who cleared their schedules to speak with me. Some had reporters literally waiting for them as they took the time to sit down with me and explore the topic at hand. Picture Carmelo Anthony after a game and having the entire New York media waiting to interview him about the latest Phil Jackson statement, or trade rumor, or

New York media gossip, and him asking them all to be patient once I told him what this interview was for, and him sitting down with me for fifteen or twenty minutes as all that media became invisible. That's the kind of eagerness I have been met with by just about every person I interviewed. These are people whose schedules are typically managed by an entire team of handlers. Who in many cases bypassed the wishes of their management team to work the interview into their schedule. They genuinely cared.

I want younger athletes to read this book and be inspired. I want them to hear directly from NBA Commissioner Adam Silver, NBA CEO Mark Cuban, and Washington Wizards CEO Ted Leonsis as they express their respect for the history of athlete activism and their appreciation for the current wave of young athletes using their voices. (Note that I generally avoid using the term *owner*, for obvious reasons; instead I usually go with *CEO*.) I want them to read about what the Los Angeles Clippers accomplished when they got Donald Sterling fired as CEO of the team after his racist tapes came out. I want them to read how the Missouri football team's announcement that they were going to boycott all football-related activities forced the university to take immediate action against President Tim Wolfe, who had been under fire from the student body for his refusal to address various racially charged incidents that had taken place on campus. I want them to read about the Oklahoma University football team who banded together for a silent protest over a racist frat video, resulting in the closing of the fraternity as a whole and the expulsion of two Sigma Alpha Epsilon students who were caught on video talking about lynchings and keeping African Americans out of the fraternity. I want them to read about how Thabo Sefolosha sued five NYPD officers for false arrest, excessive force, malicious prosecution, and false imprisonment after they broke his leg. I want them to hear the words of Russell Westbrook as he speaks out on behalf of the Crutcher family after Terence Crutcher was murdered. I want them to be inspired by hearing Carmelo Anthony discuss marching with the people of Baltimore after Freddie Gray was murdered. I want them to be inspired by hearing ESPN's Jemele Hill discuss the fact that Serena Williams has had to take on racism, sexism, and body-shaming, and how she hasn't allowed it to stop her one bit. I want them to be empowered hearing Soledad O'Brien discuss Dominique Moceanu speaking out on abuse at USA Gymnastics. I want them to feel inspired by Swin Cash and Tamika Catchings as they explain how the WNBA used their collective voices to take a stand after the murders of Alton Sterling and Philando Castile. I want all of this to be motivation for young people to continue carrying the torch of athletes using their voices.

Throughout this book, I make multiple references to my son Malcolm's Amateur Athletics Union (AAU) team, the First Baptist of Glenarden Dynamic Disciples 13u, because it is important to start telling athletes from a young age about the tremendous amount of power they have. It is also important to teach them the value of accepting guidance from the older generations, and how advantageous it is to connect with and learn from activists and elders who have already been where they are about to go, à la Malcolm X mentoring Muhammad Ali and Dr. Harry Edwards mentoring Colin Kaepernick. Preparation is key. It has grown abundantly clear that we can't expect high schools, universities, or agents to properly prepare athletes for what they will face in society; how they will be treated differently; how much more will be expected of them; how to handle criticism which is sure to come their way (especially if they decide to utilize their voice and their platform); the importance of knowing their rights, their self-worth, and the law; how to not be taken advantage of, whether by the NCAA, the NBA, agents, managers, or anyone else who doesn't value their greatness and wants to exploit them in any way they possibly can; and how to follow the financial models of people like LeBron James and Michael Jordan to create wealth and financial opportunities for their communities. I want this book to become required reading for all young athletes.

As this book goes to press, President Trump has recently launched a vigorous attack on any and every protesting NFL player, and on the league for not disciplining them. The president has sent numerous tweets demanding that the NFL force players to stand at attention during the national anthem. The majority of NFL players and CEOs seem to grasp that this is in fact a democracy and not a dictatorship, and that real freedom of speech and freedom of expression are values that make up a democracy. Trump may have unintentionally added fuel to the fire of justice.

Unfortunately, the firestorm created by the president has somewhat confused what the protests are all about. They were never about him, or the military, or the flag. They are about the killings of unarmed Black men by the police and the absence of justice for those deaths. One of the most difficult aspects of this project was interviewing the children, siblings, and other family members of those who have been killed by the police. There **were so** many times when I struggled to keep my composure as they expressed **the** devastation that still affects them today. I saw their hands tremble and **their** eyes water as they discussed the details of their losses. I saw the pain in **their** eyes as they talked about their struggles for justice for their lost loved **ones**, and their dedication and connection to each other's cases—sometimes **for** people they'd never even met before.

But I also saw how thankful they are for athletes speaking out on **their** behalf. They were overwhelmed with appreciation, couldn't say thank **you** enough. They all expressed initial shock not only at the fact that the **athletes** might be wearing a shirt that supported their loved one, or a hoodie, **but** even more when they heard the various athletes expressing personal **con**nections with their stories. How these stories made the athletes reflect **upon** their own children, as Dwyane Wade expressed after the murder of **Trayvon** Martin. Or the passion with which they publicly spoke, even in a **state as** conservative as Oklahoma—as Russell Westbrook did following the **murder** of Terence Crutcher. Many people feel that athletes exist in some **protective** bubble and aren't affected by things that happen in day-to-day society. **After** reading this book, you will see that this couldn't be further from the **truth.**

The Children
of the Movement

My son Malcolm was six years old at the time of Trayvon Martin's murder. He was a fun-loving kid, liked sports, *Avatar: The Last Airbender,* and swimming. Everyone thought he was absolutely adorable. People would look at his long dreadlocks, his big smile, they would admire his kind and playful heart, and they would comment on how respectfully he spoke to adults. He was a big kid; I am 6'10" and my wife is 6'0" so Malcolm was head and shoulders above everyone else in his class. But I had to explain to him that he will not always be viewed as a cute little kid. That as he gets older, so tall for his age, he will be looked at as a threat. He had an innocence that I had to ruin for him. He was still under the impression that everyone would be treated fairly.

The case of Trayvon Martin was disturbing on so many levels that I don't even know where to begin. According to published reports, on February 26, 2012, Trayvon had gone to a 7-Eleven before the start of the NBA All-Star Game. He was walking back through a gated community; he had been visiting a member of that very community. George Zimmerman, who was not a member of any police force but rather a neighborhood watch volunteer, called 911 to report "a suspicious person" in the neighborhood.

Zimmerman: "Hey, we've had some break-ins in my neighborhood and there's a real suspicious guy . . . This guy looks like he's up to no good or he's on drugs or something . . ." He later informed the dispatcher that the guy looked Black.

He then said, "He's just staring at me."

While on the phone with the dispatcher, Zimmerman explained that Martin was "running." When asked where, he replied, "Entrance to the neighborhood." On the recording you can hear deep breathing as the dispatcher asks Zimmerman, "Are you following him?"

Zimmerman replies, "Yeah," and the dispatcher clearly says, "We don't need you to do that."

From this tape, it sounds as if Trayvon was the one who was scared, which would be understandable. If I turned around and saw a man looking at me from an SUV in the dark for no apparent reason, I would be a little uneasy myself.

When police arrived, seventeen-year-old Trayvon Martin, who had a squeaky-clean record, no priors, and only a bag of Skittles, an iced tea, his cell phone, and his headphones, was dead from a gunshot wound.

Zimmerman wasn't arrested, even though he admitted to the shooting, because the police claimed to not have probable cause and Zimmerman claimed self-defense.

My question is, what exactly constitutes self-defense?

An unfortunate reality is that in Zimmerman's mind, he didn't have to see a gun, or actually see Trayvon doing something wrong. All he saw was that he was Black, as he repeated two times in the short 911 call. Is the unfortunate reality that "young Black male" equals "threat," and "young Black male at night" even more so?

Never mind the fact that most guidelines for how you run a neighborhood watch have a primary rule of thumb that you are not supposed to be armed.

I won't dwell on the fact that over a span of eight years, Zimmerman had called police forty-six times, or that in 2005 he was charged with resisting arrest with violence toward a police officer—that alone should have made him questionable as a self-styled neighborhood watch captain.

Nor am I going to argue that the Florida "Stand Your Ground" law shouldn't have been applicable in this case for the simple fact that, as heard in the released tapes, Zimmerman left his vehicle and went after Trayvon.

Nor am I going to make the race of Zimmerman an issue.

To quote Rev. Al Sharpton: "The race/ethnicity of Zimmerman or any citizen in this type of scenario doesn't matter, because at the end of the day, it is the race of the victim—Trayvon—that does matter. It is his race and his demographic that is consistently depicted as the threat, and negatively portrayed in popular culture."

It is this perception that I had to teach my son—the unfortunate reality that in Zimmerman's mind, he was justified and understandably afraid as soon as he laid eyes on young Trayvon. He didn't see a cute little kid who was drinking an iced tea. He saw a threat, a criminal, someone who could be on drugs or "up to no good."

I had to ruin my son's rosy view of the world we live in. I had to teach him that:

1) There are going to be people who view you as the enemy when you have done nothing wrong.

2) You are going to be harassed and accused, and some people will be terrified of you.

3) If the police stop you, try to get to a well-lit area and don't make any sudden moves.

4) Keep your hands visible. Avoid putting them in your pockets.

5) Orally broadcast your actions (e.g., "Officer, I am now reaching into my pocket for my license").

6) Always get the receipt after making a purchase, no matter how small, so no one can falsely accuse you of theft later.

7) Many times, actually being guilty has nothing to do with being viewed as guilty.

I also had to teach him about Emmett Till, James Byrd Jr., Amadou Diallo, Sean Bell, Oscar Grant, Rodney King, Eric Garner, Tamir Rice, Rekia Boyd, Philando Castile, Sandra Bland, Michael Brown, Terence Crutcher, John Crawford, Alton Sterling, and Freddie Gray.

I had to teach him these things for his own safety. I wish I didn't have to take away his innocence, but for his own well being, I had to.

I started taking my son to panel discussions to hear different perspectives. He has met Jahvaris Fulton (Trayvon Martin's brother) a few times, and each time Malcolm was hit hard. One of those panel discussions took place at the Congressional Black Caucus. I was on a program with attorney Benjamin Crump, and the Martin family came in between their own panels and listened. After the event, Malcolm went up to Jahvaris and hugged him, and I saw his eyes tearing up.

Later that day, Malcolm and I had the following exchange:

Malcolm: "Dad, I understand why you do these panels that you do where you combine different athletes and celebrities with people like Jahvaris who have lost a brother or a family member to the police, but why aren't these panels shown on TV?"

Me: "Why do you feel they should be on TV?"

Malcolm: "Because everyone needs to see how they are affected by what has happened to them, and people need to keep saying how wrong this is. I get why you have the celebrities and the athletes too, because people know them and they draw the people there because they want to hear the athletes talk, and while they are there, they hear them talk about issues like what's going on with the police and society and schools and everything you all talk about. You should keep doing these, Daddy. They are really helpful. In fact, I want to write another poem that I can perform because I want to help too."

I was very moved by the impact that Jahvaris Fulton had on my son. I was also pleased that Jahvaris then allowed me to interview him for this book, and appreciative that he spoke with me so candidly about everything that he and his family have had to deal with in the aftermath of their tragedy.

Me and Malcolm showing our support for Trayvon Martin.

Interview with Jahvaris Fulton
(Brother of Trayvon Martin)

Etan: On March 23, 2012, the Miami Heart released a statement in support of your brother. What has been the impact of that statement?

Jahvaris Fulton: It was just all shocking, to be honest. Because we never expected anybody to really say anything, let alone LeBron and the team . . . I am not sure if this has happened before. Not like this. Where this many athletes come out and support. I mean, my brother was not the first one to have this happen to him. But there was this connection to my brother that pushed them to all come out in support. So we really didn't expect it would turn into this. And definitely not with the president. I mean, President Obama, we figured had to make a generic statement about it, but he personalized it. He said, *If I had a son* . . . I feel like my brother was the tipping point. This has been going on for a while, and people have been seeing them get away with it, and they just grew tired. Like this is enough. And the terrible thing is it's happened before him and is still happening after him . . .

Millions of people watch NBA games, NFL games, hockey games, every single week. So the volume of people that have the ability to touch just by making a statement is astronomical . . . We were definitely appreciative of the different athletes speaking out on our behalf because, to be quite honest, it couldn't have happened without you guys . . . and the tremendous amount of support we received from the community. Everybody had to come together in order for it to be a movement. People around the world know my brother's name. I don't know if a lot of people know this, but in the beginning, the news outlets didn't want to run the story.

Etan: Oh wow, I didn't know that.

Fulton: We had to literally fight for this to be a story. We had to almost beg and plead for local news to cover what happened to my brother, and they didn't want to do it. But when athletes started talking about it on their various platforms on social media, and when they took that picture in the hoodies, it almost forced the media to cover it and it forced people from around the country to take notice because these athletes were talking so passionately about this. So if it weren't for you guys, I honestly think people would **never** have even heard the name Trayvon Martin. I remember one time, my **parents** were literally pitching the story to different stations and they had the **attitude** that this isn't news. Just another dead young Black man isn't news**worthy** enough for them to run a story. Now, there was one reporter who **tried to** help and I can't remember her name . . . You have to excuse me because, **as** I said, so much from that time is a blur and I'm trying not to lose it **even** recalling that time period now . . .

My emotions just flow differently nowadays and I kind of cry **at the** slightest hint of anything. But . . . she was the only one who at least **tried to** help and tried to run a story on it, but nobody really wanted to.

Etan: Dwyane Wade talked about why this hit him so hard and **LeBron** spoke passionately about it, and you saw a lot of athletes pose with **their** sons in hoodies. I myself posed on social media with my son Malcolm **in a** hoodie.

Fulton: The personal connections that I saw were really amazing to me **for a** lot of reasons. Sometimes people think that athletes are so far removed **from** things that go on in the community or that you can't relate to things **that** happen in everyday life, and I think one of the things that was so **striking** was so many athletes talked about your sons, and the fact that y'all are **Black** men, and that this could've happened to anyone, and it made you all **scared** for your children, not just outraged. That was really . . . words can't **even** express.

Etan: Tell me about all of the work you have been doing since then.

Fulton: I've been doing a lot. Currently I work for the young men's ini-tiative out of the mayor's office. Mayor Bill de Blasio here in New **York.** Our job is to create opportunities for young people of color throughout **the** city. Mentoring programs, tutoring programs, programs for court-involved youth. There's programs for young fathers . . . A lot of young people of color aren't given opportunities, depending on where they live, and **their** household income, and resources that are in their neighborhood, it's **just not** a level playing field. So, we provide those opportunities . . . and introduce them to the networks that wouldn't give them a second look, or bridge those gaps where some of these hard-working, aspiring young men and women get a better chance at life.

Etan: Talk about the Trayvon Martin Foundation.

Fulton: Both of my parents wanted to create a space that was healing for parents, so that's why my mom brings in the mothers, and they have their circle of mothers and it's just relaxation and healing. And my dad's is more about talking in actions. There is definitely still healing there as well. And the overall goal is to support other families that are like us. So many people call the office and they want to know what they should do next.

And I see my brother in so many of the people we help, and we only have so much time here on this earth and everyone should feel the need to help someone else. But sometimes it takes a tragedy for someone to step into their purpose . . . And I am starting to sound like my mother, but it's true, she always said that with great power comes great responsibility . . . Essentially, I have been given the tools, so not to do anything with them is just wrong. I wear this bracelet on my wrist and on this side it says, *I Am Trayvon Martin*, and on the other side it says, *You Are Trayvon Martin*, and I keep this as a reminder of my brother. Not to say that I'll forget, I am always reminded of him. Like I said, I see him in so many of the young men we serve. I see young men on the train who remind me of him in some way; they may walk like him or laugh or smile like him. So how could I not help these young men who remind me so much of my brother?

Etan: I've seen your family speaking everywhere: the Congressional Black Caucus, the National Action Network, the NAACP, the Urban League. That takes a lot of strength because you are pouring yourself out at a time when you are still grieving.

Fulton: I try not to do a lot of public speaking in front of audiences, because honestly, it's tough for me. But my strength with their strength only comes from above . . . My best friend's mom passed away toward the end of last year and she asked me how I made it through this, and I told her, "You should keep people around you that are good people, people you enjoy being around . . . not negative people." And I think for my family, that's something that I noticed from the beginning that we kind of did . . . The family we had just stayed around. After my brother passed, it was months before it was just me and my mother in the house alone. Every day, there was family over with us. And that was invaluable. I think if we had stayed in the home by ourselves, we probably would have gone crazy. We stayed busy, we still kept things going.

Etan: What can athletes and people in general do now to help?

Fulton: I guess now we are ready for action. I do think we have talked and talked, and I think we will always talk, but now it's time for action . . . What I like to tell people from what I have seen from my experiences is to speak with your elected officials. I have seen it. They listen to who comes in the office . . . They are the ones making the rules and making the laws, so if you could get a group to go and sit and talk with your congressperson, that can really be impactful.

This was such a difficult interview for me to do. Jahvaris shouldn't have to deal with the pain and grief of his brother being taken away from him.

Interview with Emerald Snipes
(Daughter of Eric Garner)

I first met Emerald Snipes when I invited her to a Black Lives Matter panel discussion I put on during NBA All-Star Weekend in Harlem in 2015. The year before, her father, Eric Garner, was choked to death by NYPD officer Daniel Pantaleo. She was nervous and didn't know if she wanted to speak. I told her not to worry at all, that just her presence was enough, and I wanted her to feel the love from the community. I told her that she didn't have to say a word unless she wanted to. There were over 2,500 young Black and Latino men in the audience. At one point she gave me a signal that she wanted to say something. I was glad that she did. She kept it short and sweet and really just thanked all of the young men for supporting her and said that she wanted them to make sure they listened to what all of the panelists were saying and that no matter what anybody tells them, their lives matter. She received a standing ovation. I could see that she was completely overwhelmed by the amount of love and support she received from the audience.

After a few months, she reached out to me to share that she and her sister had been invited to a town hall forum in Washington, DC, with President Obama. What she really wanted to share was her experience meeting Alton Sterling's son, Cameron, who was also invited to the town hall. Cameron told Emerald that he saw her speaking at the Black Lives Matter panel we held during All-Star Weekend, and it gave him strength. His father had been killed by police in July 2016. He thanked her for being a symbol of courage for him. She told me how she was completely blown away because at the time, she was extremely nervous about speaking publicly and didn't feel very strong at all, but here was this young man who was inspired by her. That's when she told me that she was ready to do some more speaking. "I'm ready now," she said.

After that, we started appearing at events together. We spoke at a rally for Colin Kaepernick outside of the NFL headquarters. We had a panel discussion for Harlem schoolchildren. We put together our plan for "The Children of the Movement," which in part was going to be a speaking circuit for people like herself who have lost their loved ones to the police. I had my daughter Imani and my wife Nichole sing a duet before the panel in Harlem; they sang a rendition of J. Cole's "Be Free." During the panel Emerald leaned over

ETAN THOMAS ⚡ 21

to me and said, "Okay, why didn't you tell me your wife and daughter could sing like that? We're going to have to have them do that before *every* event."

In this interview I ask Emerald about the significance of having NBA players speak on behalf of her and her family, and really the entire country, and her plans to continue fighting for justice for her father, to use her voice to inspire others, as she did with Cameron.

Etan: When you saw various NBA players wearing the *I Can't Breathe* shirts over their warm-ups before the games, what did that mean to you?

Emerald Snipes: On Facebook someone had reposted the video . . . and I thought it was Photoshopped. I didn't think it was real. And more and more people starting texting me and e-mailing me about what was going on. It was really overwhelming because I felt that my voice is being heard. I am in New York, but people in California or all the way in a different state are hearing our cry for help. And they are responding with support. That made my heart warm. I was completely overwhelmed because . . . I'm just this regular person from New York, and you want to support me? And you are going to have consequences for doing what you are doing . . . going against the dress code of your job, your livelihood, how you support your family, and you're risking all of that for my father? It was really overwhelming. I was so thankful to them for doing that because they didn't have to, and I am sure there were people telling them not to. That it would be bad for their image or that it would upset their fan base or it may affect their endorsements or if a team would pick them up the following season. In spite of all of that, they made this public statement for my father, and words cannot express how thankful I am.

Etan: Okay, so let's go back to the panel we did in Harlem during All-Star Weekend. It was absolutely amazing. Over two thousand young Black and Latino young men at Canaan Baptist Church all in *Black Lives Matter* shirts, and we had a really powerful lineup. I just wanted you to come there, listen to the different athletes on the panel speak, and just feel the support from the community. You did decide to say a few words and you got the standing ovation. They all wanted to show their support for you. Talk about that feeling.

Snipes: It was so overwhelming. That's the only word that describes it. And like you said, I wasn't planning on speaking at all, but then I heard the poems from the different poets. Your little son Malcolm . . . to be so young and to be so woke, and I saw how engaged the young men were in the audience, and I was like, *No, I have to say something. I have to give them a piece of my heart.* And these young men were so locked in and asking questions and saying that they didn't want to be the next Eric Garner, and they saw the tape and how much it bothered them . . . I wasn't too much into social justice before my father was taken from me, but I was aware of Trayvon Martin and everything that was going on. But I wanted my voice to be heard, and of course it's sad, the circumstances surrounding what is allowing my voice to be heard, and I definitely did not ask to be in this position. But I just couldn't sit there quiet and not say anything and not pour into these young men. I'm sure there were kids in that audience who have gone through something similar with a loved one. Maybe they had someone brutalized by the police or maybe they themselves have been brutalized and victimized.

Etan: It really was amazing. The fire marshal was actually going to shut it down because we were way over the building's capacity, but it's not like we could tell them no or turn them away. The funny thing was, the teachers beforehand said that three hours was way too long and that we wouldn't be able to keep their attention. But they were all the way wrong on that.

Snipes: Oh, they were definitely wrong, those kids didn't want to leave even after the three hours was over. And then the questions that they had. I was like, *Oh my gosh, these young people are really following everything and aware and woke.* All of the athletes who shared advice, shared stories, it was just a really, really beautiful event. And you did that yourself, right? The NBA didn't help you?

Etan: *(Laughing)* No, the NBA and the National Basketball Players Association weren't too comfortable with a Black Lives Matter event with all Black and Latino young men right after everything that happened with your father. Actually, a few people from the NYPD and several other organizations didn't want the event to happen. I had to fight to be able to do the event the way I wanted to do it. So I called the different athletes myself and they were all eager to support.

Snipes: I didn't know that. Wow, that makes it even more special.

Etan: Well, it was meant to be. Now, from that event, we are putting together the Children of the Movement. We saw how this can be a real support group for y'all. And all of you, at the same time, want to pour into other young people. Making sure they know their rights, that they get home safely when stopped by the police, etc. Talk about what we want to do and what our overall goal will be.

Snipes: Our main goal is basically first to help us have an outlet. We want to be able to use our tragedy and form this platform where we can help other people. There are so many young people who need help and are not getting the help they need. What about the other people whose fathers are killed by the police and there is no video and nobody knows about it? Those whose tragedies don't make the news?

There are so many people in our community who need therapy, which is what a lot of these panels will be—therapy sessions for the panelists just as much as they are for the audience. And we need that. I can't afford actual therapy . . . People don't understand how we feel once the cameras go away. We are just left there, standing there, with all of this on our hearts, our minds, our souls—like my soul hurt after my father was taken from me . . . I know there are a lot of young people who are going through that same hurt. We may not be able to help everyone, but we will be able to help as much as we possibly can.

Etan: That's a lot.

Snipes: Yeah, and people don't even think about all of that. So we have gone through this very public execution of our father, and we have to see it replayed over and over and over again on TV, the phones are ringing nonstop because everyone wants to stick a mic in your face, and then all of a sudden they move to the next story, and all you hear is silence. And that silence can be torturous. People don't understand hearing voices tell you to do something bad, or that nobody cares about you and you should slit your own wrist or your own throat, that your life and your father's life doesn't matter and isn't important and doesn't mean anything and neither does yours. People don't see that.

So what happens the next time we are confronted with the police? Some are shell-shocked and can't move, some are angry and want to lash out, some break down crying every time they hear a siren, people don't know that side. They see that we were awarded some settlement but don't take into account that lawyers cost money, courts cost money, and it's by the hour, and the city doesn't always pay when they announce they have paid. But even when you do get it, so much of it is taken before it even gets to you. And in the meantime, you have to live, you have to go to work if you can.

I could hardly leave my house, so most of us have to either do the school year over or lose our jobs. Tamir Rice's sister missed like a hundred days of school the year, or the next year, after her brother was killed. Why? Because her brother was killed! I don't want anyone to feel alone and have to go through that without some type of support. Sometimes, people just need someone to talk to. Or they want to yell and scream, or they want to go in a quiet place and cry and have someone to allow them to cry and then be there for them for support. You need to have a place for that. I want to punch something—okay, here's a punching bag, go punch it out. So that's what I want to do with the Children of the Movement: offer support—emotional, mental health, spiritual support.

Etan: And now you are comfortable speaking. Tiffany Crutcher, who had her brother Terence Crutcher taken away from her, said that she wasn't really comfortable before speaking, but now she is. And Jahvaris Fulton, who doesn't really like speaking, now sees how powerful his voice is. Talk about seeing the reactions from people hearing you speak.

Snipes: I started hearing feedback and people genuinely asking me how I am doing and how I am feeling, how am I coping and what I am doing now. Jahvaris is not comfortable speaking and he prefers to be in the background. His mother speaks and they have the Mothers of the Movement, and what they do is powerful. What I want to do is to take what they are doing, and do it for the children. The young people. Jahvaris will never have Trayvon back, and your sibling is sometimes your best friend. They are the person where, you don't even have to speak and they know what you are thinking. You can finish their sentences for them. You are protective of them. Y'all have conversations that nobody else knows about, and he will never get that back. And he lost his little brother who he couldn't protect. Could you imagine what that feels like? So the fact that he doesn't want to speak shouldn't be surprising to anyone. But also, the fact that he will show up, and just sit there on the stage and show his support, speaks volumes.

Etan: You told me the story of when you met Cameron Sterling, and how his words really pushed you into stepping up to the platform and showed you the tremendous influence you could have.

Snipes: Yes, when we went to do the town hall with President Obama in Washington, and I saw Cameron Sterling and his family sitting there . . . I went up to him and his eyes lit up. He said, "You are the one that we have seen all over the place speaking." And they actually saw the video from your event in Harlem during All-Star Weekend, and they said my words gave him strength and courage. Now, he didn't know that I was nowhere near courageous, I was a hot mess. I mean, I didn't know if I was gonna make it, to be honest. I didn't know if I was gonna go crazy, depression, I didn't want to leave my house. But after talking to his mother, she told me that he is the oldest, and everybody else is younger, and they don't have a voice. And he wants to go around and talk to people but will do it in his time and he was really emotional at the time and couldn't stop crying. It broke my heart to hear her explain where he was because I was there.

He wants to tell people that he didn't grow up without a father, he knew his father the way a father and son are supposed to have a relationship. And that it isn't fair that he has to lose his father at such a young age. He wants to tell the world that he has beautiful memories of his father. And that stories of his father from his point of view, a young Black boy growing up in the hood, and his father was killed by the police . . . He wants to turn all this anger that he has into action. He speaks very well, he is a very well-rounded young man, he's just a sweetheart.

People have to understand that a lot of times in situations like these, the children are younger. They are under ten. They don't form opinions of their own or form relationships, and they don't get the help they need. In my situation, we were all adults . . . I am the oldest so I can be the voice for my father and I can tell you who he really was. I mean, imagine having your father killed by the police, and then seeing the media justify how your father was killed. You can't imagine what that feels like. To want to save your father's good name and his reputation, but you are a child. People just don't know how that feels.

Etan: You know, I have a radio show here in DC and we were discussing the Korryn Gaines case, and the fact that she was holding her five- or six-year old son at the time when the police killed her. And they demonized her in the media. Said she was crazy, that she was holding her son captive, that the police were trying to help her son who was being abused and held against his will. Then a video came out of the little boy in the hospital bed, and he was giving a completely different account of everything that happened, saying that he loved his mommy, and his mommy was scared for him and didn't want anyone to hurt him, and I got choked up on the air. I was thinking, *What's going to happen to this little boy after the cameras go away?*

Snipes: Yeah, he is a five-, six-, seven-year-old little kid, and he was very aware and everything that he said in that video showed that he knew everything that he needed to know. It's sad that you have to tell your kids at a young age that this is what you do, this is what you don't do, and that it can be a matter of life and death. Korryn Gaines tried to do the best that she could raising him as a Black boy growing up in this world. And she didn't want her son to become a victim.

And when it comes to the media, nothing is off limits. I discovered that myself. How can it be okay to stick a mic in the face of a five-, six-, seven-year-old after they just witnessed their mother being killed by the police? And if he doesn't have the proper therapy, he could grow up having PTSD. He could flip out every time he hears a knock or a bang because he is reminded of the knock and bang on the door by the police when they wanted to knock down his front door before eventually killing his mother . . . That situation made me cry. He is going to need help, and a lot of it. And that's what the Children of the Movement is for, to help those people who need it the most. And not just children who are victims but children who go through things every day . . . We are going to use our platforms and our tragedies in order to help them.

Etan: And one of the main pieces of feedback we got from all of the young people was, "Wow, they are so strong, so courageous, seeing their strength gives me strength."

Snipes: And it's that level of support that could give people the extra push to say, "Yes, I have been through a tragedy, but you know what, I'm gonna make it." I see Emerald, I see Jahvaris, I see Tiffany, I see Alton, I see Eric, my brother, who is going to start speaking as well—I see all of these people who have been through so much, and the fact that they haven't given up or thrown in the towel will push me to follow in their footsteps. Or, "I'm in the foster care system, but I can make something out of myself and I can ignore all of these haters who are telling me I can't." I know now that my voice is making an impact on people. I know now that I can turn my anger into action. I don't want to walk around angry all day, and I don't want anyone else to walk around angry all day, because anger builds up and then it explodes. And we don't need kids exploding all over the world. We need love and support for the young people, and that is exactly what the Children of the Movement is all about.

Emerald Snipes and Erica Garner at our first Children of the Movement panel in Harlem, speaking on the pain of dealing with their father being taken away from them and their continual fight for justice following his murder.

Interview with Tiffany Crutcher
(Sister of Terence Crutcher)

When Terence Crutcher was murdered in my hometown of Tulsa, Oklahoma, it wasn't just another police shooting for me. This hit very close. I know the Crutcher family personally. I went to school with Terence's twin sister, Tiffany. She was a little bit older than me and played basketball at Carver Middle School and Booker T. Washington High School. I remember when I was in the sixth grade, Tiffany's AAU team kicked our AAU team's behinds. I particularly remember Tiffany's smile and her telling me and a few other teammates to keep working and that we were going to be all right.

I remember another game, when I was a freshman playing varsity at Booker T. Washington. I had probably one of the worst four or five minutes I had ever had on the basketball court. I remember Tiffany coming up to me after the game, putting her hand on my shoulder, and saying that I was going to be just fine. "You're only a freshman," she told me. "Nobody expects you to be ready now." It may not seem like much, but it was so genuine, and it meant the world to me at the time.

So it really hurt me to see her in the news when her twin brother became another sad Twitter hashtag. Terence was unarmed and standing beside his stalled SUV with his arms raised prior to the killing. When I saw her on TV, in tears, talking about how the police had shot and killed her brother, it hit me. Hard.

Even though I didn't really know Big Crutch personally, I knew *of* him. All I kept thinking was that she and the rest of her family shouldn't have to go through all this pain. She looked so defeated when she was forced to defend her brother's reputation.

I'll never forget how this one reporter kept asking her how she felt, and trying to get her to directly address the fact that an officer observing the incident from a helicopter said that Terence looked like "a bad dude" before he was shot and killed.

That just seemed like a stupid approach. *How do you think she feels?* Her brother had just been taken away from her. She shouldn't have to go on CNN and speak through tears while attempting to convince the world that Terence didn't deserve to die. She shouldn't have been subjected to the endless tape loop of the shooting, haunted by that voice saying that her brother looked like "a bad dude." And she shouldn't feel that, as she expressed: "Anyone who . . . may have brown skin, it just seems like they automatically criminalize or demonize." She shouldn't be experiencing this pain.

And after the death of her brother, Tiffany shouldn't have been bombarded on social media by all of the people trying to somehow justify her brother's killing. Seeing all that happen made me sick to my stomach.

Was Big Crutch a saint? Was he perfect? No. Who is? Did he deserve to die?

The answer to that last question should be a resounding no. But, unfortunately, that answer was not the most prevalent one on social media. It was so sad and frustrating to see Terence's death talked about as though he was not a real person—as though his life had been of no value. Time and time again, so many people attempt to justify and rationalize killing after killing at the hands of the police.

"Why didn't he simply comply?"

"I never have problems with the police. I just do as I'm told."

"What about Black-on-Black crime in Chicago?"

One thing has absolutely nothing to do with the other. To attempt to justify the killing of a human being by using deeply flawed reasoning is both absurd and sad. And it goes to show how little some individuals value the lives of Black people.

One of the things that was especially striking about the police videos that were released was that the officers on the scene were talking about everything so casually, almost like they were watching TV or something. This was an actual human being with a family and children and loved ones. What was going to happen to Terence's children, now without a father? What would it be like for them in the future, when they google their father's name and see all the videos and photos of him being shot by the police? And read the articles in which people attempt to justify his killing?

The media moved on to the next story as they always do, but Terence's family and friends will have to live with this reality and tragedy for the rest of their lives. And that is so sad.

I went down to Tulsa to stage a Black Lives Matter panel at the church I grew up in—Antioch Baptist—and I participated in a manhood summit alongside many powerful speakers. The next day, the Oklahoma City Thunder played a preseason game against the Memphis Grizzlies. The team donated a thousand tickets, which we gave to the middle school students who had attended the panel and summit. I gave the invocation at the game, interviewed Russell Westbrook, and watched as the Thunder and Grizzlies players all wore *TC* (for Terence Crutcher) on their warm-ups. Many players greeted the Crutcher family, offering their condolences and assistance. It was a really special weekend.

I caught up with Tiffany, now Dr. Crutcher, in New York for this interview. I am still amazed at her ability to continue fighting for justice while still grieving the loss of her brother. I honestly don't know how she does it.

Etan: All the Thunder wore the initials *TC* on their jerseys and so did Memphis. What was your reaction to their support?

Dr. Tiffany Crutcher: Well, we were definitely humbled because, you know, athletes getting ready for preseason . . . you just wouldn't think that they would stop and take the time to be that vocal. For them to speak out on our behalf like they all did, we were surprised, we were shocked. When we saw the footage of Russell Westbrook speaking out after my brother's death, and telling the world how wrong it was and that they were going to do whatever our family needs, and that they were going to be there for us, it really touched my family. It meant so much to my father . . .

And we invited all of the men in our family, because at that point we knew that we needed to come together and represent our community. But for Russell to make that comment, it's like he dropped the rope and tied a knot in it and said, "Just hold on, we got you." That knot, for me, symbolizes hope. It symbolizes love. It symbolizes the fact that we're going to continue to be there when everybody goes away.

Etan: Yeah, Russell spoke with so much passion at the press conference, it was really powerful.

Crutcher: And yourself. You flew down to Tulsa. You did the panel. You've been helping us keep Terence's name out there . . . You don't see that a lot. People are just moved by the moment and then it goes away. It's like church on Sunday: we get happy, and then on Monday, back to reality.

And so, I just can't say enough about people of your stature and Russell Westbrook's speaking out on my brother's behalf. You put yourself in a situation where it could possibly affect the organization. It could possibly affect ticket sales because you have people who think that we are anticop and antipolice and all of this. So, if you're speaking out against something that the majority do not like or agree with, it makes them uncomfortable. I heard a lot of people—and I don't tend to look at the comments—say, "Hey, we're going to boycott the Thunder games," and I'm like, *Boycott the Thunder games? Simply because of what Russell said?*

Etan: Oklahoma is a very conservative state. For the Thunder organization to be that supportive—I mean, I was pleasantly surprised about it.

Crutcher: Right. The Memphis Grizzlies sent paraphernalia to the kids. To my nieces. To my nephews. Hats and a box full of things to let us know that, *Hey, we support you, we're standing in solidarity with you.*

I was thrust into all of this chaos. But you never know how strong you are until you have to be strong. I just think that this is all what God ordained, and unfortunately Terence had to be the sacrificial lamb, but everything that you've been preparing for, I believe it was for a time such as this. I was just proud to know that I had the right people in the right place at the right time for such a tragedy as this. I mean, I just can't even explain it.

I had to fight to keep my composure during this interview. It broke my heart to see the pain in Tiffany's eyes as she talked about losing her twin brother Terence.

Etan: I've been so amazed at how you all have gone through these tragedies and then you all have this similar passion to pour into other people. Talk about that aspect of it.

Crutcher: You know, it's so different when it happens to you. Of course we see all of these other families go through this . . . I mean the Trayvon Martin case, it ate me up. I was drained, I consumed myself with this, like, *This isn't right! What are we going to do?* But never in a million years would I have thought that it would be *my* brother. Or *my* mom and dad's son. And so, it's like you're obligated. You have a duty when it happens to you to make sure it doesn't happen to anybody else. You have to be the voice for the cases that aren't publicized, that don't become a trending topic . . .

We were at the Circle of Sisters and people were coming up to us afterward, crying, saying, "Hey, can you help us? You know the police did this to my son, we've never gotten justice. They won't even answer our phone calls." And I just feel obligated . . . because people don't really realize that for the first time in Tulsa's history, a police officer has been charged or indicted . . .

We've been able to do some major things that we have never seen in Tulsa . . . We were able to get charges pressed, a week later. We were able to get a trial date within seven, eight months. An indictment. I have a huge opportunity to get these reforms passed . . . I'm fighting so hard behind the scenes getting stuff done. When I was in Tulsa last week, I ran through Tulsa like a Tasmanian devil. I met with the mayor, making demands. I met with so many people. I've put together a task force for Terence Crutcher and I just brought together some movers and shakers. We've been making it happen. We've been fighting. We've been doing a lot.

You know, that march when Reverend Al [Sharpton] came? They said it was one of the largest marches Tulsa has ever had.

Etan: That's amazing. How can people help you now? And how can people contribute, whether they're athletes or not?

Crutcher: We get moved by the moment . . . we're angry, we're outraged, and then we're on to the next thing. I need for people to speak out. Stop being silent. And let's put some pressure not just on the local government, but we need to put pressure on Jeff Sessions, on Donald Trump, and let them know that we're not going to stand for this. You have little pockets of people here and there maybe doing something . . . but we need a clear-cut and concise message that we all can stand behind or get behind. And we need to execute it precisely.

Interview with Allysza Castile
(Sister of Philando Castile)

The interview with Dr. Crutcher was conducted before Betty Shelby, the officer who murdered Terence Crutcher, was found not guilty of all charges. I had visited Tulsa for a prayer rally days before the verdict was given. I spoke on the same stage with Reverend Al Sharpton. When I returned home a few days later, I was met with the news that the jury had in fact returned a verdict of not guilty. I was sick to my stomach. My daughter Baby Sierra offered me words of encouragement:

Baby Sierra: "Daddy, I know you were sad yesterday and I know why, Malcolm explained it to me."

Me: "Yeah?"

Baby Sierra: "Yes, because you went to Tulsa to protest what happened to your friend's brother by the police and the police lady didn't get punished for it."

Me: "Yeah, I'm sorry if I was a little quiet yesterday."

Baby Sierra: "No, I understand, and I wanted to give you these flowers to make you feel better."

Me: *(Smiling)* "These are great, Baby Sierra."

Baby Sierra: "Okay, and I just want to let you know to not give up and just like you tell us, if you fall down, get knocked down, or fall short, pick yourself up, dust yourself off, and keep going."

Me: "That's fantastic advice."

She was absolutely right: as devastated as I was, I couldn't stop. Tiffany later told me that she had absolutely no intention of stopping anything. How she was going to continue to push to get the laws changed so that this doesn't happen to someone else's brother or son or father. How she wants the mayor to turn his condolences and his heartfelt apologies into action toward police reform. She said that Tulsa has the opportunity to be the change that every other city in the country wants and needs. She vowed that the entire

Crutcher family would continue to be part of the solution and agents for that change.

Shortly after I returned from Tulsa, Philando Castile's cousin asked if I would be interested in interviewing his mother and his sister. Philando had been killed by police in Minnesota on July 6, 2016. I said, "Of course." She told me how uncomfortable his sister Allysza was speaking in public about this, but that she wanted to be a part of *We Matter* and really get the message out about her brother. This was a very difficult interview for me. I could hear the pain in her voice. She broke down twice during the interview and I started getting choked up myself. To be honest, I started getting choked up at some point during all of these interviews. When Jahvaris pointed to his bracelet and said that it's a reminder of his brother; when Emerald talked about how the media just goes on to the next story and they are all alone— and that she was nervous to leave the house for a long time. How they need counseling but can't afford it.

The reason I am so passionate about this project is because you hear firsthand from the victims how much it helps them when athletes use their voice and their platform. You hear how appreciative they are. You also get to hear about their personal loss, who the victim was to their family.

Etan: Talk to me about what Philando meant to you as a brother.

Allysza Castile: My brother was my best friend. We were ten years apart so I came in the picture as a baby and he was already ten years old. Our little baby pictures, he's holding me like I was *his* baby. I didn't really have a father figure so my brother was that father figure for me. He showed me how to fix a bike, how to defend myself, talked to me about boys, birds and the bees, everything. He was always there for me, and was a very loving, kind, warmhearted, sweet-spirited person. You never heard him yell, never heard him raise his voice. We would talk and joke and also have serious conversations about what was going on in the world . . . As soon as I came home I would immediately go find him and say, "What you doin', big head?" and he would say, "What your lips doin'?" That was like our thing that we would say to each other. I lost a lot, a lot was taken away from me. I didn't just lose a brother, I lost a friend, a mentor, a father figure, a teacher, a confidant. I used to talk to him about all my problems and issues and would get his perspective from a man's point of view. Even though we were ten years apart, we were just very close . . .

I remember the day before, he asked me if I watched the video of Alton Sterling and I was like, "Naw, bro, I am so tired, I can't watch that," and we sat here and we talked about it . . . If you go back on my Facebook, I made a post that said I was so tired of this. Then I woke up the next morning to it knocking right on my front door. I would have never imagined this would happen to my brother. He was just talking to me about this and how we have to be careful and how the police are killing us and we had to be aware and know what was going on and . . . it sucks. It really . . . I don't talk about this much because I am very emotional and I just start crying at the drop of a hat, but . . . that was really my best friend and it's hard for him to not be here and me not seeing his beautiful smile and lighting up a room . . . Okay, I'm sorry, can we take a break . . . ?

Etan: Take all the time you need.

Castile: He was my brother and I thank you for doing this entire project. It's so important, I just need a minute to pull myself together . . .

My brother's job where he worked, those kids were his kids. He didn't have children himself, and he treated all of those kids with the love and care that you would treat your own children. I didn't know the depths of how much he impacted their lives until after his death. I saw all of the kids pouring out their hearts. There was a white family at this press conference and the daughter said to me, "He was like a brother to me too." And I cried and they were crying . . . After his death, that's when all of these things came out.

I remember seeing on the news this little boy who was around eight years old, and he was at a little press conference thing and he was telling the media in his little voice, "Phil was my best friend and he got killed by the police and it's not fair." And it was really crazy to hear all of these little white kids saying all of the things my brother did for them. "He helped me, he walked me to the bus, he made sure I had a ride and wouldn't leave until my ride came and I was safe, he was my protector, he helped pay for my lunch when I didn't have any money." They knew him and loved my brother, like genuinely loved him. Hearing them say things like he had rainbows in his heart, and he knew all of these kids' names and allergies, and . . . if they were getting picked on or bullied, he was there for them and helped them. Not just in his supervisor position, but he genuinely actually helped and cared for these little kids. One of his supervisors was saying that one time the power went out and he manually wrote down all of the kids' lunch PIN numbers and said, "We'll take care of all of the administrative stuff later and enter it into the computer system later, but the kids have to eat first." That just shows his heart.

Etan: What did it mean to you when you saw all of the support from the greater sports world on behalf of your brother, particularly from the WNBA who were in the middle of their season at the time? The Minnesota Lynx, your hometown team, showed up at a game in black shirts with the phrases *Black Lives Matter, Change Starts with Us*, and *Justice and Accountability*, along with an image of the Dallas police shield and the names *Alton Sterling* and *Philando Castile*. And they continued to make that statement and it spread throughout the entire WNBA. Talk to me about what that level of support for your brother meant to you.

Castile: It really touched my heart. If I could personally meet each and every one of the WNBA players, I would give them all a hug and tell them individually, "Thank you for speaking out and supporting my brother, it was just so brave." Some people in the spotlight are afraid to speak out, but they weren't at all. They used their voices and their outlet and told the entire world that what happened to my brother and to Alton Sterling was wrong . . . I can't thank them enough for showing their love and support to my family and every other family who lost their loved ones . . . They all spoke from their hearts and said what was needed to be heard. They could've all lost their jobs, they were getting all kinds of backlash, but they still stood strong for my brother, and not everybody on the team was Black. There were all the white players and the players from all over the world who were saying, "No, this was wrong and this can't happen," and . . . I just love them for doing that for my brother . . .
I'm about to start getting emotional again.

Etan: That's okay, take your time.

[Short break.]

Etan: One of the things that makes what the WNBA did so remarkable is the fact that the WNBA players aren't paid as well as the men, so they aren't as financially set as their male counterparts. I really thought that was brave for them to do.

Castile: That was just the heart of a warrior for them to do that, in the face of everything that was going on. I heard some of them were actually getting threats that someone was going to hurt them, which is just absolutely crazy, but in spite of the threats, the backlash, their employer actually telling them to stop, they continued. They told the world what happened to my brother. They actually told the media, "We're not going to answer any of your questions, so don't even ask, this is what we are talking about." Me and my family were watching it in amazement like, *Wow, look at these strong sisters.* And for the police to say that they wouldn't police their games? That was just beyond absurd. But I just commend them for standing up and not caring about any of that, staying focused on what is right and what is wrong.

Etan: Do you pay attention to the other cases?

Castile: Oh yes, how could I not? I feel so sad for Terence Crutcher's sister because they just let this woman off for murdering her brother. I don't even know what to say, my heart is literally broken because of this . . . We all saw the tape, he was not being aggressive in any way, he had his hands up, his car was broke down . . . and she said she was scared, he looked like a big bad dude. Well, if you are that scared, maybe you shouldn't be a policeman. These are people's lives, these are human beings who have families and loved ones, these aren't just targets . . . They shouldn't be able to be the judge and jury and use the excuse, "I was in fear for my life." It's not fair. There are no second chances once you take someone off the earth. *You* get a second chance, you don't even get punished, but that person is no longer here, no longer breathing and taken away from his family, and that's not fair.

Etan: Were you as surprised as I was to see so many white people speaking out for your brother?

Castile: I think it's very important for them to speak out. What happened years and years ago with slavery, it's not their fault. We know that. But as time went on, they benefited from slavery in a way that cannot be denied. They benefited from Jim Crow in a way that cannot be denied. So for them to now, from that state of privilege, to speak out and say that this is not right and this is not fair, means a lot. They don't have the same interactions with the police that we have. The police don't treat them the way they treat us. And everybody knows that. Either you are going to be part of the solution or you're going to be part of the problem. We have been speaking out and crying out for years . . . People hear it more when *they* say it. That's just a fact. It resonates more with other white people when they hear them speak about how wrong it is. For them to make the statement that "Black Lives Matter" even though that's not what the police are showing us. For them to say by the thousands like they did that what they did to my brother was wrong . . . I can't even find the words to explain how important that is. The community of Falcon Heights, they were having meetings with the mayor and were demanding that my brother have a monument as a reminder to everyone about what happened, and I really appreciate them for doing that. They saw my brother as a human being.

Etan: *Everyone* should be outraged when this happens. Nobody should be okay with it.

Castile: That's right. Listen, I don't want to see this happen to anybody else. I don't want anyone to feel the pain and the hurt that I have felt. That my family has felt. I have a gun license as well, because I am scared. And I shouldn't be scared to drive in my car with my gun that I bought that I have a legal right to have . . . This is messed up, that I honestly don't feel safe. How would you expect me to feel right now? People seriously have to question why Black people get nervous and scared whenever a policeman gets behind them or pulls them over. We saw what you did to Sandra Bland, we saw what you did to Alton Sterling, we saw you on tape carrying Freddie Gray's lifeless body to the back of a truck and then reporting, "Oh, he somehow broke his spinal cord, but we don't know what happened." Broke his spinal cord? And you expect us not to be afraid?

Etan: And just to reiterate, y'all have every right to bear arms just like those gun-loving, NRA-supporting, Second Amendment–spewing Republicans.

Castile: And it's messed up because when I go to the gun-range shows by my house, the white guys have the guns on their hips and they walk outside to the store. Let *me* try to do that. Walk outside with a gun on my hip. You know how quick someone will call the police on me? But they won't call the police on *them*. Open-carry state or not. Permit or not. License or not. Legally purchased or not. They won't ask any of that with them, but with me they automatically assume. There can't be laws for them and laws for us. We don't have Black Codes anymore, at least we're not supposed to. And did you hear the NRA come out and support us at all even after it was made clear that Philando had a license and a legally purchased gun? They didn't say a thing. Not even an RIP tweet. How is that even possible?

Etan: Well, I am doing something with Emerald Snipes, Eric Garner's daughter, called the Children of the Movement where we will have the children and siblings of the victims go around and speak at different places.

Castile: Oh wow, that sounds amazing . . . And I want to keep my brother's name alive. We established the Philando Castile Relief Foundation, and basically it's to help victims and families who have been affected by gun violence in particular from the police, or police brutality in general. Whether it's helping them with a meal, or getting them a stipend, helping them with bills, or emotional support and therapy and counseling, because people just don't know the turmoil that we go through. They don't know how much some people just need love and support. We let them know how difficult the process is going to be. How they are going to have to listen to the lawyers, and the police and the media tear down their loved ones and attempt to convince everyone from the judge to the jury to the public that their loved one basically deserved to die. They will demonize them and it's going to literally break their hearts to hear. I would love to join your Children of the Movement. I think that is a wonderful idea. That's what I want to do—to keep his legacy alive and do what he would have wanted us to do. He wouldn't have wanted us to be walking around moping, sad. He would want us to be doing something. Fighting for justice and for humanity. We want to make sure this doesn't happen to anybody else.

Athlete Activism Matters

Now that they occupy a position where they can be more than symbols of
black achievement, where they can actually serve their communities in vital
and tangible ways, while also addressing the power imbalance within their
own industry from a position of greater strength, they seem most at a loss,
lacking purpose and drive . . . [C]ontemporary black athletes have abdicated
their responsibility to the community with treasonous vigor.
       —*William C. Rhoden,* Forty Million Dollar Slaves

In his book, Mr. Rhoden takes the readers on a captivating journey
with the Black athlete, from the plantation to nineteenth-century boxing
rings, from Tom Molineux, "who represented the beginning of the African
American athlete's march across time," when he literally won his freedom
from slavery with his fists, to Jack Johnson and Andrew "Rube" Foster, the
founder of the Negro League. Rhoden talks about the athlete-activist fore-
parents like Jesse Owens, Althea Gibson, and Willie Mays. I think his book
should be required reading for every athlete at nearly every academic level.
It touches on the unfortunate paths and states of mind that have overtaken
the realities of some Black athletes of today. It could serve as an example for
so many athletes of what *not* to become. That said, I respectfully disagree
with the overall notion that the Black athlete today is simply "lost," as Mr.
Rhoden labels us in his book.

    Painting the entire, illustrious roster of current Black athletes with this
broad brush is just wrong. If he would have said "some" Black athletes of
today are lost, I wouldn't have had an objection. But to say "the contemporary tribe," as he calls us, "with access to unprecedented wealth, is lost," is
completely inaccurate.

The book's subtitle, "The Rise, Fall, and Redemption of the Black Athlete," indicates that Rhoden is convinced that the Black athlete's willingness to advocate for social and economic justice has diminished since the sixties—and perhaps disappeared—and that there currently exists a "vacuum in leadership" that has led to Black athletes becoming a "lost tribe."

Enter the Trayvon Martin shooting . . .

When a national tragedy such as this occurs, it affects everyone who has kids. This is a parent's worst nightmare. It is an unfortunate reality that the stereotypes that exist in society can have deadly consequences. Martin was nothing more than a young man wearing athletic shoes, jeans, and a hoodie. He posed no immediate threat and committed no crime, yet was viewed as a criminal, and the only thing that went through George Zimmerman's mind as heard in the released police reports was that something had to be done to eliminate this threat.

As I mentioned earlier, my first thoughts after this tragedy were of my son Malcolm, who was six years old at the time. I was devastated. Couldn't sleep. Hugged him close. Many Black parents had the very same reaction. "How can we protect our sons?" became a question in Black communities and households across the country. Even President Barack Obama said in a national address that the killing of Trayvon Martin requires a national "soul-searching." "If I had a son, he'd look like Trayvon," the president added.

Mainstream America simply did not feel this same sense of terror and horror upon hearing this news. So many Americans don't have the same fear for their children's lives, which is understandable because their experiences with the police are completely different than those of the Black community.

Philando Castile did everything by the book. He followed all of the instructions and commands, but was still deemed a threat and killed by the police. What Bill O'Reilly and many others in mainstream America can't understand is that when your face or your skin is the threat, that will lead to a much different experience, one they cannot relate to. It doesn't matter what your economic status is, if you are an athlete, whether you have graduated college or earned advance degrees, etc. That could have been anyone's son.

This tragedy did not fail to hit home for many athletes. For some reason, people seem to think that the problems and issues of society don't have the same effect on athletes. People seem to think that there is an imaginary bubble that we all live in that protects us from any harm—but that simply is not the case. As expressed by countless athletes, entertainers, professionals, activists, authors, journalists, Trayvon could have been *anybody's* son.

Commentator Geraldo Rivera said on *Fox & Friends* that the hoodie Martin wore when he was killed was as much responsible for his death as the man who shot him, and mainstream America seemed to agree with his assertion.

This prompted athletes from all over to join in the protest.

Dwyane Wade and LeBron James, arguably two of the top players in the NBA, but more importantly also fathers, decided it was time for them to speak out, as did many others around the league.

In a show of solidarity, LeBron James posted a picture of all the Miami Heat wearing the team hoodies with their heads bowed and their hands stuffed in their pockets. Among the hashtags James linked to the team photo: *#WeWantJustice.*

James told the media "It was very emotional, an emotional day for all of us, taking that picture. We're happy that we're able to shed light on the situation that we feel is unjust."

Dwyane Wade also posted a picture of himself.

In an interview with the Associated Press hours before the Heat played the Detroit Pistons, with this tragedy weighing heavily on him, Wade explained, "This situation hit home for me because last Christmas, all my oldest son wanted as a gift was hoodies. So when I heard about this a week ago, I thought of my sons. I'm speaking up because I feel it's necessary that we get past the stereotype of young Black men and especially with our youth."

In a further demonstration of support, several Heat players, including Wade and James, took the floor that Friday night with messages such as *RIP Trayvon Martin* and *We Want Justice* scrawled on their sneakers.

Other players around the NBA were also affected by this tragedy and aimed to show support. Carmelo Anthony tweeted a photo of himself in a gray hoodie, with the words *I Am TRAYVON MARTIN!!!!!* over the image.

The National Basketball Players Association issued the following statement:

The National Basketball Players Association (NBPA) offers its condolences to the family and loved ones of Trayvon Martin in their time of need. The NBPA is saddened and horrified by the tragic murder of Mr.

Martin and joins in the chorus of calls from across the nation for the prompt arrest of George Zimmerman.

The reported facts surrounding Mr. Zimmerman's actions indicate a callous disregard for Mr. Martin's young life and necessitate that he stand trial . . . The NBPA seeks to ensure that Trayvon Martin's murder not go unpunished and the elimination of the injustices suffered by the innocent.

A tragedy such as this doesn't escape any Black parent.

As this stance by the Miami Heat proves, contemporary Black athletes are capable of carrying on the tradition of their brave brothers and sisters before them who led the way in challenging racial injustice in the world outside the athletic arena (all while potentially facing the petty and insipid criticism of reactionary media).

Now, back to *Forty Million Dollar Slaves*.

There is a common myth that Black athletes today are disconnected from the Black community, and that the retaliation athletes face from the reactionary side of the sports media has fractured the "common cause" that once united all Black athletes standing for social justice. Many contemporary sports writers, analysts, and commentators agree with Mr. Rhoden's assertion that after decades of Black athletes who faced the most dire consequences—loss of livelihood and death threats—we have now entered a period where an unspoken code encourages contemporary athletes to avoid "rocking the boat," lest they risk losing their lucrative sponsorships and opportunities to compete professionally.

Furthermore, for Black professional athletes who do remain connected to their communities in significant ways, Rhoden focuses on the harsh reprisals that they are likely to face at the hands of the largely white sports media.

Yet, as seen with Dwyane Wade, LeBron James, and the rest of the Miami Heat, this dynamic did not prove true. They didn't receive any ridicule or censure from the team for injecting themselves into a national tragedy and using the company logo to do so. Instead, they drew praise and support from the entire organization, including Heat coach Erik Spoelstra.

The decision made by Wade, James, their Heat teammates, and other athletes to take a stand after the tragedy of Trayvon Martin should not be dismissed as singular and nominal. These are not the actions of a group that is, to quote Rhoden, "isolated and alienated from their native networks" or that possesses an "ignorance of the issues impacting a vast majority of African Americans across the country."

Bill Rhoden and those of his ilk should apply the same vigor and thorough analysis to uncovering the positive efforts of contemporary Black athletes to improve their communities and stand up for what they believe in that they do in generating criticism.

I wanted to ask someone who I have a great deal of respect for about this topic—Michael Eric Dyson. He is a sociology professor at Georgetown University, a *New York Times* opinion writer, and a contributing editor for the *New Republic* and ESPN's *The Undefeated*. He has authored or edited at least eighteen books to date dealing with subjects such as Malcolm X, Dr. Martin Luther King Jr., Marvin Gaye, Hurricane Katrina, Nas's debut *Illmatic* album, and Tupac Shakur. He is also a season ticket holder for the Washington Wizards and an avid NBA fan. I have introduced him to guys from my AAU team when we've run into him at Wizards games, and I have given them assignments to read some of his work.

Interview with Michael Eric Dyson

Etan: What are your thoughts about the rise of athlete activism?

Dr. Michael Eric Dyson: Well, I think that's happening more in your sport than in others. I think that basketball is a more liberal, open-minded enterprise, not only from the players but some of the owners. Not all of them. We know about Donald Sterling and his retrogressive views . . . But still, I think that the leadership of the NBA has been far more willing to engage in the exploration of social issues and the elevation of social conscience . . . whether LeBron and the Miami Heat tweeting out a picture of themselves in a hoodie or the *I Can't Breathe* T-shirts . . . One of the reasons that Kaepernick's gesture was so widely denounced within football circles is because despite the fact that, what, 69 percent of the players are Black, it's still an overwhelmingly white sport in terms of the front office, in terms of many of the culturally conservative and politically conservative ideas that are spouted in those general manager offices and often by the largely lily-white ownership.

What you see is the reproduction within the NFL of the same conservative ideology that is taken up often by players. Now you have the Bennett brothers stepping up and being honest and open-minded. Martellus basically said, "Look, I'm not going to the White House and I'm not going because Donald Trump doesn't represent an open-minded approach and a tolerant disposition toward varieties of minorities, and I'm not gonna pretend that I second that kind of belief." And Michael Bennett essentially said, "Look, the reason Kaepernick doesn't have a job now is because he led a one-man protest."

Etan: Well, we do have a lot of examples of NFL players who have spoken out.

Dyson: Yes, but I do think that overall the NFL definitely . . . in one sense discourages the kind of outspoken expression that some of the players have adopted. Of course, they have their independence—you mentioned [Richard] Sherman, and [Eric] Reid . . . but in one sense, if you named them then they're the exceptions . . . By and large, that league does not encourage the kind of independent thought and assessment of social issues that athletes might be encouraged to adopt, and then by adopting to engage in a kind of a serious form of social resistance . . . I do believe that the NBA may in fact be a bit more tolerant and I was beginning to say part of it has to do with who watches it.

But number two, there's no question that there have been tremendous expressions of social conscience, but let's be honest . . . there has been a transition from the sixties and seventies, when players like Kareem Abdul-Jabbar and Jim Brown and Muhammad Ali took stands in bold fashion for vulnerable populations of which they were a part. Ali against the war in Vietnam, Jim Brown with Kareem supporting him but also speaking out about racial injustice . . . So, there was a different temperature in the culture where it was easier for athletes to speak up in more unexpected ways because they were true representatives of their communities and there were fewer athletes who were Black breaking into these sports.

Think about it—Jackie Robinson broke the color barrier in baseball, and baseball as a result had a far greater amount of Black players. But now, those numbers have dwindled, whereas Latino players are 23 percent of Major League Baseball. Now, many of the Latino players are immigrants who are grateful to be in this country and feel no need to point to its flaws and are perceived to be more compliant with the wishes of ownership and general management than Black players, who rightfully believe that as American citizens they have rights and should be treated like men as well . . .

Etan: Interesting point.

Dyson: But the transition from the sixties and seventies to now is one of . . . social conscience to social service. Let me tell you what I mean. The NBA, the NFL, maybe even Major League Baseball, they do a great deal of investment into the communities in terms of rebuilding homes, visiting people in hospitals, children, especially those who are sick. Make-A-Wish Foundation. That's social service, but it's not social conscience or social protest in the sense of the sixties and seventies . . . In one sense, it is more acceptable for athletes to be involved in a project of charity to the community than it is to point to fundamental forms of injustice in that particular community.

Martin Luther King Jr. believed that charity is a poor substitute for justice. So, there's no doubt that the athletes of this generation continue a noteworthy tradition of social conscience and social protest to a certain degree. LeBron James, Dwyane Wade, Chris Paul, Carmelo Anthony. And, let's be honest, even they were far outstripped by the women in the WNBA. They are usually overlooked because they are subordinate to the men in terms of gender awareness, because of the persistent sexism in this culture. But when you think of a woman like Swin Cash and what they did to rally their forces to speak out against police brutality and injustice and how Black people and brown people were being mistreated, you definitely can't claim that the current athlete doesn't engage in political social activism.

Etan: I agree.

Dyson: However, there is a legitimate point to be made that what the league did to absorb some of the social protest and redirect it, and some would say *deflect* it, is to offer programs of social outreach and social upliftment as opposed to social protest.

Muhammad Ali suffered for the stance he took. It cost him money. One of the few players that it costs money now, it seems, is Colin Kaepernick, in terms of the sacrifice made and the economic benefit that was denied to him. Very few athletes in this day and age are being denied a living and an economic opportunity because of their social conscience. So they have to be more savvy because, let's be honest, there's a lot more at stake . . . The leagues have grown. The economic interests have deepened . . . Therefore, when a LeBron James or a Carmelo speaks out, it's even more noteworthy for the courage it takes to sacrifice a potential payday . . . But I'll still say this: the transition from social protest and social conscience to social service has lessened the need of the leagues to be held accountable, politically.

Etan: That's true, but you can't say that it doesn't exist altogether, right? In William C. Rhoden's book *Forty Million Dollar Slaves*, he writes that "black athletes have abdicated their responsibility to the community with treasonous vigor." The evidence simply does not support that claim in any way or fashion. Come on, Dr. Dyson, "treasonous vigor"?

Dyson: I think what Bill Rhoden is acknowledging is partly what I'm trying to explain in terms of that transition from social conscience and social protest to social service. On the one hand, I think that you're absolutely right. Many athletes continue to speak up and speak out, but partly, I think, this has a correlation with so many of the young athletes who may not necessarily be encouraged to speak out during their careers—in fact, who are discouraged from speaking out. "Look, you're going to lose your contract, keep your mouth shut. Keep your nose to the grind." Now, this has been said to every athlete of every color. But especially to Black and Latino athletes who have more at stake because their peoples and communities are subjected to some of the horrible consequences of injustice in this culture . . . So you're feeling that generational tension and the assault upon younger people and not understanding that if you've been on Twitter and use social media . . . and you're promoting Black identities and ideas, that is a different expression, but one that may be equally valuable.

For instance, when LeBron James gets the agents and companies to hire his young men from his neighborhood, and then he gives them an opportunity to be taught by the best; and then, when they are ready, puts them in positions of authority, gets rid of the white infrastructure, and then puts in place his own African American colleagues and peers, who he's lifted by virtue of his fame, to positions of authority . . . now that's a tremendous racially transformative practice. It's not often acknowledged, but that's every bit as important, at the end of the day, to do as LeBron speaking out in public against certain forms of racial injustice toward the vulnerable.

Etan: Good point. We have to examine the long-term solutions. Not just episodes and tirades, but how do you create systemic change and long-term progress?

Dyson: Now, let's be honest, many younger athletes have not been groomed in the same way as their predecessors. Meaning, earlier athletes who went to college, had the opportunity to interact with other colleagues and people from the NAACP and the Urban League, from social protest organizations or civil rights organizations at an earlier stage in their lives—resulting in an acute awareness they possessed because they were more part of a broader community. And because of the isolation of some of the athletes, who may not be as intimately familiar with the political strategies being deployed by the civil rights organization, or have been taught to be hostile to them by white money interests that have an investment in keeping them apart. White agents are not going to encourage their athletes to be socially focused. I'm sorry, they're not. And they're going to warn them about the consequences of it . . . It makes sense that there would be a diminishment of social conscience among these athletes and a greater sensitivity toward the economic consequences of their protests and a discouraging of them from engaging in social protest.

Etan: That's also a good point. Let me ask you this: do you think that sometimes there's a certain romanticizing of the sixties? Most of the athletes were not like Ali and Bill Russell and Kareem.

Dyson: *(Laughing)* Oh, there's no doubt about that. I write about this, especially in my book *Race Rules*, where I discuss this very topic. There's not only a romanticization of athletes from the civil rights era, but all the leaders and Black figures from the civil rights era. Most Black people were not involved in the civil rights movement. Most athletes were not actively engaged. There's always a small remnant, a redemptive remnant, of people who change the stakes of the conversation and the parameters of progress for all of us . . . So we end up looking back through the haze of nostalgia that creates a false impression, that most of the time in the sixties they were involved in protests, movements, and marches. The March on Washington was an aberration in the sense of that great a gathering, that big of a commitment expressed by people across the board. Most of these marches were much smaller, and most of the time they weren't marching but strategizing, thinking, critically engaging their communities. Trying to encourage conversation, change, and protests.

So, yeah, there's a huge nostalgia piece about this . . . Let's be honest, there was a greater likelihood, when you have limited opportunities and when segregation prevailed, for Black athletes to protest social barriers, because they were denied. And the denial to those Black athletes of things that they knew they should've had access to was a metaphor for how other Black people were being denied. Lawyers, doctors, painters, engineers. So, athletes and entertainers were the front line of social protest in the forties, fifties, and sixties because they had opportunities that most other people didn't have. And as a result of that, they bore a burden . . .

Now, a lot of people did what they could. They couldn't take off their jobs, they couldn't afford to—they were poor so they did what they could. They cooked food for the movement. They were sacrificial. So I'm not dissing them, but I am saying that, through the haze of nostalgia, we pretend that every athlete over fifty was profoundly involved in the social movement . . . We didn't know what they were doing and some of them were outright like O.J. Simpson, saying, "I ain't no Negro and what are you talking about? And I've got it made and I don't want to be involved in that racial protest myth."

Etan: Exactly.

Dyson: So it is unfair, and I think illegitimate, to demand that of young athletes—these kids are basically trying to find out who they are. Exploring their opportunities in a culture that often didn't support them, just like with hip-hop in the eighties. You know, think about hip-hop's emergence in the seventies and eighties . . . "Look, y'all are ridiculous. I don't even want to support y'all." Now that they've become famous, they're rich, all of a sudden you want them to support your community and to be outspoken. You haven't engaged them. You haven't trained them. You haven't loved them. Allen Iverson was demonized by a great deal of people in American culture and some in Black communities. "You're wrong, you got the wrong dress, you got the wrong tattoos," and so on. Now everybody's got a tattoo . . . So things change. They transform. We get nostalgic and romantic and we deny that each generation has to find its voice, its outlook, its way, its means of expression.

Etan: So, not a "lost generation."

Dyson: Definitely not. There's probably as many athletes today who are involved in social protest and social conscience as there were earlier, but there were fewer athletes in the fifties and sixties than there are now. But the progress of those men and women has indeed made possible the expansion of opportunity for some of these younger people. And therefore, there is an expectation that they would engage in socially redemptive kinds of practices. But let's be honest, it's always against the grain. It was against the grain in the sixties and seventies and it's against the grain now.

Etan: A lot of young people took a knee. Does seeing these young people engaged the way they are give you a bright hope for the future?

Dyson: It's absolutely tremendous. In one sense, they're learning from their elders, social media, greater exposure on cable channels. Think about it: in the forties, fifties, sixties, and seventies, television is in its infancy, then it comes into its own. We ain't got no cable TV. When Ali is doing what he's doing, the eyes of the world are on him because there were fewer options . . .

Now it's even more remarkable that these young people do what they do, because there's a proliferation of options. There are options galore. How many channels you got on cable now? Six, seven hundred? Ain't nobody had a Facebook.

There's been a tremendous transformation. A proliferation of outlets, which is both good and bad. Good in the sense that now, young people have many more ways to consume information and absorb knowledge. And, in turn, to express themselves. If Russell Westbrook or LeBron or Swin Cash and other people are tweeting and posting on social media, they have immediate access to a nation of followers and listeners. Many of these people have fifteen, sixteen million people following them, and they're getting their message directly to the people.

It's heartening because many of them are then educating themselves . . . Young activists are encouraging younger people to become involved. So there's a beautiful consequence of transmitting that tradition from one generation to another. Hopefully, each generation digs deeper. I know a lot of people say, "Well, they have historical amnesia because they weren't there," but they learn like any other people learn . . . We have to acknowledge that there are varieties, means, and ways for young people to get educated. But we shouldn't dismiss them. We shouldn't denigrate them or demonize them. We should elevate them and celebrate them . . . So yeah, it's refreshing and rewarding to see young people educating themselves about a myriad of social issues, and then doing whatever they can to make sure that things are changed.

Interview with Dwyane Wade

I was glad to be able to sit down with Dwyane Wade, who I have grown to know personally. We both had fatherhood books come out around the same time. His book, *A Father First: How My Life Became Bigger Than Basketball,* is a very good read. We've appeared on panels together, including the one at the Congressional Black Caucus and during NBA All-Star Weekend in Houston. Which is why it was no surprise for me to hear how the Trayvon Martin tragedy affected him personally.

Etan: Talk about the decision to wear those hoodies as a team.

Dwyane Wade: It really hit home for a lot of guys on the team. Obviously, being African Americans, we have to go home and talk to our kids about this situation and answer their questions and concerns and calm their fears. It was a very difficult conversation to have because it's something that could happen to us. Being in Florida at the time and knowing that he was a big Miami Heat fan, we felt we had to make a statement and shed more light on the situation and figure out what we could do. We didn't want this to be another incident that goes unseen and unnoticed and unheard. We wanted to really broadcast this to the entire country and the world, because we know in the NBA and being who we are that we have this massive global platform at our disposal, so we utilized it to broadcast this message. And it hit home with a lot of other people, especially when they saw us talking about how much it hit home with us.

Etan: I remember seeing you talk about your sons and how much they loved hoodies, because at the same time I was talking about my son Malcolm about how much he loved hoodies.

Wade: That's definitely what it was. African American kid, tall like all our kids . . . Whatever the situation may be, we all wear hoodies. And for that to be the reason given as a justification—and why this child Trayvon Martin won't be able to experience the fruits of this life and won't be able to experience life, graduate, get married, have kids, just live—is really sad. He was taken off the face of the earth, and for what? Because of his hoodie? Because he didn't have the right to be walking in the neighborhood he was walking in? For a lot of us, it was a talking point for us to have to sit our kids down and discuss how there are things that we don't think about and you take for granted and how it can easily end in tragedy. I remember having the conversations with my boys, and they didn't really understand everything exactly, but it was important to let them know and answer all of their questions and talk with them about everything that was going on.

Etan: There is this misconception that the management or the organization would tell you not to speak out on issues like this because it could be bad for business. Or that the owner of the team would come down on you hard as far as fines or suspension or even being traded if you do something like this, on what turned out to be a very divisive, controversial case. But that didn't seem to be what happened here with the Miami Heat organization at all. Also, it seemed to me that even if the organization was against it, by you all collectively doing this, you kind of forced their hand to go along with it.

Wade: I think it's just a different day. With social media being as powerful as it is, you become in essence a reporter. So it's hard for someone to tell you not to do things or say things that you want to do on your social media platform. If the only outlet was the local media, then maybe teams would have more control over what goes out and what doesn't, but with social media, you pretty much say what you want to say. But with us, the Heat were always supportive and never tried to deter us from getting involved. The coaches were the ones who took the pictures for us.

Etan: The coaches?

Wade: Yeah, they were supportive because they knew that we were passionate about it . . . I've honestly never been in a situation where the organization didn't support what the players collectively wanted to say or wanted to do.

Etan: Now take me to the Excellence in Sports Yearly Awards (ESPYs) and you and Carmelo and Chris Paul are all standing there making your statements, calling for community involvement and activism from players while addressing the systemic debasement of Black and brown people in America. What brought you all to collectively make that statement and use that particular platform of the ESPYs?

Wade: Well, you can't be in the position that LeBron is in, that Melo is in, myself and CP, and really care about criticism and what people say about you. As you know, we all have to deal with critics, all athletes have been for our entire athletic careers. Fifty percent of people are going to praise you and the other 50 percent are going to criticize you no matter what you do, and the flack that we've even taken just for being friends . . . that's just the nature of the beast. So you just have to be true to yourself and who you are and you have to do things because you want to do them. Because it makes you happy, and makes you satisfied, not because it's going to please other people. For us, this was a moment that was bigger than us; it was bigger than basketball. This was a moment that we could come together and use our power and speak on something that we all felt was important, and really lead the charge and challenge other athletes . . . using the platform of the ESPYs to do it.

Etan: Many times, people almost purposely misconstrue and twist the message.

Wade: For us, everyone had their own message that they wanted to bring to present and focus on. We wanted to talk about the killings by the police. We wanted to talk about police brutality in particular. And at the same time, we understand. CP said on stage that his uncle and grandfather are police officers, so he is definitely not antipolice. But he also acknowledged the police brutality and murders and he listed them: Trayvon Martin, Mike Brown, Freddie Gray, Alton Sterling, Philando Castile. So we asked ourselves the question: what message did we want to come across, taking into consideration that while we are the brotherhood, we all go about things in our own particular ways? So we all sat down and we all wrote the particular message that we wanted to present to the world. And if you listen to everyone's speeches, everyone said something that was near and dear to their hearts, to their communities and their families. My overall point was that enough is enough and I'm tired of seeing all the murders, always picking up the newspaper or turning on the news and seeing that another person has been killed by the police.

Etan: What is it going to take to change what's going on? There are so many young people who have developed a distrust for the police as a result of everything they keep seeing. The murders, the brutality, the beatings, the videos on social media. What do you say to them?

Wade: I definitely understand it. And I have had conversations with young people and I have had conversations with police officers. And one of my messages to the police officers was, "Listen, you guys understand that there is a distrust of police officers, and me myself, if I see a police car behind me, it's a very uncomfortable situation. Even me being an athlete and I know that I haven't done anything wrong." And I told the police officers, "Listen, if you really want to begin to change this, you have to work toward bridging the gap." We are having all of these town hall meetings and panel discussions, let's sit down as a community—police officers, the community leaders, and the youth leaders—and let's have these conversations and allow everyone's voices to be heard. You need to know what the people in the community are feeling and how they view you and why they view you that way. It's not like they don't have legitimate reasons or they just don't like you because they just don't like you. They have reasons. Experiences. Things they've seen. That their family and friends and loved ones have seen and experienced. And vice versa.

The community needs to hear from the policemen. Hear the things they've experienced and seen and heard. As in any relationship, the best way to really understand someone's perspective and where they are coming from is to first listen to them. Not listen to disagree with, but actually listen to understand their perspective. And both sides need to hear verbalized what the other side expects. Right now we are dealing with two sides that don't understand each other at all. And that doesn't lend itself to a successful or productive relationship. That was my message to the different police departments in different cities as I was meeting and talking with them.

Interview with Carmelo Anthony

As a Syracuse graduate, I have to admit that I do have a little bit of a bias for Carmelo Anthony. I am proud of what he has accomplished on the court, but even more proud of who he is *off* the court.

So, I'm waiting after the Knicks played the Wizards to interview him. Knicks president (at that time) Phil Jackson had just floated something in the newspapers that maybe Carmelo would be better playing somewhere else. All of the media were waiting to talk to him, and then Carmelo emerges from the training room. He looked at me and smiled and gave me a hug. We briefly talked about Syracuse, and then I told him about this book and what I was doing, but in the middle of my explanation, he stopped me to say that I didn't have to sell it, that he would be more than happy to talk because it's something that needs to be covered.

Etan: You were in Baltimore marching with the people after Freddie Gray was murdered by the police, and in Brazil you went to a favela, a slum. Talk about how you haven't been afraid to speak out—and even more than just speaking out, really being among the people, almost like Muhammad Ali.

Carmelo Anthony: I was always a part of that growing up. I was always on the other side of the fence, with the people. Everything that we have ever done growing up in my neighborhood in Baltimore, I was taught that you had to be about the people. The community. And the Freddie Gray situation really hit home for me personally because that happened in my backyard. To turn on the TV and see people that I know going through that . . . I felt the same pain that they were feeling. I felt the same heartache that they were feeling. It was really a horrific situation . . . Seeing that image of how they were carrying his body to the police van, over and over and over, it was just really terrible.

Etan: Were you afraid of any backlash that may have come your way?

Anthony: No, none at all. I have always kind of stayed away from politics and everything, but this was a situation where I could not be quiet. I wouldn't be able to look at myself in the mirror if I didn't say something, so I decided to put my all into this . . . I wanted this family to receive justice for what had happened. I wanted there to be peace. I didn't like seeing my city burning. I understand the anger and the frustration, but we have already suffered so much as a community, and the destruction was just painful to see taking place. We did a peaceful march. If people want to still criticize a peaceful march, then they're gonna criticize anything we do and we can't be worried about them. I was there for the community, *my* community.

Etan: What was the reaction from the people when you were out there marching with them, rallying with them?

Anthony: It was unbelievable. They felt like there was hope. They had somebody there who was fighting with them and fighting for them who was already out of that situation but hadn't forgotten about them . . . They felt like there was some hope for justice. Because you have to remember, at that time, a long time had gone by and nobody had provided any answers whatsoever about Freddie Gray's spinal injuries sustained while in police custody. They wanted answers and for somebody to be held accountable for what had happened. And they weren't getting any answers. So for me to come there fighting for justice, it meant a lot to the people to know that I was just as frustrated as they were . . . They had every right to demand answers and to be upset. We just gotta go about it the right way.

Etan: I've seen you wearing Muhammad Ali shirts, I saw you on the *ESPN* cover wearing the Black Panther–esque beret. Were you influenced by Muhammad Ali and the Black Panthers?

Anthony: I was always educated about that. I read Muhammad Ali and Malcolm X and the Panthers, and really examined the things they were saying. I didn't just read it and glance over it, I really examined it, you know? And, my dad was on the Puerto Rican side, part of the Young Lords Organization, so that's in my genes. To go out and get the information, stand up for what you believe in, fight for what you believe in, and not to just talk, but to do action. Anybody can talk, but the Malcolms, the Alis, the Young Lords, the Panthers, they were about action. Putting together programs that would help the community, help the youth, empower and educate the youth. That's how you really create change and make a difference . . .

The system is broken. That's something I keep repeating over and over. And it's like, they don't want to teach us what we need to know to survive, so we have to educate ourselves and educate our youth. You can't know how to deal with the police if you were never educated on how to deal with them, and at the same time, the police have to be educated on how to deal with people, and neither one is happening . . . When I was growing up, we knew all the police by their first name, we even gave them nicknames, that's how familiar we were with them. And when the white police came into our neighborhood, the Black police said, "Yo, we got this." That doesn't happen anymore.

You gotta know the community that you are policing. That's like me playing on a team but I don't know any of the players. How is that gonna work? You got these police that know absolutely nothing about the places they are supposed to protect and serve. That doesn't even make sense.

If you had community policing, I don't believe Terence Crutcher would have been executed the way he was.

Etan: Your platform as an athlete, it's like a blessing, but can it also be a burden?

Anthony: It only becomes a burden when you say something and you don't follow through . . . But when you say what you're gonna do and you follow up, there is no burden because it's a part of who you are as a human being.

Etan: Tell me about what you did in Los Angeles. You got the men's USA Olympic basketball team and the women's team all together right before y'all went over to Brazil to play in the Olympics, and y'all had a town hall meeting in South Central Los Angeles. It was called "Leadership Together: A Conversation with Our Sons and Daughters." Sounds like it was really powerful.

Anthony: So I put together this town hall, and I knew that I had all the best basketball players in the world together in one place, so in LA I wanted to get in front of the youth, the police chiefs, the commissioners, the mayors, and bring them into one place and have a dialogue. I wanted the police to hear from the youth and I wanted the youth to hear from the police. And one of the main things that came out of that discussion was that there is a lack of trust. We don't trust the police . . . because when we see police, we run, automatically, they get scared, they get defensive, they think something bad is about to happen to them. And the police needed to hear them say that and express that fear that they feel.

Then, I also wanted the youth to hear the police's story, because they never get an opportunity to be exposed to their side or their perspective and *their* fear. The difference is, they're scared but they have guns, you know? We're scared, and we have nothing. And everyone needed to hear everyone's perspectives. And also, the youth needed to hear the police officers say out of their mouths that they didn't agree with everything that was going on and that they weren't in support of some of the murders that were happening around the country. It was good for them to see that not all police officers were bad . . . It was really touching.

Etan: So what was the response from the youth after this forum?

Anthony: You had some of the youth that were relieved to be able to get that out and talk about that because they don't have any platform to be heard. And they want to be heard. People gotta understand, when they take away all of your resources, you become hopeless, and voiceless. Kids need to have a voice, they need to have someone who will listen to their concerns just to know that somebody cares, but all that is happening is that they're taking away their resources and opportunities and showing them that their lives just aren't important to them. When I was coming up, we had rec centers, parks, after-school programs, basketball courts, football fields—you had all these different things that you could go do. But now, and this is in communities across the country, it's like they are taking all that away. Closing parks, closing rec centers.

Etan: And did you see a change in the police?

Anthony: Yeah. A lot of them came up to me afterward and said, "Hey, we need more of this because honestly, we don't know what they're thinking. We're just out there trying to protect and serve and we don't know what their fears are and what their mind-sets are, and we don't hear these conversations." They really wanted to get across that all police are not bad. But it was really good for everybody all around

Etan: D Wade and I talked about the ESPYs and how everyone had their own specific messages that they wanted to convey. Talk about what your specific message was.

Anthony: My message was, first of all, how four athletes at the top of the game could come together and give you one message, four different ways. And we just said, "Why don't we just go out there and just say it? We don't have to do too much scripting and planning. Let's all go out and say exactly what's on our hearts." And we had all of the best athletes from around the world in one place at that time, and for them to hear that, it was just really powerful. It also put the pressure on a lot of people to step up to the challenge too . . . I wanted to put the pressure on the other athletes to step up and do what they can in their own networks and their own communities.

The problems and issues are not new. If we talk to our parents and grandparents and aunts and uncles, they'll tell us they've been fighting this fight for a long time . . . But urgency for change is at an all-time high, and we ain't got no time to be worried about no criticism, or endorsements, or what this or that person is gonna think. People's lives are at risk, so we all have to do what we can.

Interview with Bill Russell

Bill Russell is a pioneer. He is on the Mount Rushmore of athlete-activists. I remember learning about him at a young age. His eleven championship rings during his thirteen-year career are the most of any NBA player to date, but what I marvel at is his courage and what he stood for, at a time when Boston wasn't exactly shy about its racism.

I remember reading his memoir *Go Up for Glory*, and being enthralled by every word. From dealing with racism as a child growing up, how his parents were victims of racial abuse, how during games at the University of San Francisco he and his Black teammates were verbally attacked with the most disgusting and vile epithets you can imagine. When a hotel owner denied him and other NBA all-stars rooms in a very segregated North Carolina. While with the Celtics, he and his Black teammates were refused service at a Lexington, Kentucky, restaurant, and he and the other Black teammates refused to play. He was active in the Black Power movement and supported Muhammad Ali as soon as the champion refused to be drafted into the army. It was an absolute honor to interview Bill Russell for this book.

Etan: After the Cavs won the championship in 2016, in the midst of their celebration, the camera caught you speaking to LeBron and him listening very intensely. What wisdom were you passing on to him and how did he receive it?

Bill Russell: Well, the first thing I told him was congratulations . . . Then I spoke with him about the responsibility of being great and that he had to be willing to accept that responsibility. I told him that no leader can be great without his teammates. No matter how great he is. And LeBron was very receptive to what I was saying, he thanked me, told me how much he appreciated my advice, and how much he respected me. He is going to go far because he is always willing to learn and doesn't think he knows everything, even though he is one of the greatest, if not *the* greatest, player on the planet.

Etan: One of the things that a lot of guys reference when speaking about you is the situation that happened while you were playing for the Boston Celtics before an exhibition game in the 1961–1962 season in Lexington, Kentucky.

So you and your teammate were denied service in a restaurant because it was whites-only. And you said (and of course, I am paraphrasing here), "Oh, okay, this is a whites-only restaurant? Our Black money is no good here? Well, fine." And you and the rest of the team flew back home without playing in the exhibition game. I can't imagine the amount of courage it took to do that, and the level of scrutiny you must have received upon returning to Boston, a city that isn't known for being a very welcoming and warm place for Black people.

Russell: *(Laughing)* Well, that's one way to put it. It was simple. I said, "If we can't eat here, we can't play here." We made the point clear that we were human beings and had to be treated with the dignity of human beings the same way you treat everybody else . . . So it was simple . . . And I'm not going to name names, but at least half a dozen very high-profile white players came to me and said to me privately, "You guys did the right thing, and we have a lot of respect for you. Now, don't expect us to say any of this publicly *(laughing)*, because if this all blows up, you're on your own." When we returned to Boston, the reaction from the press and a lot of the so-called fans was exactly what you would think it would be. Boston was not exactly a liberal oasis. In fact, a couple of writers said that the league should've suspended every single one of the Black players who refused to play, for insubordination, not fulfilling the obligations of their contracts . . . They said that the NBA should banish us because we—and get this—we hurt the feelings of some of the white players.

Etan: Hmmm.

Russell: Yeah, that's exactly what I said: *Hmmm.*

Etan: But you stood strong with it . . .

Russell: I didn't care what none of them said. I didn't care one bit. I didn't need their approval or their pat on the back . . . Let me tell you about where I come from in Louisiana. Louisiana at that time was all about the separation of the races. It was just a different time. And my mother would tell me to be careful, because if you were doing something wrong it would reflect negatively on all of us, and if you were doing something right, it would reflect positively on all of us, and if you went along with something that was wrong, it would affect all of us. So that's all I was focused on, doing what was right.

Etan: That's some great wisdom that was passed down to you. How was it to win championships for Boston, and then to come home and find out that people have broken into your home, ransacked everything, and actually defecated in your bed? These same fans that cheer you when you are winning championship after championship. I honestly couldn't imagine having that happen to me.

Russell: Well, one thing you have to always remember is that the majority of the country are decent folks. The majority of white people are decent folks. And I was always very careful not to stereotype people based on the actions of a few, or of a little more than a few, as was the case in Boston *(laughing)* . . . A lot of the stuff that went on, in my mind, I knew that they were individual acts and not a reflection of everybody in Boston, because I would see and still see today what many people really think and believe—that Black folks are responsible for all of the actions of other Black folks, and that's just ridiculous . . . And it's just as crazy for me to think that all white people were responsible for the ones that treated me and my family so poorly, broke into my house, destroyed my property for no reason at all.

When I was with the Celtics, I was still very much connected to Louisiana. So one time in the off-season, I went down to see my friends and family. Now, this guy who was my barber's former boss sent for me. And I said okay. So I go to his house to ring his doorbell and the lady that answered the door said, "You have to go around to the back. You can't come in here through the front door." And she said it like I was ridiculous for even thinking that I could come through the front door like white folks. So I turned around and went home. And he called my father and told on me like I did something wrong.

And this was after Eisenhower had invited a lot of athletes to the White House, and I was one of the guys he invited and all of us went in the front door. Now I am saying to myself, *The president of the United States invites me to come to the White House and he didn't suggest that I go around to the back, but a regular Joe invites me to his house and you expect me to go to the* back *of the house? You must be crazy (laughing).* Just because I said that I don't put all white people in the same boat doesn't mean I don't still recognize that too many white people looked at me as less-than, and no matter what they thought, I wasn't about to allow them to treat me as less-than.

Etan: That's great how you made that point. I have been quoting you since I was in high school, especially when you said, "I refuse to allow you to reduce me to a clown used to entertain your circus."

Russell: Well, at that time, the most prominent Black athletes were the Globetrotters. I refused to play for the Globetrotters although they offered me the most money. I was publicly criticized by Abe Saperstein for refusing. He said I was out of my mind. But I told him and everyone else that I am a basketball player, and not a clown. In fact, I'm the best basketball player there is.

Etan: My grandfather always said that he felt embarrassed as a Black man when he would watch the Globetrotters do their routine.

Russell: Well, your grandfather was a smart man . . . Jackie Robinson had been my ultimate hero because, of course, he was a great baseball player, but more importantly, he didn't take no mess from nobody. Up until Jackie, no matter how good you were, you had to say that you were lucky to be able to play with these guys. Even in the cases where you were actually better than them . . . And when Jackie came along, he showed that we could walk with our heads up. We didn't have to be in a demeaning posture in order for you to accept us, or we didn't have to make you laugh, or entertain you, we could play on your level . . . That's why I will always admire and respect someone like Jackie Robinson, because that's what he represented for all of us.

Etan: So who were some of the people who mentored Bill Russell?

Russell: My father, first of all. That's why we left Louisiana. He said, "We can't stay here, because I love my children. And if some of this stuff that is happening around here happens to one of my kids, I will kill one of these people. And then, my kids will have to grow up without a father." One of the things he always stressed to me was to always demand respect. You don't allow anyone, no matter who they are, to make you feel less-than. You always hold your head up high, and you always walk with pride knowing that you are special. My father also stressed that I had to always conduct myself in order to command respect. And those lessons really carried me all through my entire life. They guided my actions. I have tried to always conduct myself in a way that my mother and my father would never be ashamed of. My mother was a really proud woman. So between my mother and father I had a foundation that prepared me for life.

Etan: Powerful. I wanted to ask you about the summit in Cleveland in June 1967 . . .

Russell: Well, Muhammad Ali and I had a special connection even before all of that. We both won gold medals for the Olympics before we turned professional . . . Now, I came along with the educated athletes. Most of the times, they went to college and got degrees and everyone had their various experiences. And we all respected each other because we all knew what we had to go through in order to rise to the top of your profession. And so we supported each other . . .

Our organizations that we all played and worked for were constantly saying bad things about Ali, and we all heard it, and it bothered all of us the same way. Especially the ones like me who knew him personally or had a personal experience with him . . . And we understood how a large majority of the prominent Black athletes at that time, especially if you stood up for yourself and for your people in any way, were almost immediately given the reputation of being bad guys. There was so much that I respected about Muhammad Ali. I admired his professionalism, of course he was the greatest boxer around, and it took awhile for the nation to recognize that, but he was. I know in my case, and Jim Brown's case and Kareem's case, they would have never approved of us supporting Muhammad Ali. And there were some other Black athletes who didn't support what Muhammad Ali was doing because they didn't want it to mess up their situation. But as soon as I found out about it, I knew that I had to support my brother. I wasn't going to have him out there standing by himself.

Etan: So what is your advice to younger athletes now who want to follow in your footsteps and stand up for what they believe in?

Russell: My first piece of advice would be to learn your trade and put into practice what you have learned. And never be afraid to stand up for what you believe. But also, every Black athlete cannot be a Jim Brown or Kareem or Ali—you have to be who you are. But if you choose to stand up, you can't be worried about the negative press or criticism or the people who will start to attack you on all fronts . . . You have to be strong enough to withstand that, ignore it, and keep your eyes on the prize. If you are not strong enough to do that, you might as well go sit in the corner somewhere and just be quiet . . . Let me also say this . . . when you are a prominent athlete, there is much more to it than playing the game. There is a responsibility that you do have to your community . . . What you say or don't say can bring about change or no change. You can have an effect on people you don't even know. You mind if I tell you another story?

Etan: You are Bill Russell, you can tell me as many stories as you wanna tell me *(laughing)*.

Russell: *(Laughing)* Well, okay. I remember when I was in college, a few of the coaches would send guys into the game for no other reason but to pick a fight with me. They didn't play much, weren't really that good, to be honest . . . but their sole purpose for being sent into the game was to pick a fight with me so that I would get thrown out the game . . . And I knew what they were doing and I understand why they were doing it. So I had to develop a way of taking care of them without being thrown out the game and allowing them to achieve their goal. I had to have self-control. And I also developed some of the sharpest elbows in the NBA *(laughing)*, but I didn't let their plan work.

Etan: I am trying to wrap my mind around the level of self-control you had to have your entire career.

Russell: Self-control is just a part of life. Doesn't mean you stop doing what you're doing. It just means that you maintain the self-control not to allow them to sabotage you . . . When I was in the third grade, we moved into the projects. The first time I went out to play, they ran me home . . . My mother said, "You better always stand up for yourself." And she took me throughout the neighborhood and made me fight every last one of those kids. Now, I was physically afraid of my mother, but I learned so much from her and my father. But the point was always to never let anyone think that they can get away with making you feel less-than, never allow anyone to knock you off your game or keep you away from your purpose.

The Kaepernick Movement Matters

Seeing all of the venom spewed at Colin Kaepernick takes me back to the 2003 invasion of Iraq. Today, even Republicans admit that there were no weapons of mass destruction, no direct connection to 9/11, and no true reason to invade Iraq. But back in 2003, it was thought to be anti-American, even treasonous, to speak out against the Iraq invasion. I was playing for the Washington Wizards in the nation's capital at the time and simply couldn't keep quiet about what I saw as blatant disrespect to our troops—sending them in harm's way because of deliberate lies perpetuated by then-president George W. Bush. I began reciting my poems at rallies and marches around Washington, DC. Sometimes thirty or forty people came. At other times, hundreds or even thousands showed up. I delivered each poem with the same tenacity, no matter the size of the crowd.

Here is an excerpt from my poem "Hoodwinked":

A poet once posed the question
What father and son benefited the most from 9/11
Unable to overcome his grip on your mind
You helplessly became his next victim

He had the perfect strategy
His tune you would all soon sing
He pumped terror into the minds of the multitude like unleaded gasoline
He tricked y'all
Had you all shook
Scared of your own shadow
On the run from the sun thinking it was coming after you

Heightened terror alerts
From green to yellow
From yellow to orange baffled your mental stability
You actually believed he could keep you out of harm's way
He had you nestled in the palm of his hand
A herd of blind sheep led astray
The truth never set you free from his grasp
Even after you learned of his lies
Continuously rising like the tide of an ocean
His mountains of deceit never bothered you
Why?
Y'all had to know he wasn't keeping it real
Stealing your joy with scare tactics
He peeled away at your emotions
Fear is the final frontier of the unenlightened masses who believe every-
thing they hear
Accepting as true all of the lies that Fox News tells you
Using their "fair and balanced" strategy to cause commotions in your
rhythmic patterns
He scattered your brains
Played on your ignorance like a fiddle
Making you tap dance to his tune of fear
He was Geppetto pulling your strings
Holding you down and making your soul cry during an election year
A tragedy like Romeo and Juliet
Y'all gladly drank from his cup of poison

I attempted to get my message out to the papers, but nobody wanted to cover it. Then, at one particular antiwar rally, I performed a poem called "The Field Trip." I named some ten Republicans I wanted to take on a field trip to see the results of their policies. Soon the story of the rally was everywhere.

The Kaepernick controversy reminds me of the hate mail delivered to me at the MCI Center (now the Capital One Arena). Before the rally, I would get a few letters here and there, but after it I started getting boxes. Some of the letters were supportive, but a lot of them were filled with anger and hate.

Today, I take my hat off to Colin Kaepernick for everything he is enduring, especially now in the age of social media. Every Tom, Dick, and Harry can develop what I call "Twitter courage" and type a hateful, evil condemnation of the player.

In September 2016, Kaepernick reported that he had received death threats as a result of his decision to kneel during the national anthem. That shouldn't surprise anyone. Muhammad Ali, Mahmoud Abdul-Rauf, John Carlos, Tommie Smith, and countless other athletes who have taken stances viewed as "unpatriotic" have received similar threats.

Isn't it interesting that many of the same people who are currently calling Kaepernick "unpatriotic" disrespected President Obama and First Lady Michelle Obama for eight years?

Isn't it also interesting that those same people who describe Kaepernick's stance as disrespectful to veterans haven't expressed anger toward George W. Bush, who sent those brave soldiers whose lives are precious and should be valued to die for a lie? Isn't it interesting that these same conservatives have voted against better health care and aid to vets after they come home?

A lot of people have a confused interpretation of patriotism. If you're not offended by the fact that one out of two veterans who have returned from Iraq or Afghanistan knows a fellow soldier who has attempted suicide; or by the half a million vets who don't have insurance; or the thirty-nine thousand who are homeless—but you are offended by Colin Kaepernick taking a knee during the national anthem—then you have greatly misplaced your patriotism.

It's beautiful how Colin Kaepernick's message is spreading and resonating with so many other athletes, from high school football teams to Howard University cheerleaders.

At first, only 49ers teammate Eric Reid joined Kaepernick. But then more teammates, including Antoine Bethea, Eli Harold, Jaquiski Tartt, and Rashard Robinson, joined in, raising their fists during the national anthem before a game against the Carolina Panthers.

Next, Jeremy Lane of the Seattle Seahawks sat during the national anthem. Kansas Chiefs cornerback Marcus Peters raised his fist, and told reporters he supports Kaepernick's efforts to raise awareness about our broken justice system. On Sunday Night Football, Patriots tight end Martellus

Bennett and safety Devin McCourty also raised their fists for the national anthem.

Although he lost two endorsement deals, Denver Broncos linebacker Brandon Marshall also took a knee, and said he would continue to kneel.

What's almost more impressive is how this message is affecting high school athletes, who, as we know, are greatly influenced by professional athletes. They are watching, learning, and taking stances of their own because they have their own experiences with injustice. Some have bravely faced down adversity, hatred, and threats of physical harm.

In September 2016, a Brunswick, Ohio, high school football player named Rodney Axson Jr. was threatened with lynching and called the N-word by his white teammates after he knelt to protest racism.

In Seattle, Garfield High School's entire football team and coaching staff took a knee while the national anthem played before their Friday-night game on September 16, 2016.

They were not intimidated by a number of public figures who all used their platforms to discredit, condemn, and ridicule Colin Kaepernick and other athletes for having the moral courage to stand up for what they believe in. One would think they would be just as vocal in condemning social injustice and the countless murders at the hands of the police that have gone unpunished. More than two dozen Black people were killed during encounters with police in just the first six weeks after Kaepernick began protesting. Where is their condemnation of that?

They were silent when police murdered unarmed Terence Crutcher in Tulsa, Oklahoma; he was guilty of having car trouble and expecting the police to help him out. They had nothing to say when the Charlotte police killed Keith Lamont Scott, a mentally impaired Black man allegedly guilty of reading a book in his car. In both of these cases, the officers went out on paid administrative leave. As Colin Kaepernick said in a postgame interview, "There are bodies in the street and people getting paid leave and getting away with murder." They should be outraged at that and not at whether Colin Kaepernick and other athletes are sitting or standing during the national anthem.

As a wise saying goes, *Justice will not be served until those who are unaffected are just as outraged as those who are.*

Here I am listening to Esaw Garner, the widow of Eric Garner, during a Black Lives Matter panel discussion in Harlem.

Interview with Eric Reid

I applaud all of the athletes who have had the moral courage to withstand the backlash, the criticism, the outrage, the venom, and all of the hate, and have used their platform to speak out and bring awareness to an issue that has plagued our country for far too long.

Kaepernick's teammate Eric Reid was the first one who truly stood by him. Reid listened to Kaepernick's reasons and concerns, saw the backlash that he was getting, and said that there was no way on earth he was going to allow his teammate to take this burden alone. When I interviewed Reid, he expressed how police murders hit close to him, especially Alton Sterling's, which happened in his hometown of Baton Rouge. Not only was Reid's support of Kaepernick courageous, but he shared his passion as well.

Etan: What led to your decision to join Kaepernick in taking a knee during the national anthem?

Eric Reid: I had a couple of discussions with him leading up to it, and he told me how he felt, and I felt the same way regarding a lot of the issues that were happening in this country, particularly with police brutality. I just felt that people were losing their lives over traffic stops and nobody was being held accountable for that. The way that things kept playing out was, you would have the initial report, they would say it was under investigation, and nothing would really happen. All of these families would be forced to deal with another loss of life, and nothing seemed to be changing, and I was growing very frustrated with the entire justice system. So, since my personal beliefs and thoughts were in line with his on this subject, I wanted to show some solidarity and some support for my teammate. He was getting a lot of backlash and I couldn't just not support him when I felt the same way that he did.

Etan: Initially, it seemed like you were the only one supporting him. After a while, more and more players from across the NFL began joining him in solidarity, but he was kind of out there by himself at first.

Reid: Well, the way it went down was that he wasn't standing for about three games before anybody recognized what he was doing. It wasn't until he dressed and put shoulder pads on to play in the game, and that's when the media recognized it, and then I believe I joined him the week after. I think it was just a product of the time of the year. Guys were concerned with making the football team, and they didn't want to do anything that would put themselves in a position to not make the team, and I can't fault anybody for that. You have to do what you have to do to provide for your family. It's a tough position to be in, to be honest, because you are at your employer's discretion; our contracts are such that we can in fact be let go for any reason, even if it has nothing to do with our actual performance on the field. I believe that a lot of guys wanted to show support from the jump, but they also had a legitimate concern about job safety and job security.

Etan: So Kaepernick began this stance by sitting during the national anthem, and then he changed to kneeling. I was reading where you all had a meeting with Nate Boyer, who was a Bay Area native and former Green Beret and later wrote an open letter in support of you and Kaepernick. Talk about that meeting and how it helped Kaepernick shift from sitting down during the national anthem to kneeling.

Reid: So we were in San Diego, getting ready for our preseason game. Kap told me that Mr. Nate Boyer was coming and asked me to join him in that meeting, and I said of course, because our whole purpose or goal from the beginning was to keep the conversation going about the issues, in hopes that we would see some changes in the system. So we had a meeting for like two hours and we were all being very candid with each other. We were explaining how we felt as members of the Black community and he explained how he felt as a member of the military and the veteran community, and he told us that quite frankly that he and some of his friends were quite pissed when they saw Kap sitting down during the anthem and took it as an insult to their years of service, their sacrifice for us . . . But then, after he heard why we were doing it, about our frustrations with the system . . . he said he had no problem with it whatsoever. He served to protect our freedom of speech, and he commended us for speaking on a subject that needed to be discussed.

So as the conversation moved along, we got on the subject of the actual gesture of sitting down. And myself, I agreed with him that there was probably a better way to put that message across, because we knew that when you do something like this, people are going to find a way to attack you, so we can't give them a reason . . . We came up with taking a knee as opposed to sitting down. We felt like in many ways, taking a knee is in fact respectful—people get on their knees when they pray—and we felt it would be a better way for us to . . . maybe increase the chances of them being able to hear our actual message. I prayed about it and I sought guidance from my pastor, and for me, this felt like the right thing to do . . . My faith talks about being a voice of the oppressed, and that's all I was trying to do.

Etan: Tell me about the backlash you all received.

Reid: I didn't pay much attention to the hate. I saw some pretty terrible things on Twitter, but I didn't let it bother me too much, and I knew that if anyone wanted to approach me man-to-man in real life, I had no problem with having a discussion with them about this, and I did have many discussions with many people. I think that anger is a weak emotion, and if your first reaction to seeing something is anger, I believe that you lack the ability to communicate and you are very closed-minded. I think that was a lot of what was happening. People saw headlines, they saw that we weren't standing for the anthem, or however the media chose to phrase it, and they grew angry and mad about it without actually paying attention to why we were doing it.

Etan: You have talked about how close to home the Alton Sterling murder hit for you, especially being from Baton Rouge. If you could speak with Alton Sterling's son, what would you say?

Reid: I would say that I was moved to tears when I found out what happened and that I struggle to find words to describe how sorry I am that that happened to his father. And that it shouldn't have happened . . . We are one of the richest countries in the world. And the people who are supposed to be protecting us are killing us. And I would let him know that there are a lot of people out there who are fighting to get that system changed because it makes no sense for people to continue to lose their lives over nothing . . . The police officer enters the situation, ultra-aggressive based solely on the appearance of the suspect. And it shouldn't be that way. I have police officers who are my friends. I believe . . . they signed up for that job to protect and serve. It doesn't say, *Do whatever you can so you can get home safely*, it says to protect and serve, and if they are not protecting and serving *everyone*, then they are not doing their job . . . I hope that all of these families know that there are people who are fighting for them and fighting for this system to be changed.

Etan: The lack of empathy . . .

Reid: That was probably the most mind-blowing part for me—that so many people lacked the very human emotion of empathy. How could you watch a family hurt so much and simply write it off as he should have listened to the officer, or he didn't have the right facial expression or tone of voice, and actually use that as a justification for a man losing his life? . . . People don't value God's creation. God made us and gave us life. And you look at loss of life and don't bat an eye at it. I still don't understand how people hide behind the law. You can't just say that this was wrong; you have to say, well, it was legal. I don't care if it was legal or not. Slavery was legal. Segregation was legal. The Holocaust was legal. Legal has nothing to do with it being right or not. And . . . to have to reexplain it and reexplain it, and you still not get it? These families have lost members and will never be able to see them again for the rest of their lives. Alton Sterling's son now has no father. For the rest of his entire life, he will never be able to have a relationship with his father. That should bother you as much as it bothers me.

Etan: Does it test your faith?

Reid: It does, and the thing that I always come back to is that the Lord's wisdom is almighty and it surpasses all human understanding. And I am sure that so many things happen in the world that I simply don't understand. Yes, I get frustrated. Yes, I get angry. Yes, I begin to lose faith. But I have to lean on my heavenly Father for strength to continue fighting. The Bible tells us that one day we all have to take that knee before God and give an account for our life, and people will be punished. I saw something the other day that said, if the punishment for sin was given immediately, people wouldn't sin. But it's given in the afterlife, and people will have to deal with what's coming. So that's what keeps me going. My faith, and Judgment Day, knowing that God will punish and reward people based on what they have done in their lives. And that's a far worse punishment than any jury can give any of these policemen who feel they got off scot-free. But here on earth, we are going to keep fighting for what is right.

Etan: What gave you the courage to be able to take a stand like that?

Reid: The answer again is my faith. Jesus walked this earth, He was ridiculed, He was mocked, and He was killed for doing His Father's business. And if He could give that perfect example and lose His life for doing what was right, I can handle some backlash from the media. I can handle some people hiding behind their keyboard and calling me names and telling me to leave the country because that's not real . . . So to me, it didn't feel like it took much courage just to take a knee for what was right, when I follow Jesus who gave His life to save mine.

Interview with Torrey Smith

Some football players took heat for not supporting Kaepernick, but many people didn't know about the internal discussions that took place throughout the entire NFL. My friend Torrey Smith, who once sat with me on a fatherhood panel with five of his fellow Baltimore Ravens, called me shortly after Kaepernick took his knee and told me about those discussions. Smith had been a 49ers teammate of Kaepernick's when the controversy broke out. You hear a lot of the Kaepernick critics saying that he was a "distraction" for the team and that he was "splitting the locker room" by taking such a controversial stance, but what I hear from the actual players is quite the opposite. Kaepernick's teammates voted to give him the Len Eshmont Award, named after the navy veteran and original member of the 1949 49ers, and given to the player who best exemplifies courage and inspiration. In this interview, Smith discusses his overall appreciation for his teammate's courage and the tangible ways it changed even what the 49ers did in the community. He also talks about the dialogue nationwide that was sparked and the effectiveness of that dialogue.

Etan: You don't seem to mind mixing it up on social media.

Torrey Smith: I'm never afraid to debate with anyone about anything. I feel that that's a right that we all have. Oftentimes, with athletes in particular, there is this thought that we shouldn't speak up about certain things, and I just don't agree with that. I think it's important to use your voice, and that goes for any and every person.

Etan: Isn't it interesting, though, that when people agree with you, they praise you for speaking out, but when they don't agree with you, then you hear, "Shut up and play and just do your job"?

Smith: *(Laughing)* It's the definition of hypocrisy. But that's just how humans are in general. People are all about what you can do for them and agreeing with you and being on your side when it is convenient or when it benefits them. Probably one of the biggest problems in our society is that people can't disagree and be at peace. There's always conflict. And people don't listen . . . I have always tried to listen to people who I don't agree with. To pay attention to their points and understand their points, and then form an opinion. And even if I don't agree with you, I can respect your opinion and your perspective, and I feel that when you are an athlete, people don't feel that way. They feel like if they don't agree with what you say or your perspective, then it just doesn't matter. You're just a dumb jock and you don't know what you are talking about.

Etan: There has been a burst of NFL players speaking out these past few years—not just Colin Kaepernick. How do you explain this new wave of athlete activism, particularly in the NFL?

Smith: I think, and this is just my personal opinion, currently there are conversations going on in the locker room that have never been had. I don't want to say never, but the depth of those conversations among different groups of people has been a game changer in these past few seasons. The way that police brutality has been brought to the forefront. Or racism, or Donald Trump as president, or bigotry. And you have people talking in the locker room who will view these topics with an open mind, and others who don't. You have people who are pro-Trump and like the fact that he is not like other politicians and isn't politically correct and doesn't play by any rules, and we have guys who are passionately against him and everything that he stands for. Guys that have said, "No, call it what it is." But we are having the conversations together. And we are learning from each other's perspectives to where guys are saying, "Wow, I didn't think about it like that." You have people who are personally affected by these police shootings on both sides.

Etan: Talk to me about what happened after Kaepernick took his stance. Did you guys start discussing those issues more, or was it basically just about whether he stood or not?

Smith: I think it was a combination of both. You had some people who were offended and some people who understood it. None of us knew that he was going to do this . . . This was something that he did on his own and he had been doing it for a few games, but no one noticed it. And when people caught wind of it, he spoke about it, explaining his positions and reasons, and I will always commend him for doing that . . . Even myself—we had a long talk and there was a point where I was going to do it with him, and I came to the conclusion that there were other ways to battle this. But I respect his way. So I gave him my support, told him how much I respect him and that I was going to continue to fight my way. But I didn't think that it was something that I would do. I was already active in the community for years and in the social justice space. I remember asking my dad what he thought about protest and if I were to take a knee. His opinion mattered because he served in the army for over twenty years. He told me that he didn't care either way and he fought for that right. He understood that it wasn't about the military and we have racial issues that need to be addressed. He supported my decision either way.

But what he did definitely pushed the conversation to the forefront, and down the line we will realize how important what he did really was.

Etan: He specifically said that this wasn't about the military. It was like the first thing he said. It's like that didn't matter.

Smith: Because people only care about what's important to them. "I think it's offensive, so I'm not going to listen to you. In fact, I'm going to call you selfish. And that you're against America. Even though you didn't say that." There are so many things history-wise that I personally wouldn't have known if it weren't for him doing that. From . . . talking to my dad about different things that happened in the military in terms of how African Americans were treated, or learning how at Pearl Harbor, Black soldiers were actually segregated in certain spots on that day.

Etan: You mentioned that down the road people are going to look back and appreciate this more. What do you mean by that?

Smith: I don't want to knock anyone who has been progressively in the forefront for many, many years, fighting these battles he has articulated, but what he did was help elevate that to a level that people wanted to reach. Or bring the attention to these issues in a way that people have been trying to for decades . . . Down the line, I think we will be able to appreciate that more as individuals and as an entire society, because things will be affected from the top down because of him.

Etan: It seems like the fans in San Francisco were pretty supportive for the most part, but San Francisco is also a very progressive place and these are issues that are commonly discussed and fought and addressed on the regular out there. But there were other cities and other fans who were irate.

Smith: I think that's exactly what happened, and what's interesting about this and what I learned from it, there's never a right way in their eyes to protest. You sit down on the bus in the front, people get mad; you protest and demonstrate and march, people get mad; you riot, people get mad; you take a knee or sit down during the national anthem, people get mad . . . But the way Kap did it, in terms of his actions, it got people talking.

Etan: You said that you decided not to do it necessarily Kaepernick's way but that you were going to fight the same fight your own way . . .

Smith: One of the things me and my wife believe very strongly and what we try to exhibit is taking care of your home and your household first. Educating yourselves and your children and preparing them and then branching out to help the community and mentoring kids and giving them the resources they need . . . After-school programs, computers, new books, technology. And we also teach them the things that people don't teach them. How to be a man, how to carry yourself. Knowing yourself, being yourself, and being comfortable in your own skin, and knowing that everyone in society is not going to always treat you the same . . . It's important because we have to be able to talk to our youth about how they have to react and respond when they interact with the police . . . There are different biases or flat-out racism that we have to deal with. That is just reality.

Etan: Very true. What are you doing in terms of directly fighting against police brutality?

Smith: Since Kap has brought that conversation to the forefront, I have been asking myself, *What would be a win? How do we win in this situation dealing with the police, because as long as the police officers carry the guns, there will always be deaths?* What we have been doing lately is visiting different police academies. Every away game we have been talking to a different police chief of that city to figure out what are they doing, how they are training their officers, so that I can go back and tell other people what they are supposed to be doing. We ask them, "Why don't you tell the things you are telling us to everyone in the public and in the community? Why is that not being communicated in terms of transparency?" There is a serious lack of trust by the community, for the most part, of the police as a whole . . . and a lot of the reason is the lack of communication and transparency . . . And honestly, certain things should be the same across the board. There needs to be some type of standard, and people need to understand or it needs to be explained to them exactly how the process works.

Etan: When you talk about what "we" have been doing, is that the team or your foundation?

Smith: No, this is the team as a whole. Our team owner has set up these meetings at these different police stations in the different cities after Kap took his stance and brought this to the forefront. The team donated a million dollars to grassroots programs who are trying to fight police brutality . . .

And let me say this: not all of the police departments had good policies, to be quite honest, but the San Jose police chief in particular was very impressive. If you could imagine what would be the ideal way that a police department should be run, he is it. And really, we have all learned a lot. It was good for me to see the good and the bad so that I can relay the information to the community and especially to the youth and say, "In this particular city, this police department has this policy, so you have to know that this is what they do." It's vital to have this information. For us to have these team events, and panels on a small level, I'm sure it will continue to grow as we all learn more about this. We will really be able to bring about change because we have communicated to some of the police departments our thoughts and opinions on their policies . . . We are having dialogues with them. And it really was all started by Kap taking that stance.

Interview with David West

It's important to note that Kaepernick isn't the first modern-day athlete to take a stance of this nature. Like Mahmoud Abdul-Rauf, whose interview appears later in this book, NBA veteran David West is another athlete whose protest actions have been largely forgotten. Many are unaware that David West has subtly been protesting the national anthem for many years, even before Kaepernick. I personally noticed him standing last in line and about three or four feet behind his teammates while the national anthem was being played before games back in 2004 when he was with the New Orleans Hornets. When I would see him, I would let him know that I respected him and the stances he was taking, and he would say the same thing to me. As the years rolled on, I would run into him at panel discussions and different events and hear him express his concerns about a wide range of issues that plague our society. He has a deep passion and articulates the specifics so well that it would leave the crowds mesmerized.

West took time out of his in-season schedule with the Golden State Warriors to talk with me about some of these particulars. They fall right in line with everything that Kaepernick has so eloquently discussed, and sometimes even go deeper.

Etan: You have been protesting the national anthem consistently for some time now. It may have gone unnoticed because it wasn't as drastic as taking a knee like Kaepernick. Talk about your reasons for standing behind the rest of your team during the anthem.

David West: During my second year in the NBA, we had a team meeting where we were asked by the owner to put our hands over our heart while standing for the national anthem. I raised my hand and simply stated my position. I told them that I wasn't going to do it . . . So me standing at the end of the line a step or two behind my teammates was something that I did solely because of that meeting. It had nothing to do with some publicized event . . . I wanted to recognize that there is something outside of this world that we are living in called *sport* or the NBA. That was always a reminder to myself. I see guys go through certain rituals before the game. Well, for me, that was something simple that I could do in that moment to reflect on how lucky I am to be doing something that I love; but at the same time recognizing that there is a greater seriousness to life outside of this little bubble called the NBA.

Etan: Did anyone attempt to talk you out of it? If so, what was your reaction and what was their reaction? Did you ever fear criticism from the media or fans?

West: I never feared criticism from the media or fans because I've always felt like I speak from a position of clarity. I speak from a perspective of honesty. I try to be as truthful as I possibly can in my declarations. Oftentimes when I speak out, it's not about me. It's not about David getting himself out in front of the camera or trying to be a lead activist. When I was outspoken about Donald Sterling and was one of the first people to call it what it was—straight-up racism—there was no other way to palatably express what he said in what he was trying to convey in that message. It was straight slave-plantation ideology and I wasn't ashamed nor afraid to say that . . . There is this logic that we will somehow lose out or we will be looked at as less-than if we speak about what is happening in society. I think that's false.

What I've found is that the fans appreciate intelligence. They appreciate the social engagement. It actually makes them feel better that the people they are supporting give a damn about what's going on in the world. I've actually had a greater response from people who appreciate athletes saying positive things because they know the type of weight our words carry with young people. Teachers are some of the biggest supporters. I've heard them say, "Thank God you said what you said," "I appreciate your words," etc. That's a constant I hear, because they appreciate us showing a different dimension . . . Now there is hope that you don't have to be one-dimensional. You don't solely have to be a dumb jock. You can read books, you can be socially and politically engaged . . . In order to present the greatest version of yourself, you must have different dimensions to who you are. Your professional experience, your personal experience, your societal experience, and your ability to critically think and express your thoughts through language help convey your message . . .

When it all comes down to it, you cannot be afraid to speak your truth, particularly when it comes to historical context. You cannot be afraid to tell history as it actually occurred, not what we want to feel about it, and not what we want to extrapolate from it or revise it . . . That in total is why I speak and why I don't have a fear of being criticized.

Etan: Here's a quote from a powerful interview you did with the *Undefeated*: "I can't start talking about civility and being a citizen if [you] don't even think I'm a human being. How can you talk about progress and how humans inter-relate with one another when you don't even recognize our humanity? We got to somehow get that straight first so we're on the same playing field." Those are powerful words. Can you talk about this in more detail?

West: I believe historical context is the most important context in this nation as it pertains to African Americans, African people in America, Black people, colored people, Negroes, people of color, or whatever other name or term that you want to endear to us. The root of all of these issues isn't just slavery. A lot of times people on both sides say we use the slavery card . . . When we are talking about police brutality, for-profit prisons, prisoner slavery, the death penalty, death row, undereducation, miseducation, mass incarceration, all of the different civic and social issues that we deal with as a group, in this country in particular and in most places around the world, you're going to find us at the bottom . . .

All of the socioeconomic indicators indicate that our group is lacking the most in this country. And those same socioeconomic indicators can be cut, copied, and pasted, and put on Black people in just about every other part of the world. We already know the degree to which Africa itself has been looted, destroyed, and robbed for hundreds of years continuously . . . The constant rape of the resources and the consistent torture and torment of the citizens of Africa mainly rest on this idea that we are not a part of the human family.

All of these ideologies have a contextual place in history where we know these ideologies grew from . . . To treat these people to the degree that they were treated, you must make them something other than what *you* are. So if you classify yourself and create sciences that put yourself in the elite status in terms of humanity, where does that leave those who you exclude from that class? That leaves them equal to or lesser than animals. Therefore, you can justify the treatment of those "things" or those "others" and do with them as you please. From this particular beginning, this is where you have the system that is currently in place now.

So you want to know how Tamir Rice gets killed in less than two sec-onds? It's because hundreds and hundreds of years ago, people began propagating these ideas that we were something other than human beings. That somehow we were not deserving or given the rights of humanity under God . . . The biggest fight we have is to restore ourselves as human beings on the field of humanity. And when you see what happened in Ferguson with Mike Brown and you listen to the language that Darren Wilson used to describe Mike Brown, that was a dehumanizing narrative. His size . . . his superhuman strength. This is Racism 101. This is Archaic Racism 101 being used in 2015. That's what we are dealing with . . .

If you want to address and get to the root cause of some of the social ills like mass incarceration and the crime that we face in our communities, start with education. Though we know that Black-on-Black crime is no different than white-on-white crime, nor any other kind of crime, because people that live in close proximity of one another tend to commit crimes against each other. What is shown and displayed via images speaks to a negative narrative that reinforces old stereotypes and generalizations. Other people have been trained and taught against us. They have been miseducated about where we sit and fit on the map of human existence.

Etan: What role has education had in your development and consciousness and awareness?

West: When I was younger, I struggled in school. Education wasn't something that I really knew the importance of . . . . As I got older, I realized the importance of staying in school and learning a method. I think that's what I learned in college—figuring out ways to research and develop intellectually. I also figured out the best way to manage my own thoughts, articulate my own ideas and my own sentiments in the best way possible.

Developing a *consciousness* is a key portion to your education. Your consciousness and your cultural awareness are of the utmost importance because it is in that cultural awareness that you are able to maximize the most of yourself . . . I think that's important particularly as we move forward and face the task of continuing to tear down these oppressive ideas and systemic roadblocks created specifically against our best interests.

Etan: Talk to me about the importance of your community work, and the level of influence you have as an athlete.

West: I was once in a bookstore in Charlotte, North Carolina, and I met an elder there. He began to tell a story about Malcolm X. He said oftentimes when people would meet Malcolm they would be overwhelmed and overcome with emotion. They would ask him, "What can I do?" and "How can I help?" Malcolm would always calm them down with his response. He would simply tell them, "Do your best work." Whatever it was that you felt like you could positively contribute to the struggle of Black people in this country for fair treatment and justice under the law, do *that* . . .

That always stayed with me. As I got older, it has never been about what people see. A lot of people don't know this, but I've volunteered and coached AAU basketball every year since I've been in the NBA. I give up a big portion of my off-season/summer to literally travel with and coach kids for free in the gym as a part of my service to them . . . We feed and have fed countless numbers of folks. I visit and have spoken in juvenile centers all over the country. I'm constantly engaging young people through various initiatives . . . What I do, I feel is what I best can do.

Etan: What do you say to the people who say that athletes should stay in their lane and just shut up and play?

West: I think that's kind of a dead issue. There is an obligation to speak if you are informed. There is an obligation to be informed as a taxpayer. For me, that has always made sense. If you are paying taxes at the highest rate in the land, you need to know about what's going on. And if it just so happens that you want to make a comment or two about what's going on, you have the right to do so.

You commonly can turn on the TV or radio and hear someone stating an opinion of what they are: as a father, as a husband, as a wife, as a mother, as a taxpayer, as a citizen, as a veteran, as a licensed driver, or whatever it is. They use those classifications to qualify their statements that they make about what's going on in society, but somehow athletes are exempt from that group. I don't think that standard should exist. If you're someone who is informed and has an opinion, you have the right to speak out. You're a citizen of the country. You're a taxpayer.

Interview with Shannon Sharpe

Shannon Sharpe is a former NFL tight end who played for the Denver Broncos and the Baltimore Ravens. He now cohosts *Undisputed* with Skip Bayless. Sharpe has been right to call the NFL on its hypocrisy and apparent blackballing of Colin Kaepernick. When Kaepernick's character is questioned and when he was accused of being a distraction for his team, Sharpe used his platform to point out players who have been convicted for domestic violence, drugs, DUIs, and so on, yet still get tryouts and are signed to teams—while Kaepernick remains unsigned. Sharpe also highlighted the blatant fabrications about Kaepernick, such as that he turned down this or that job offer, or that he refused to be a backup quarterback. With every rumor, Sharpe has been right there to separate fact from fiction.

Etan: So Kaepernick takes a knee. I want you to help us unravel why someone who is Black, who is Native American, who is pretty much anything but white, would feel a little differently about the flag.

Shannon Sharpe: I don't think that the issue was that white America couldn't understand; I think their issue was more of, "How could someone make millions of dollars and have the audacity to complain?" Their point of view was simply, "If you are making money, just make your money, be grateful, and be quiet." Colin Kaepernick said, "Yes, I'm making money, and a lot of money, but what I see going on is unacceptable." They made it about everything other than what he specifically said it was about. He specifically said it wasn't meant to disrespect the flag, or the military, or the veterans. He specifically said it was about the police brutality, the racial and social inequities, the political process. He listed his reasons.

Etan: It was almost as if he was invading their sacred football time. "Just shut up and play."

Sharpe: Of course, I get that myself. If I mention anything outside of the athletics lane, I hear, "Stick to sports." Mainstream America can look back at historic figures like Muhammad Ali, Jim Brown, Kareem Abdul-Jabbar, Bill Russell, and John Carlos and Tommie Smith, and respect them for taking a stance that was very unpopular at the time, but despise a current athlete for taking a stance they disagree with. They will say, "Well, that was a different time, they didn't have civil rights, they were fighting segregation, for voting rights. But now, everything is so good for you, why are you complaining?" So they don't value when a Colin Kaepernick invokes the courage of a John Carlos and a Tommie Smith to make a gesture that will be cemented in time.

Etan: Do you think it's difficult for mainstream America to understand and recognize that there actually *is* a problem?

Sharpe: They say the blindest man is not the man who can't see, but the man who *chooses* not to see. When something happens to an African American, and it is caught on tape, what is the excuse that is immediately given? "You don't know what happened leading up to that, and you don't know what happened after that." But let them show a Black person—not even shooting, but swinging on a policeman—there will be no, "Let's wait and see what the facts say or the investigation brings out." They would say the video speaks for itself.

But the video never speaks for itself when it involves an African American being brutally attacked by the police, repeatedly shot by the police, beaten, kicked, punched, tased, tortured, in ways that the public would lose their mind if they turned on the TV and saw a dog being treated that way . . . And then you see tapes of whites not obeying, not complying, sometimes even having a gun, sometimes after shooting people, but they don't lose their lives. They're taken into custody peacefully. You go out of your way to deescalate the situation. During the Kaepernick uproar, I spoke about the Florida State student who had killed two people, stabbed a Good Samaritan who had tried to intervene, was literally gnawing their face. A female police officer tased him . . . and they took him alive.

We saw Walter Scott, who was wanted on child support violation. He didn't kill anybody, didn't rob a store at gunpoint. He was running away, fleeing. He posed no threat to the officer, had no weapon, and the officer shot him in the back, and he hung the jury. So yes, as Kaepernick said, we definitely do have a problem that needs to be addressed and I am glad he used his platform to address it.

Etan: I didn't hear any of the critics address *any* of this. All they said was that he disrespected the flag, the military.

Sharpe: Let's talk about history for a moment. A history that apparently a lot of people have chosen not to remember. There were so many Blacks who fought for that flag overseas, but when they come home, they were second-class citizens . . . Frederick Douglass said it best: what does the Fourth of July mean to a slave? I would encourage everyone to read that speech or listen to it, because it is powerful. What does the slave get to celebrate? What freedoms did the Blacks who were fighting for that flag really have? I want rights too.

Etan: I just don't get why this is difficult for some people to understand.

Sharpe: No, people *choose* not to understand; they understand perfectly . . . I'm going to share a story, and I have never shared this with anyone else. I was probably ten or eleven, and this white kid told me that I had a hole in my jeans, which I did, and I told him, "You got a hole in your shirt and your jeans and you are dirty." You know what he told me? He said, "I may have a hole in my shirt, and my jeans, and I may be dirty, but at least I'm not Black." The worst thing was being Black. President LBJ said this—if you can convince the lowest white man that he's better than the best colored man, he won't notice that you're picking his pocket. Hell, if you give him someone to look down upon, he'll empty his pockets for you. I used to think that we were heading in the right direction; I definitely never said "postracial America," but I thought we at least were inching toward the right direction. But social media has allowed you to get a glimpse into someone's living room from thousands of miles away . . .

Now people have no problem tweeting or posting their racism. There used to be a time where people would hide behind their white sheets with their racism . . .

Etan: Isn't it interesting that the very thing the veterans fought and died for is the right to be able to sit or stand for the flag?

Sharpe: It used to be stressed that we utilize peaceful protest, but now they don't even want us to do that. Protest is supposed to make people uncomfortable, because if it doesn't take you out of your comfort zone, you won't be able to hear what I'm trying to get you to hear . . . They want to tell you how to protest in the way that is going to make them the least uncomfortable and generate the least amount of attention, which is exactly the opposite of what a protest is supposed to do.

Etan: So what would your advice be to athletes who want to use their position as a platform like Kaepernick?

Sharpe: A lot of times, you are going to have to stand alone in the beginning. But do not become frustrated, and do not become deterred. Realize that you are standing for something that is greater than you. There is a chance that you won't be around to receive the benefits from it, but know that your work doesn't go unnoticed . . . You know the rules. History will be the judge of Colin Kaepernick, not what the critics say now. And thirty, forty, fifty years down the road, he will be talked bout the same way we talk about Ali, Russell, Kareem, and all the rest of the historic Black athletes. Mark my word.

Standing Up to Police Brutality Matters

It was my junior year in high school in Tulsa, Oklahoma. I was on my way to a basketball game against one of our biggest rivals, Central High School. One of my AAU teammates, Demarco Hawkins, played on Central and for two weeks had been talking noise about how they were going to beat us. I was driving in my maroon 1978 Monte Carlo. I was proud of my car. My dad had bought it for me the summer before and I had saved up so I could get it painted, tint the windows, and install a new stereo system. It had whitewall tires and I kept them clean. That was "The Carlo."

So I'm driving down Pine Street and I see flashing lights in my rearview mirror. I looked at my speedometer to see if I was speeding—I wasn't. (I was and still am notorious for driving slow. My grandmother always tells me that I drive like an old person.) I checked to see if I had my seat belt on, which I did. I hadn't violated any law. I pulled over. Sirens blazing and lights flashing, the policeman just sat there. Then the backup car came. Then the backup to the backup. I heard a tap on my window. The policeman asked me to step out of my vehicle.

I asked, "Do you want to see my license and registration?"

He replied in a very sharp tone, "I ask the questions and give the orders here, boy, you just do as you're told."

I looked at him confused, but I obeyed his orders. He told me to sit on the curb and hand over my license and asked if my registration was in the glove compartment. I gave him my license and told him, "Yes, it is, but don't you need a warrant or something to be able to search my glove compartment?" He looked back at me with eyes that could kill, so I just turned away and shut my mouth.

As they searched my car, then huddled and talked, I heard one of them say, "I have seen his face before. I'm almost positive it was from a mug shot. Let's review some of these books and see if it matches. Are you running his plates? He's clean? I have seen him somewhere, I'm sure of it."

I glanced over and saw one policeman standing to the side, not conferring with the group. His main concern was obviously me and only me. He had his hand a few inches from his hip like one of those old Wild West movies when they are waiting to see who draws first.

To this day, I can vividly see the cars passing by, their drivers rubbernecking. I saw people looking at me and shaking their heads; I remember one little girl peering at me through the back window of her family's vehicle. I was embarrassed.

Forty-five minutes of this went by—them checking, huddling, talking—all while I am sitting on the curb like a criminal. I wasn't handcuffed, but I still knew better than to even think about making any sudden movements.

Then I heard one of them say, "Wait a minute, I know where you probably saw him and he had my gym bag in his hand. He plays basketball." See, they had seen my face in the papers but they thought they had seen me in a mug shot. So all seven of them started to go back to their cars, except for one guy who came over to me. "You're free to go, stay out of trouble," he said, patting me on the shoulder. I thought to myself, *ARE YOU SERIOUS!!!! That's an apology? No "I'm sorry for treating you like a criminal for almost an hour"? "For having you on the curb, embarrassing you in front of all these people"? "For wasting your time and making you late for your game"? "For dehumanizing you"? Nothing?* I looked over my shoulder and saw the same policeman who had been focused on me before. He had not moved. He was obviously waiting to see what my reaction was going to be. I wanted to cuss out every last one of them. I wanted to call them every name I could think of. I wanted to go *off*. But I didn't. Had I had chosen differently, I probably would not be writing this right now. I probably would not be here.

Driving to my game, I was so mad. I was late. Walked in while coach was giving the speech. Didn't say a word to anyone. Put on my uniform. Played like a man possessed. Dunked the ball every time I touched it. Blocked every shot. Fouled hard anyone who came close to me. After the game, I walked straight to the locker room, changed my clothes, and went home. Didn't really say anything to anyone.

My phone was ringing off the hook that evening. Me and my brother had our own phone line in the house and I told him to take the phone off the hook for the night. I remember replaying what happened in my head almost all night. Lying there, just me and my cat Gingy. It was like she could sense something was wrong. I remember her massaging my shoulders, which is something she did, and purring as if she was trying to calm me down. I remember lying in bed, my heart racing, and seeing the cops' faces in my mind. Them huddled up, talking. The one cop with his hand close to his holstered gun on his hip. The little girl looking at me through the back window. The nosy people shaking their heads as they passed by. Before I knew it, the sun was coming up and it was time to get up and get ready for school.

I remember being in speech-and-debate class the next day and talking to a girl I called Little Brandy. I remember just venting. Telling her what happened. What I should've told those cops. How could they do me like that? Treating me like a criminal. I had rights, they can't just hem somebody up like that with no probable cause. My speech-and-debate teacher, Mr. Bland, pulled me into his office. He listened to me vent—didn't interrupt, just listened. And after I was done, he said something that would change my life: "You should put all of that anger, all of that hurt, all of that passion, into a speech."

"A speech?" I replied. "Man, I'm not thinking about writing no dag gum speech, right now I'm pissed."

"This is the perfect way for you to express yourself. This could be your original oratory. You're always going around here quoting Malcolm X, even when Malcolm X has nothing to do with the conversation or the topic. This could be your chance to speak on a topic that you are passionate about, like Malcolm X did."

Well, that was the selling point for me and that's exactly what I did. I went home that night and wrote the speech Mr. Bland told me to write. I told the story of how I was treated by the police. I told how I felt. I talked about stereotypes, perception, racism, prejudice. I talked about how whenever I went down to Woodland Hills Mall I was followed around in the stores. I talked about white people crossing the street when I walked by or locking their doors. I talked about being treated like a criminal even though I had done nothing wrong. I put all of my anger and frustration and passion into the speech just as Mr. Bland told me to do.

I started performing the speech at different speech tournaments around

Tulsa, and I was winning. A lot. I won regionals, districts, state. Started going to national tournaments. Made it to the final round at Harvard University where I was competing against students from Ivy League prep schools from around the country. Many at first looked at me like I didn't belong there, but after they heard my speech they shook my hand and thanked me. So while Booker T. was winning state basketball championships back to back in 1995 and 1996, we also won the state championship in speech-and-debate. The newspapers picked up the story. I had a spread on the front page of the sports section in the *Tulsa World*. "More Than an Athlete," the headline read.

The Tulsa Police Department sent me a letter apologizing for what happened and saying they would do an internal investigation. Now, I don't know if anything ever came from that, but just the fact that they acknowledged it was a huge step for me at sixteen years old. I had found my voice. It was at that point that I realized this basketball thing was something I could use to my benefit. People would listen just because of the fact that I played basketball. I had access to the media. I could talk about issues like Malcolm X did. I could raise awareness, and I had to thank Mr. Bill Bland for opening my eyes to that.

Interview with Russell Westbrook

In light of how personal the Terence Crutcher case was to me, I was so pleased to see so many athletes speaking out about the murder. Athletes from all over the country voiced their disapproval:

Rajon Rondo: *Tell me this, how does an unarmed black man whose car is stalled and needs help get shot and killed by police officers, while the NY and NJ bombing suspect who actually shot at police officers gets apprehended and is alive? I guess being black is worse than being a terrorist.*

Dwyane Wade: *We must come together MORE! We must show our strength as a Black Community MORE! Or we will continue to wake up to stories of US being shot down like WE don't matter. We must show that we matter to each other MORE! We must all do MORE! #TERENCECRUTCHER #WEAREMORE*

Iman Shumpert: *Take a good look at my daughter Iman Tayla Shumpert Jr. The moment she was born was the day I saw the world a lot different. All day I wonder how can I raise her the right way and teach her the right lessons. I can't explain to her what's going on these days between the badge and the people. The badge was made to protect us, not scare us. #stealthefear #stealfear #weprayforpeace*

Through watery eyes, Tiffany Crutcher had explained to me how much it meant for players like Russell Westbrook to speak out on her brother's behalf. Even though Westbrook was an NBA superstar, an MVP candidate, an icon, he took the time to speak out passionately—and he did so in very conservative and pro–Betty Shelby, pro-police Oklahoma.

I played with Westbrook on the Oklahoma City Thunder in 2010. I have seen him grow and mature. When I was there, some of those guys were young kids. It was James Harden's rookie year. He actually came up to me the first day, shook my hand, and said, "Nice to meet you, sir. I grew up watching you play." I was like, "You grew up watching *me* play? I'm not that old."

Westbrook was talented, but young. Very young. So when I saw a press conference in September 2016 at which he spoke with fervor and fire about the Terence Crutcher murder, I felt proud. I caught up with him soon after that.

Etan: After Terence Crutcher was killed by the Tulsa police, you came out immediately and expressed your outrage and disapproval.

Russell Westbrook: I think it's important as an athlete, and specifically as a Black athlete, to be able to support something like this. To be able to support a family that's in need. I don't have an answer; in fact, nobody has an answer. If they did, we would be able to fix it, but somebody has to figure out something because this can't continue to happen like this.

Etan: Were you worried about any backlash from people who had a different opinion or just didn't like that you spoke up against this?

Westbrook: Not at all. I think that as an athlete and having the platform that I have, I have the courage and the confidence to be able to speak out and not worry about the backlash, to stand by what I stand for no matter who disagrees with me or not.

Etan: Did you receive any backlash?

Westbrook: Not that I saw, but I was definitely ready and prepared for any that would've come my way or any questions that the media would ask me about the situation, because it was a horrible situation and I definitely stand by everything I said.

Etan: Have any higher-ups ever told you not to be vocal or speak out on potentially divisive or controversial issues?

Westbrook: Definitely . . . but I was brought up a little differently, me growing up in the inner city, and for me to have experienced and seen some of those things day in and day out and night in and night out, this really hit home for me. I felt it was important for me to step up and say some things that I felt needed to be said, and by someone who has the platform that I have. Something has to change. So I'm going to use my voice as much as possible to be able to relay that message.

Etan: I guess I can understand some agents being overly cautious, but it really depends on the particular CEO for the particular team. Here with the Thunder, for instance, y'all have Ayana [Lawson, director of player services], who is absolutely great in community relations, and you have general manager Sam Presti, who at least from what I experienced is nothing but supportive of athletes using their voices . . . Does having that type of a supportive team help in you being so comfortable and willing to speak out?

Westbrook: Yeah, it definitely does help, but I wasn't really thinking about all of that at the time. I was just saying what was on my heart.

Etan: Did you get a chance to meet the Crutcher family? I saw that y'all wore the *TC* on your warm-up shirts, which I know the family really appreciated.

Westbrook: I think it's important. A lot of people don't think about the families when something like this happens. The children, aunts, grandmothers, sisters, cousins. I think it's really important that we think about how the family feels, because they are the ones who lost their loved one in a horrific way. It's important for us to be able to support a family in need the way they are right now. I can't even imagine the pain and everything they're going through. It's important for us to show them that we support them, have their back, and represent the family, because we know it's a tough time for them and for Tulsa.

Interview with Anquan Boldin

I cannot tell you how many TV and radio shows have invited me to appear in order to criticize athletes for not speaking out on crucial social issues. These critiques of athletes are not new. They have been articulated for years—in barbershops, bars, on social media, in various articles and blogs, from the everyday fan to the most celebrated scholars. But many are misguided and inaccurate.

What happened in Ferguson, Missouri, on August 9, 2014, was another catastrophe that affected so many people, including athletes, and especially those with kids. The death of Mike Brown, the young Black unarmed teen who was shot and killed by Ferguson police officer Darren Wilson, was a national tragedy.

According to a preliminary autopsy report, Brown was shot a total of six times—twice in the head and four times in the arms. Many questioned how someone could be struck in their right palm unless their hands were up. In addition, why would a police officer shoot someone in the top of the head . . . and then leave him lying dead in the street for hours? Some view the shooting as a public execution.

This is a parent's worst nightmare. Couple this with the apparent mishandling of the situation by the St. Louis Police Department. Wilson wasn't being charged with anything, but was put on paid administrative leave in an undisclosed location. This resulted in two weeks of unrest; police clashed with demonstrators in what resembled a war zone in a foreign country.

People were simply searching for answers, but couldn't find any. An entire community hadn't had the chance to breathe following the Eric Garner choking incident by the NYPD. Many were still healing from the deaths of Trayvon Martin, Jordan Davis, and countless others. On August 14, 2014, *USA Today* released FBI statistics that confirmed racial disparities in police shootings across the United States over a period of seven years. Data showed that a white police officer killed a Black person nearly two times a week in the United States, which was more than twice the rate of young white people killed by police. Nearly 18 percent of the Black victims were under the age of twenty-one.

President Barack Obama addressed the nation on the tragedy of Mike Brown's death, the violence that had occurred, and the overall issues that needed to be addressed—which included excessive police force and the people's right to assemble peacefully. He condemned those breaking the law, reassured them that he understood their frustrations, promised that he was doing everything he could to bring about justice, and spoke to the overarching issue: "In too many communities . . . too many young men of color are left behind and seen only as objects of fear."

Countless athletes—and entertainers, rappers, activists, authors, journalists—stood in solidarity with Brown and the people of Ferguson, and used their positions and their platforms to voice their disapproval and push for justice.

A group of players from the Washington NFL team (and, yes, I am referring to them that way for a specific reason—out of respect for Native American people), in a show of solidarity before their preseason game against the Cleveland Browns, entered the field through the tunnel with their hands up, referencing how Mike Brown reportedly had his hands raised in surrender when he was killed.

Wide receiver Pierre Garçon posted a photo on Instagram of himself and over a dozen other players from Washington with their hands up in the submission pose. He included the caption: *#HandsUpDontShoot We are all #MikeBrown.*

Kobe Bryant tweeted a link to an ABC news story about racial tensions in Ferguson. Allen Iverson tweeted a link to an Instagram post of him wearing a T-shirt that read, *Mike Brown.*

Garçon and his teammates had the courage and felt the responsibility to stand up for what they thought was right. The significance of the public demonstrations of solidarity by the entire secondary of the Washington football team and many other athletes should not be minimized. They are carrying on a great tradition of athletes and activism, and I applaud them for that.

Around this time, I was also very interested in what NFL wide receiver Anquan Boldin was doing with criminal justice reform. I saw him testifying to Congress on different occasions and was part of a coalition of athletes he brought together at the *Players' Tribune* offices in November 2016, in order to further the discussion on how we can affect change by utilizing our voices, our positions, and our platforms. What really impressed me was everyone's passion for bringing about real change. And not simply by raising awareness—which, don't get me wrong, is very important too—but by actually pushing for laws to be passed that directly address myriad topics under the umbrella of criminal justice reform. After the meeting, I caught up with Anquan and asked him about his passion around this issue and what he planned to do next.

Etan: Talk to me about when you testified in front of Congress about criminal justice reform and how that whole process started.

Anquan Boldin: It started when I did some work with Oxfam. My second trip with them was to Senegal. The problem in Senegal was that people were being taken advantage of as far as mining. The laws were so corrupt, it literally made me sick to my stomach to learn the details of what was going on . . . So I had a chance to testify before Congress about that, and we were able to get a number of mining laws changed . . . So doing that gave me the chance to see just how powerful an athlete's voice really is.

Etan: What happened to push you to go into criminal justice reform?

Boldin: Well, my cousin was killed by a police officer. He was in a church band, and he was coming home from a gig, and his car broke down on the side of the road. He was on the phone with roadside assistance, and this officer pulled up in an unmarked vehicle. He was dressed in jeans, white T-shirt, and a hat. So he pulls up, he doesn't know the call is being recorded because my cousin is on the phone with roadside assistance and they record all of their calls . . . He asks my cousin, "Hey, is everything good?" And my cousin is like, "Yeah, I'm good, I'm on the phone with roadside assistance." The cop says, "Are you sure?" My cousin responds, "Yeah, everything is good." He says it again, "Are you sure?" Then the only thing you hear is, *POP POP POP*. And then a couple minutes later you hear three more shots—*POP POP POP*. And he tried to act like my cousin was trying to escape from him or whatever, but my cousin was already dead. And the lady on roadside assistance just starts screaming, "Oh my God, what happened? Oh my God!"

So, that's what started me off on social activism and fighting for criminal justice reform—because what happened to my cousin had happened to a lot of different people. We never received justice for him killing my cousin. The officer is on house arrest. Still hasn't actually gone to trial. So I don't want for any other family to have to go through what my family has had to go through. I had a chance to testify before Congress about changes that needed to be made . . . And this second time I went, I wanted to take some guys with me. So I took Malcolm Jenkins, Andrew Hawkins, Josh McCown, Glover Quin, and Donté Stallworth . . . These were guys that I knew were well-respected in the league, and had been doing a lot of work in their communities. I wanted to bring guys who were serious about this work and also guys who didn't know how powerful their voices were. I wanted to show them the entire process and experience that I had with Oxfam America and the effectiveness of using my voice. We went in and got meetings with different congressmen and senators and were able to make an actual difference and get laws changed. That's power.

Etan: What has the reception been as you have come across different guys and have been showing them exactly what they can accomplish and achieve?

Boldin: A lot of guys were very surprised. They just didn't know that this was possible—to dialogue with actual lawmakers about making changes to the police system as a whole. We want to figure out ways to cut down on recidivism, which is a huge problem and a tremendous issue. Job training, rehabilitation, education. We wanted to come up with tangible solutions. Not just voice our concerns or tell sad stories, which everyone had, but we wanted results, and we got them. And out of that, we have built a coalition of athletes who are willing to come forth. There is so much curiosity.

Etan: Talk to me about Josh McCown. People know him as an NFL veteran, currently quarterback for the New York Jets, but they don't know his passion for this other work. And with him being a white player, it adds a different dynamic to everything.

Boldin: Josh isn't just another player to me, he's more of a brother . . . Now, bigger than me and him and our friendship is the issue at hand. So the public isn't solely hearing Black athletes discussing the unfair treatment in the criminal justice department and the need for police reform . . . Now you are hearing a white athlete speak on the same issues and fighting for justice right along with us. He will be able to reach certain demographics . . . whose ears are automatically going to be closed when they see a bunch of Black NFL players discussing police brutality and pushing for criminal justice reform. That's just a fact. And he knows this and discusses why that fact frustrates him as well, so I am really glad that he has joined us.

Etan: Do these topics divide the locker room?

Boldin: *(Laughing)* Of course you will get different opinions and different positions even within the racial dynamics. But the reality is, some guys on both sides just don't want to get involved. They don't want to talk about it . . . And I can respect that, because this isn't for everybody. You have to have this passion in you.

Etan: Talk to me about the players coalition. Your numbers are growing of like-minded NFL players who are focused on using their influence to push political leaders to make legislative and policy changes. Really great work you all are doing. What are some of the changes you want to bring about?

Boldin: In a perfect world, it would be equal across the board for everybody. The only way I truly see that happening is if you get man's heart to change . . . The only person who can do that is God. So where do we go from there? I think you have to deal with the laws that are in place that are discriminating against certain types of people. So that's the endgame for me . . .

So particulars: one of the things we have been pushing with criminal justice reform are mandatory minimums. Guys are getting these long extended sentences for drug-related offenses and that is just unbelievable to me. You now have guys sitting in jail for drugs longer than guys who have murdered someone in cold blood. That's absurd. And we're talking about nonviolent drug offenses . . . small amounts of drugs.

The way that has affected the African American community is just unreal. You have these guys locked up for decades, you have kids growing up in single-parent homes, you take the man out of the home, it's a ripple-down effect. Another thing we are trying to get changed is . . . for-profit prisons. This only leads to quotas being met by police officers in an attempt to keep prisons at capacity. I mean, how ridiculous is that? And then there's the recidivism. For guys who have been locked up, once they get out of prison, what do they have to fall back on? How do you reenter them into society?

We are also fighting to reform juvenile justice and end police brutality and racial bias in police departments. But criminal justice reform you can hit from so many different angles, because so much is wrong with it. And it hurts my heart to see so many of us—meaning Black and Brown people—being affected by this unjust system. So if we don't fight for it, who will?

Interview with James Blake

Enter James Blake. In August 2015, the former pro tennis player was standing in front of the Grand Hyatt in New York City, minding his own business, waiting for a car to pick him up and take him to the US Open tournament, when he was mistakenly tackled and handcuffed by plainclothes NYPD officer James Frascatore.

I remember seeing this story on the news and thinking to myself how great it was that he was using the fact that he was an athlete, and had access to the media, to tell everyone exactly what had happened to him. In June 2017, he published the book *Ways of Grace: Stories of Activism, Adversity, and How Sports Can Bring Us Together*, and more than two years after suffering the police harassment, his ongoing court case against them remains a national news story. This all takes me back to my own incident with the police while I was in high school, so I appreciated the opportunity to speak with Blake.

Etan: Take us back to what happened to you in New York.

James Blake: I was standing there waiting for my car to take me to the Open and it was a little strange because I had just received an e-mail through my website from an old friend who I was actually on the wrestling team with in high school, and we had this great exchange . . . Then I saw this guy out of the corner of my eye, running toward me, and he kind of looked like the guy I went to school with. He had a similar build and similar-shaped head, so I was thinking, *Wait a minute, is this him?* So I was actually smiling as the person was running toward me, but I quickly realized this wasn't someone who was coming for a friendly encounter or a high school buddies' reunion. I remember seeing the guy running toward me split the two doormen and I thought that was kind of weird. Why wouldn't he just go around them if he was joking around? It seemed kind of rude to just run right through them, and then of course five seconds later he picks me up and slams me to the ground. I had no idea what was going on, and I am so thankful now I get choked up sometimes just talking about it, because the whole thing could've been so much worse.

I didn't fight back or anything. I was so startled I didn't do anything. And he never identified himself as an officer or said "NYPD" or anything, but of course once he pulled out the handcuffs, I put two and two together . . . He screamed, "Keep your mouth shut!" and that was it.

I said, "I am complying with whatever you say 100 percent."

So he picked me up, put me in cuffs, and walked me ten or fifteen yards down the street, and I remember being completely baffled . . . I remember trying to communicate the fact that they definitely had the wrong person, and I said, "I don't know who you are looking for or what you are looking for, but it definitely doesn't have anything to do with me. If you want to tell me what you're looking for, I'll dispel it very quickly." They asked for my ID, and I told them where it was, and I told them, "The other thing you might want is my US Open credentials in my back pocket, because that's where I was going, so you can check that out if you want to find out what I am doing here in New York."

Now, the cop that did this to me just kept saying, "Okay, we'll see, we'll see," very dismissive. Then one of the cops asked me if I was working at the US Open and I said no, I was actually a player and I was going for an event there. They never took my badge or looked at it in any way, but they eventually told me that they had information that someone had been delivering things to me for the last two weeks or the last three weeks, and I said, "Well, let's go up to my hotel right now and I can show you my plane ticket, because I just got in this morning on the red-eye."

They kept just being dismissive and repeating, "We'll see, we'll see." So the fifth officer on the scene, which I believe was the highest-ranking officer, he started actually talking to me like a normal human being and . . . actually appeared at least to be listening to what I was saying. He kept looking at his phone, then looking at me, and I don't know if he was looking at Google Images or if someone had sent him a picture of who they were looking for or something to do with my ID, but he kept looking a little confused like he was thinking that something was not right here. He was the only one who actually apologized. None of the other ones did . . .

And I realized how incredibly shaken I was, because I didn't even think to get anyone's badge number or anyone's name or anything like that. I was just lucky that I had the resources I had to get a lawyer and have someone look into it, and I was unbelievably lucky that there was video of it, because if there wasn't it would've been my word against theirs and five cops would've said the exact same thing, that nothing happened, because before they knew there was a video, they put out a statement saying they were looking into the matter, and it only lasted less than a minute and they were not even sure if I was actually in handcuffs.

Etan: So they weren't taking any responsibility for what happened?

Blake: No, so I was really lucky that there was a video, and we found that out after I decided to go to the press. The interesting thing about that is the only reason I even decided to go to the press is after I spoke to my wife, she said, "What if that had happened to *me*?" You go through, you're a big boy, an athlete, you can handle it, take everything on your shoulders, but when she said that, I realized that I wasn't just doing this for me. So when I went to the press, I found out also that they had never filed a report. There was never going to be any trail or any record or any type of report that they just tackled someone at noon in the middle of Manhattan, so I was happy that there was an actual video because I know without a doubt that if there was no video, all of the policemen would've stuck to the same story that nothing happened and moved on, and that would've been it. I probably would've gotten a little bit of newspaper coverage because of who I am and because it was during the US Open, but other than that, absolutely nothing would've been accomplished.

And what's interesting is even before the video, I told my friends what happened and some people close to me, and their reactions were, "Oh man, that's terrible," but not really fully understanding. But then after the video came out, they said, "Oh my God, we had no idea how brutal that was or how serious you were about that." I remember saying to a few different people, "You're friends with me, I don't exaggerate, I told you what happened, but it still took the video for you to believe that something like that happened the way I said it happened." So I can imagine how the general public after first hearing about it and before the video was released probably thought . . . there is something else to the story because why would the police just tackle someone for no reason? . . . Like I said, I was really fortunate that there was a video because I don't know what the outcome of all of this would've been if there wasn't one.

Etan: So Officer James Frascatore of the NYPD didn't identify himself as a policeman?

Blake: No, he never said anything, which I am sure is a breach of protocol, and I think that's really one of the reasons why there can be so many miscommunications, if cops don't have accountability and are allowed to go unpunished when they clearly handle situations completely the wrong way. I think about this often, I think about how lucky I am that I'm not the type of person that gets freaked out by a situation like that. There have been plenty of times where a fan has run up to me and inappropriately given me a hug or . . . some type of overzealous fan appreciation, so I wasn't freaked out or anything. I honestly just stood there and smiled. I think most people's reaction when someone is running up to you is that you're going to put your hands up, you're going to defend yourself, you're going to try to run or something—that's just a regular instinctual reaction—and in talking to a lot of police officers who in my opinion do things the right way, they all agree that if I had done any of those things, it would've been a whole different story.

The injuries I did get would've paled in comparison. I have nightmares about what could have happened and I don't even have to say them, you know what could've happened. I think about how poorly he did his job, and there is just no accountability . . . You have to identify yourself as a police officer, and he never said it at the beginning. The only time he let me know that he was a cop was after he had handcuffed me . . . and he could see that I was visibly shaken, and he said, "You know you're safe with us, right?"

I looked at him and said, "No, I don't."

And he said, "Well, you are."

And you think that made me feel better? After he had just tackled me to the ground? I didn't feel safe at all. Like I said, after he pulled out the handcuffs, that was the only time I realized that he was a cop. After I saw the second or third cop come up after I was already handcuffed, I could see their badges on their belt buckles. But the officer who tackled me didn't have any badge, or I didn't see any badge. He was just this man who tackled me for no reason.

Etan: He did everything wrong, while you had to do everything perfectly right or your life would've been in jeopardy. That's just not a fair dynamic.

Blake: That's why I always say there needs to be some type of accountability in these situations. If I'm a cop that is doing my job the right way, I'm not afraid of accountability . . . Same as a doctor or fireman or any other profession. If you are doing your job the right way and you make a mistake, that's one thing. If you do your job in a completely negligent manner, well, that's what malpractice suits are about, and there should be that same accountability for a cop who is holding life-or-death situations in their hands. They need to be trained well enough to do what they're doing; they need to be able to handle those situations, and if they can't, there are plenty of other jobs out there that don't require life-or-death decisions to be made. So I definitely agree with you: it's more than a little unfair that the onus is on me or on the citizen in general, and that's why it's so frustrating to not have the accountability.

Etan: The officer who tackled you, James Frascatore, is the defendant in at least four earlier lawsuits alleging excessive use of force. These are repeated allegations, but it doesn't appear that the NYPD is doing anything to correct it. Am I wrong?

Blake: The more I find out about his history, the more frustrating this entire situation becomes, because it didn't just happen to me. I want him fired. The fact is that he has these previous offenses, but when I talked to the people who are there to prosecute him, the civilian complaint review board, they said none of those cases have been closed really. There is one that they paid out like $40,000 from the city, but he faced no consequences even mone-tarily, because that was paid out from the city and the others are still open and pending. I can't go into the court and present these priors as evidence just like they do with criminals when they have a long list of priors and their punishment is typically greater, but I can't use his priors because they are just delaying it and delaying it and delaying it, just like they are with mine, which happened in September of 2015, but he hasn't seen . . . any form of repercussions . . . He continues working and getting a paycheck since that day and will continue to get a paycheck. This is not going to make him hes-itant to do this again.

There is no deterrent. They are showing him that he can do this and he's going to get desk duty for a while and still make just as much or more money than he was before, and then be right back on the street like it never happened . . . The past precedent for a case like this is losing a few vacation days, and that's it, because it was set when it was just the police officers trying the other police officers. So it was their decision and their rules and they were obvious-ly very lenient. Now, when you have this complaint review board, they have to keep going on that past precedent. So when I asked for termination, they said that would make us look foolish, because it would make us look like we are favoring you just because of who you are . . . And I told them that we need to change that precedent because these things are reoccurring and there have been multiple offenses and mine was actually caught on tape. Losing ten vacation days is just a ridiculous punishment.

Etan: Isn't that interesting that they said they can't ask for termination be-cause it would look like they were giving preferential treatment, when this case would not have been in the news or brought to the public if you weren't who you are?

Blake: Right, which is what I said. I understand there have been cases that have been more severe, with worse injuries and more gruesome than mine, and those are just two of the pending cases on him. There are actually others, and add to that history and those precedents my case, which is actually on tape, which could be the tipping point and a lightning rod because that video is out there. That video has been on YouTube, it's been on CNN, it's been on *Good Morning America, The Today Show*, so people have seen it and people have seen how egregious this mistake was, and yes, the fact that I am who I am definitely made that possible. That's why this can help so many others who don't have that kind of access and that media availability. They can get something out of this by showing the public their dedication to getting one of the bad officers off of the street and showing the world that they are dedicated to running a clean department, etc.

You have so many officers who are doing it the right way, and guys like this have to know that they can't get away with these kinds of things. He has had more complaints than 90 percent of the police force have had in their entire career. In a twenty-five-year career, I believe the stats are that most police officers have less than four complaints and he has had five in like seven months. So why would you keep someone with that record on the force, and what message does that send to the world about the integrity of the police department as a whole?

Etan: So you're not going to drop this is what I'm hearing, and you're going to continue to push for termination instead of the regular protocol of losing vacation days.

Blake: Yes, I'm approaching this in a two-pronged way: in speaking with the city, and the city in my opinion is doing the right thing; in the meetings, they have been repeating that they want to do the right thing, they want to help, and they want to promote things together. They have expressed that they want a positive to come out of this situation and they are going to start a fellowship. This is going to happen soon—it hasn't yet, but they have ensured me that it will happen soon. They are going to fund a two-year fellowship so if someone comes straight out of law school, they will be instructed to handle cases like mine, where there aren't any major injuries but there is a civilian complaint.

This is good because these complaints, as I said before, are often not taken to completion, because they are usually dragged out and the people just drop it. I think around 45 percent of these cases don't even go to completion. So there will be someone specifically staffed to focus on these kinds of cases, and it will be on the city's dime. They're going to implement that and continue it for six years . . . and then review its effectiveness after the six years, so I am excited about that. The other part of that is the accountability for the officer, through the civilian complaint review board. And that has been so frustrating because it's not even a trial for criminal punishment or anything like that. It's just internally, for him to keep his job basically. So it was supposed to be in November initially. They adjourned it, they said it was going to be in January. I was just in New York to deal with that, it was supposed to be January 9; they adjourned it again without even telling us . . . He has to testify in some other case and they said he would have a tough time being truthful in this case because of the other case . . .

Sounds like a pretty lame excuse, to be honest. They told me they were just asking for fifteen vacation days and . . . that they feel that that's a win. I told them absolutely not. I want to go to court, and we have an actual trial, and if he gets off then, I'm going to publicize it as much as possible that this is what happened, because he should be held accountable to go through the process of at least resembling some form of justice. I will definitely publicize this as much as I possibly can and utilize every last one of my resources to do so.

Etan: That's why it's important for somebody in your position to speak out. They implemented an entire new program based on your case being brought to the public and you not simply being silent about what happened to you.

Blake: Honestly, my initial reaction wasn't even to think on those terms. I was so vulnerable at the time that I just wanted to forget about it and never think about it again. I just wanted the whole thing to go away, but thinking about it through my wife's eyes, that this could happen to someone . . . in a situation where the cop is completely in the wrong and the outcome is fatal, I later saw that I had the opportunity to do something instead of being selfish and brushing this under the rug and never talking about it again, I have the opportunity to help more people that this could happen to. And I have had so many people since then come up to me and say, "This kind of thing happened to me," "This kind of thing happened to my brother," "This kind of thing happened to my cousin."

And the other reaction I am getting from people is just utter disbelief that this actually happened to someone that they know. And even if they don't personally know me, they may be a tennis fan or they read my book and they don't know Walter Scott and they don't know Terence Crutcher and they don't know these other people who have been actually murdered. But now they have a personal connection to a case because the other cases just seemed so far away. For some people my case made it hit home for them and showed them that this could happen to anyone. And this made me realize that I needed to let people know that, yeah, this stuff still happens and happens way too often.

Etan: How could people think that this doesn't happen?

Blake: Well, one of the things you have to understand is the cops are the ones who are directing the media. With my case, and typically in most cases, they are the ones directing all the rhetoric, all the sound bites, all the press clippings, and it makes you realize how tremendous their PR machine really is. The way they handled this situation was really incredible. So, this happened on September 9. We tried to get the video from the hotel and they said they couldn't release it to us, but they could release it to the police if they got a warrant, so they kept telling us no, they can't give it to us. No, they can't release it, and we eventually said, "No, we are going to subpoena you if you don't give it to us," and they said, "Okay, we'll give it to you." They kept stalling us, this is after we subpoenaed them. "We'll give it to you, we just gotta get it all together and finish paperwork, etc., etc. Give us a half an hour we'll get it to you."

This is after we were done being cordial and nice, after we served them with a subpoena. So, in that half an hour they released it on their own, purposely on September 11 because they knew we couldn't make a big media thing against the police on 9/11. And in the days leading up to that, they kept saying that they couldn't release the picture of the person who they were actually looking for because this was an ongoing investigation, etc. "But rest assured, the person looked just like him. This wasn't racially based, just the person looked a lot like James Blake and it was an honest mistake that anyone could've made." Those were their talking points. Then they finally put out a picture, and sure enough, the person did resemble me, but then I find out that this person in the picture has been in Australia, has a famous sunglasses business there, and hasn't been in the States for like ten years.

But they wanted to control this PR by finding a picture and putting it out. I even wonder if they just found this picture on Instagram or Facebook or Google Images and found someone who looks like me. So people who haven't been following the story saw that and thought, *Well, yeah, the person does look like him and that was on the news so it looks like just an honest mistake.* And that's just how they have so much control over public perception through the NYPD's PR machine. If you're James Blake the plumber or James Blake the electrician, you have no chance of getting anything accomplished when you're up against this kind of a machine. You're completely at their mercy. You're supposed to trust the police. They're supposed to have your best interest at heart. Protect and serve, and a lot of people don't have that trust because of these certain officers that do their jobs the wrong way, and if I was a police officer who did things the right way, I would be just as upset at a civilian getting tackled because it makes their job tougher.

It makes the good cops' jobs tougher because now I'm scared. Every encounter I have with the police, I'm not going to go into it in a trusting way or think that they have my best interest at heart. I'm going to be scared that they're going to do the same thing again. And a lot of people who have been in a situation like this where they are a victim of police brutality are going to feel the same way, and that's completely unfair to the good cops.

Etan: Mayor de Blasio and NYPD Police Commissioner Bratton called you to apologize. You said that you appreciated their apologies, but their apologies weren't enough. You pointed out that had you been somebody else who wasn't a famous tennis player, you wouldn't have received an apology. It is really important for you to be doing what you're doing, so my hat's definitely off to you, sir.

Blake: No thanks needed. This is what I honestly feel I have to do, like I have no choice . . . I don't want to have one meeting—you guys apologize, take a couple of pictures—and then move on with my life as if nothing happened, because I know there are enough people who are not getting this type of treatment and something has to be done to change this.

Interview with Thabo Sefolosha

During my time with the Oklahoma City Thunder, one of my teammates was Thabo Sefolosha. My daughter Imani played with his daughters. My wife was very pregnant with Baby Sierra at the time, and his wife, Bertille, would come over to the house and help her. We were close. Thabo has a quiet, reserved demeanor. He is one of the most laid-back guys I have ever met. In the locker room, he would sit in the corner icing his knees and just listen to all of the guys debate about whatever the day's topic was. Which is why, when I saw how the news outlets, even the sports news outlets, were reporting Thabo's nightclub incident on April 8, 2015, how the police described him as though he had taken on an entire police force by himself, I knew that couldn't be the real story.

Other former teammates chimed in, like guard Reggie Jackson, quoted in the *Detroit Free Press*: "I think a lot of people fear Black males so it's scary. I'm not gonna lie, it's kind of unfair at times as a Black male. Only thing I feel protects us is probably the celebrity status and being an NBA player, but nobody is off limits when you see what happens to a former teammate like Thabo."

I had a particular issue with the absence of coverage on ESPN when this took place. It was almost as if they were acting like nothing had happened. Like Thabo was just missing in the Eastern Conference Finals because he hurt his leg by accident or something. It was weird. They just weren't reporting it and discussing it. The NYPD were actually on tape breaking an NBA player's leg, and it wasn't big news. I couldn't understand why. Especially given that there was a league-wide movement of players speaking out against police brutality and killings after Eric Garner was murdered. I was watching in hopes of a show discussing what had happened to my former teammate and someone I considered a friend—but nothing. It was as if there was an intentional media blackout.

I remember watching *Mike & Mike* and they were discussing how the Hawks would be able to guard LeBron without Thabo, and they barely mentioned Thabo's situation. They brushed over it, saying something to the effect of, "Well, he won't be available because of the situation we all know about." I literally repeated out loud, "*The situation we all know about? You* mean where the police broke his leg!!!"

I was glad to be able to sit down with Thabo and have him tell in his own words everything that happened, the action he took against the NYPD, and how this can serve as an example and inspiration to other athletes.

Thabo Sefolosha was a great teammate and a great person. Much respect to him for suing the NYPD after they unjustly broke his leg.

Etan: What happened in New York City?

Thabo Sefolosha: I was coming out of the club, and it was the night of the stabbing of a fellow NBA player, and as I was coming out, I see the yellow *Do Not Cross* line, so I go to the opposite side and I just stand there. So I am already many feet away from what was going on. One of the officers rushes at me and says, "You cannot be here, you gotta get out of here now." So I kept moving. I wasn't running away or even jogging away, and I still to this day don't know if that's what he expected me to do, but I was walking away. And he keeps pressing me in particular, and I'm looking around at all the people who are just standing around, but he is telling me to leave as if I did something wrong. I told him I was moving and I was following his orders. You can talk to people nicely. Just because you are an officer doesn't mean that you can talk to people that way. And he is just getting more and more agitated, and I have no idea why because I am following his orders . . .

So I kept going and there were three or four officers around me at this point, and there was an SUV parked there and I asked the lady if it was okay if we come in the car. So, as I am entering the car, this homeless guy comes up to me and says, "Do you have something for me?" I looked around to where the officers were because I knew that anything would be like a reason to do something, and I saw they were looking back at me, and I said, "Hey, I am just giving this guy some money," so I go and make a few steps and one of the officers jumped in front of me and pushed the homeless man away from me.

Etan: Oh wow.

Sefolosha: That was my reaction as well—I was shocked that he would actually push a homeless man who did nothing but ask for some money. So . . . I said, "Here, take this money," and that's when one of the officers grabbed my arm and said, "That's it, now you're going to jail."

Etan: They didn't say anything to your teammate who was with you?

Sefolosha: No, no, no. Just me. And my teammate was actually behind me, so he was closer to the yellow line. But once the one policeman grabbed my arm and said I was going to jail, I was so shocked I thought he must be joking . . . I didn't break any laws. I was literally complying with everything they were telling me to do. So I put my hands behind my back. I actually turned my back to him with my hands behind me, and I just kind of assumed the position because I was seeing that as ridiculous as this entire thing was, they were serious. One policeman grabbed my other arm and started pulling me to the left. And while he was pulling me, the one grabbing my arm on the right side started pulling harder, so I am being pulled in both directions.

Eventually somebody comes from behind, kicking me in my leg, and steps on my leg real hard, breaks my leg, puts me facedown on the ground, and puts me in handcuffs and takes me to the precinct. It was just crazy the way it escalated. The entire response from them was just uncalled-for all around. I understand that there was a lot going on with the stabbing and everything, but I wasn't a part of that, I wasn't doing anything wrong, and they singled me out.

To this day, I don't know exactly why; there could be a racial element to it. I don't like to call people racist, but there is a racial element in a lot of things in this country.

Etan: And your teammate . . .

Sefolosha: Yeah, he is white too. Pero Antić.

Etan: Right, and just to paint the picture of Pero, and you tell me if this is an exaggeration or not, but he is a big, bald-headed, tattooed, menacing, *Sons of Anarchy*–looking white guy.

Sefolosha: Yeah, he's pretty much like you described.

Etan: And they said nothing to him the whole time?

Sefolosha: Not until the end, and then they were looking around like, "Well, what do we do with *him*? Okay, well, let's arrest him too."

Etan: And they charged you with interfering with an ongoing police investigation, disorderly conduct, and resisting arrest, but you were offered a plea deal. Why did you reject it? And did that plea deal involve an admission of guilt?

Sefolosha: So the deal was exactly that. I would've had to do one day of community service, and after six months the charges are completely dropped. So there wasn't any admission on anybody's part of any wrongdoing. And that was the part that was completely unacceptable for me, because most people will say, "Oh, he didn't really want to go to court because somewhere he probably did something wrong and accepted a plea deal of community service." Also, I thought it was an easy way out for them for them to say, "Okay, you do one day of community service and we'll act like the whole thing didn't happen." Why would I have to do community service? You broke my leg, I didn't break yours. You violated me. I didn't violate you. I am supposed to just accept this and say it is okay? There was no way I was going to take that deal.

Etan: The media coverage was terrible.

Sefolosha: Yeah, but in the bigger picture, I was lucky. If the police want to do something to you, they have the power to. For me, it was breaking my leg. For other people, they were shot to death. And people will, in most cases, take the side of the police no matter what. Even if they see a video tape, they will say, "Well, maybe there is something we didn't see before the tape," or, "Let's wait until all of the facts come out." That's what happens, and people will believe whatever the police report says. And the media won't give the other side much of a chance to tell their side of the story before they make up their minds . . . Never mind if we are looking at the tape and see that I am in no way resisting anything. If the police say it, then it must be true.

Etan: That's just not your personality.

Sefolosha: People who know me know my personality and my character. But what I was worried about was the people who *don't* know me personally. Who only see me on the basketball court. Who will believe anything that the police and the media tell them . . . I couldn't allow people to think that I actually did the things they were saying I did.

Etan: So they still don't want to admit that they did anything wrong, even to this day?

Sefolosha: No, no admission whatsoever. And that's the problem . . . There are a lot of things that are wrong with the way they police in America as a whole. They have the authority, they have the power, they have everything on their side . . . If I would have done anything wrong, it would have been all over the news and all over their report and everyone would have said, "Well, he should've done *this* and they wouldn't have broken his leg," or, "He should've done *that* and none of this would have happened." But since I did nothing wrong, they had no choice but to settle. And the DA was trying her hardest to make me look bad and excuse what the police did to me . . . For her, it was just about winning the case for the police. It wasn't about truth or justice or any of that, just win at all cost. And they just made stuff up. The report early on, before we even got to court, was saying that I punched an officer in the face, and then they had to scratch that because once the video came out, you saw that didn't happen. And in a case like mine, no officer is going to lose their job or have a serious punishment.

But what about the people who get killed and they don't have a lawyer to defend them, or there is no tape, or they are not famous? What happens to those people? How easy is it for the police to get together . . . and say this is what happened, and nobody can do anything about it?

Etan: What has been the fan response to the police settlement? I know many people were wondering why you settled for four million dollars when you sued for fifty million.

Sefolosha: Well, it wasn't necessarily about the money, it was the principle . . . And after the settlement, people started saying, "Okay, well, maybe he didn't do anything wrong or they wouldn't have settled. Maybe he wasn't the one at fault." I feel like now, a lot of people are looking at me differently and not looking at me like I am a criminal or a bad person.

Etan: What advice do you have for young people if they have an encounter with the police?

Sefolosha: The main piece of advice would be to know your rights in your particular state. You can read it on the Internet, you don't even have to ask you parents or teachers to tell you. You need to know what the police can and cannot do legally . . .

Etan: I wish I had seen the same uproar in the media when you settled that I did when you were arrested. That bothered me.

Sefolosha: People want to believe the police, they want to look at them as the good guys, but everyone has to be held accountable . . . So I think that's the biggest issue—just not holding the police accountable. People's lives get taken away from them. People get traumatized, PTSD, scarred for life. They actually broke my leg. People have their entire lives changed and nobody is being held accountable, and until they start holding the police accountable, there will unfortunately be more cases of tragedy.

Coaches and Management
Using Their Voices Matters

In 2003, I made the choice to use my voice as a platform to speak out against the invasion of Iraq. I was playing for the Washington Wizards at the time in the nation's capital, so I was right in the middle of the heart of the activism. I wrote a few different poems and speeches about what was going on and began performing at local poetry spots. As I began performing more and more, I started meeting more like-minded people who would invite me to different rallies and events and demonstrations throughout DC. So I kept performing. Kept writing. Kept speaking out. I was now beginning to get standing ovations for my poems and speeches.

I really wanted to get my message out. I told the DC newspapers I wanted to write something for them about this topic and was met with a resounding no. John Mitchell of the *Washington Times* said he would love to print something on the topic, but there was no way that his conservative newspaper would ever be supportive. Steve Wyche at the *Washington Post* said that while they weren't anywhere near as conservative as the *Times*, the chances were pretty much slim to none of them ever running this story. I was thoroughly disappointed. I talked to these guys every day after every practice and every game. They were usually begging for some type of a story or inside scoop or something about the ins and outs of what was going on with the team, but when I had something meaningful to discuss, something that affected our entire country, they didn't want to touch it?

So I kept speaking at different events across DC. Some rallies had all of twenty-five people, others had hundreds, but whenever I got a chance to speak at a rally, I did. Then one day I was invited to a rally at the National Mall. I had no idea how enormous of an event it was until we got there. Malcolm was in a stroller at the time and my wife Nichole was pushing him around with the baby bags and formula and snacks and rattles and toys and everything else.

So we get to the Mall and there are literally thousands of people there. Dr. Cornel West was speaking and a person with headphones came up to me and asked me if I needed anything and said that I was on next. I was like, "Y'all got me following Cornel West? Could you put someone in between us or something?" He said he had seen me before and that I would be just fine.

So I performed a poem called "The Field Trip" and the crowd went crazy. Dr. West came up to me and gave me a hug and—I'll never forget it—said, "You young brothas gotta carry the torch. That was brilliant."

Dr. Cornel West called my poem "brilliant." I was interviewed by Amy Goodman, the host of *Democracy Now!* I ran into sportswriter Dave Zirin, whom I had met at an anti–death penalty rally, and he asked me why hadn't I talked about this to any of the newspapers. I told him that I tried but nobody wanted to touch it. He informed me that he was working for a small paper called the *Prince George's Post* (*PG Post* for short) and he would be happy to write it—and he did just that. The title was "The Anti-War Speech Everyone Is Talking About," and soon it was everywhere.

This was during the summer, so we had not officially begun practice yet. The next week I was at the Verizon Center working out and received a message that Mr. Pollin, the CEO of the Washington Wizards, wanted to speak to me in his office. When I heard that, I remember saying, "Well, I guess this is the end for me." I didn't really think this one through at all. Abe Pollin didn't ask anyone to talk to him in his office and definitely not in the off-season.

As I enter his office, Mr. Pollin has this big smile on his face. He shakes my hand and begins to tell me that his son attended the antiwar rally and was raving about my speech. He said he read the text and was really impressed. We then began to have a lengthy conversation about politics. We covered Iraq, the Bush administration, child malnutrition in Africa, Vietnam, inner-city schools . . . We even debated the gentrification processes taking place throughout the city. He told me of his dedication to building housing units for people at a range of different incomes, not just the high-income bracket.

Needless to say, I was very impressed. We looked up and an hour and a half had gone by. He told me to keep standing up for what I believed in and said not to be surprised if I received a tremendous amount of criticism, but that he respected the stance I was taking, and any way he could help or support me, to just let him know.

I went home and told my wife what had happened and she was just as surprised as I was. It was extremely refreshing to have someone in his position offer words of encouragement and support.

There is a notion, especially after the apparent blackballing of certain players like Mahmoud Abdul-Rauf, Craig Hodges, and now Colin Kaepernick, that athletes will be punished by the powers-that-be if they speak out. But I didn't suffer any repercussions whatsoever. Now, I don't know if my experience in DC was the norm, but I had no management pushback at all. As reflected in the following interview with the current CEO of the Wizards, the organization is continuing its fine tradition of supporting players when they speak out on issues that are important to them and their communities.

It was great to hear Ted Leonsis express so much support for the activism of the Wizards players.

Interview with Ted Leonsis

Etan: After everything happened with former Los Angeles Clippers owner Donald Sterling getting caught on tape making racist comments in April 2014, I noticed that you were one of the first NBA CEOs to condemn him. What prompted you to speak publicly?

Ted Leonsis: I acted organically, not coached and not handled. It was an authentic response . . . because his comments were just not acceptable in any way, shape, or form . . . I think the league acted accordingly, and Adam Silver had the same reaction that I did. When I watched Adam address this situation, I was so incredibly proud.

Etan: You said, "There should be zero tolerance for hate-mongering. Hate speech demonstrates an ignorance that is unacceptable, and I implore all of us to help eliminate any form of discrimination. I have full confidence that Commissioner Silver will conduct a thorough investigation and act accordingly upon his findings." And you issued this response almost immediately after the tape was leaked.

Leonsis: And I meant every word of it. Again, that was my natural, unfiltered, uncoached, unhandled response. That's what I felt in my heart, and I felt led to make that known . . .

You know, we expect so much from our athletes in the NBA . . . so if we are asking them to be exemplars and leaders in the community and really hold them to this incredibly high standard, why would we say, "Be with the people, but don't have an opinion on issues that directly affect the people"? Why would we tell them, "Don't get political"? . . . These are really experienced, intelligent people who probably know a lot more about what is going on in the community than we do . . . They know I am not going to attempt to silence them. I know a lot of players have their agents telling them, "This may be bad for business," or, "You're alienating this group if you do that." And my position, or my advice if I am asked, is, the worst thing for anybody is inauthenticity.

Etan: Do you think players on the Wizards now feel that they have that freedom and support from you and the entire organization?

Leonsis: Without a doubt . . . I think this next generation of players, the thing that is going positively for them is, they make a lot of money, and money gives people freedom . . . it gives them independence. So before, the prevailing notion—whether true or not—was, *If I talk about this subject, I may lose my sneaker contract or some other endorsement or sponsor.* Now, not so much.

Etan: Last summer, Philando Castile and Alton Sterling were killed by police officers. It was really a horrific time. Wizards guard Bradley Beal came out strong about those murders.

Leonsis: It was also very personal to Bradley. It was organic; he gave an honest, not-coached, not-handled opinion. And when I read it, I said, "Good for Bradley. He is letting his voice be heard." Bradley was definitely authentic and he had our full support as an organization.

To me, the only time I would ever get involved, or offer advice, is if I felt that someone had put you up to it. Or if I knew someone felt really strongly about something, and their manager or agent advised them to keep silent because it may hurt their chances of being successful with the Wizards. I would assure them that they have the freedom to speak their minds and to be passionate about whatever it is they are passionate about . . .

And I think these have become really big platforms for people. And each generation of players, their cognizance around the opportunity is becoming better all around.

Interview with Mark Cuban

I was part of Mark Cuban's first draft class in 2000. Myself, Courtney Alexander, Donnell Harvey, and Eduardo Nájera. Mark Cuban changed the way NBA CEOs conduct themselves. He was outspoken, argued with the refs, argued with David Stern, got fined, and kept arguing. One time in the Dallas Mavericks locker room (he was always there and had his own locker, something that I am pretty sure wasn't commonplace in the NBA), I asked him why he always argued with and criticized the refs. Didn't he know he was going to get fined?

He said it didn't matter, that if something was not right or fair, someone needed to speak up about it. "So let them fine me. Nobody is above being criticized, not even David Stern."

I was like, *Whoa, okay, this cat is different.*

I was very excited to interview Cuban. He has been outspoken about the Trump administration since the election. He has been an NBA CEO who doesn't dissuade his players from using their voices and speaking out. In fact, right around the time I was speaking out about the war in Iraq, Steve Nash, then on the Mavericks, was doing the same.

Steve Nash is a nineteen-year-career, two-time NBA MVP recipient with a dazzling highlight reel of passes that will keep him regarded as basketball royalty for a long time. But he also made a huge mark with his willingness to use his voice and his platform. After the US invasion of Iraq, Nash began wearing a T-shirt during warm-ups that read, *No War. Shoot for Peace.* He verbalized his perspective to reporters: "I believe that us going to war would be a mistake. Being a humanitarian, I think that war is wrong in 99.9 percent of all cases. I think it has much more to do with oil or some sort of distraction, because I don't feel as though we should be worrying about Iraq."

Nash's comments incited a backlash from the media; some journalists were outraged that a professional athlete had the audacity to criticize President George W. Bush, especially after all the newfound patriotism following 9/11.

ESPN's Skip Bayless, then of the *San Jose Mercury News*, not only told Nash to "shut up and play" but suggested that basketball players "are paid money because they serve as an escape." Dave Krieger of the *Rocky Mountain News* said that athletes "seldom know what they're talking about." But just as Abe Pollin did with me, Mark Cuban continued to give Steve Nash the support and freedom to speak his mind and stand up for what he believes in, as he continues to do today with the present-day Maverick players.

Etan: You have been very critical, to say the least, of Donald Trump. We talked to Steve Kerr and you don't really see that a lot with coaches, and you definitely don't see it a lot with NBA CEOs. So, what really pushed you to come out so strong in this election?

Mark Cuban: I was never really into politics all that much. Back when we drafted you to the Mavs, it's not like I was out there taking a stance in the

2000 elections, or the 2004 elections, or even the 2008 elections for that matter. And when Trump entered into the presidential elections, when he first got in, I was for it, shockingly enough. I thought he was honest, open, authentic, wasn't a politician, spoke his mind, wasn't scripted, and because of that, he put my quotes in his book and showed the world that I supported him. And I was really anti-Cruz. I thought Ted Cruz would be dangerous, plus he was smart, and that was a bad combination, so I said I'm gonna help Donald and see what happens. And the problem was, the more I got to know him . . . *(laughing)* the worse it got. So that led to the point of, do I say something or not say something? And seriously, the more I got to know him, the more it bothered me that if this guy wins, it's not going to go in the direction that I think this country should go.

Etan: So there were things that you did like about Trump at first?

Cuban: Well . . . I think corporate taxes should be lower. Put this all in the context of: there are things that we need to accomplish socially, and we have to figure out how to pay for them. But I'm a believer that with a little bit less taxes—not a lot, but a little bit less—the economy can grow more and that creates more tax revenues. It's not about reducing total revenue, it's about *increasing* total revenue . . . For every dollar you put into the government, instead of 90 percent going to the people who need it, 70 percent goes to the people who need it. When you try to start and run a business, there are so many rules that you need to spend a boatload of money on lawyers and accountants instead of just doing your business. And that's all the way down to the local level.

Etan: One of the things I did like about Trump—I do have the ability to point out something positive—was when he said that you can't become a lobbyist if you were recently working for the government.

Cuban: Exactly, and I like that he wants to reduce two regulations for every one you create, because it reduces the friction. My attitude is that we do need to help people, but if we are going to help people, let's do it the right way. The government right now has gotten so big and disconnected and bureaucratic that it doesn't accomplish the job it needs to do . . . And it's a little bit of a disconnect that he just wants that money to flow right back into people like me and my pocket.

Etan: The 1 percent.

Cuban: Right. And in reality, I'm not worried about it getting back to me. I just don't want the government to keep getting bigger and bigger, because it just won't work at some point. In his mind, the more money I have, the more money I will have to invest, and if I invest wisely, I can build bigger businesses that will benefit more people. It doesn't always work that way, of course. But if business invests more, you'll get a greater return on that money than what the government can. But there are still obligations that we have to our citizens and people who are disadvantaged, and I definitely believe that people should work for it, I don't believe in just giving anybody anything. So we may agree in the tactics, but strategically, we are just in a very different place. So I don't want people to think I am just some full-time, biased Trump-basher and critic . . . There are some concepts of his that I as an Independent can agree with. Now socially, that's a whole different story. What he wants to do with immigration, the EPA, rounding up immigrants that are illegally here, his implementation of ideas are so lacking and so *not* thought through, and ultimately so not presidential.

Etan: Talk a little more about the social part, because I could name quite a few problematic areas of his platform—the Muslim ban, the rhetoric, the racism, xenophobic rants, misogyny.

Cuban: That's the part that's appalling, to be quite honest. He has absolutely no leadership skills, no management skills whatsoever, and you see it with all the leaks. A good leader . . . would go office to office and say, "Listen, if you have an issue, bring it to me." He would ensure the people who work for him that he will hear their grievances and take into consideration their concerns, and they would come to some common ground . . . The reality is, if you believe in the economic stuff we just talked about, if he were a good leader, if he had the communication skills, he could go out and say, "You know what? I was a little abrasive during the elections, but I want to bring people together and here's how I think we can accomplish that." And he probably could get a lot more than the people who voted for him to support him. But to your point, he doesn't know how to deal with people. He is like that athlete you grew up with who passed school but never really did the work, where they would sit in the meeting and they would say, "What do you think?" And they just fake it till they make it. That's him.

Talking politics with Mark Cuban. He was as spirited in discussing Donald Trump as he is on the Mavericks sidelines cheering for his team.

Etan: So let's talk particulars. The Muslim ban: your thoughts?

Cuban: There are two sides to it. If you want to "keep us safe," just picking these six or seven countries is not keeping us safe. That does nothing. Now, if you want to improve the extreme vetting program for all refugees, then just say that. "I want to improve our system, and we are not picking out specific countries, or religions, or ethnicities. But anyone who is a refugee from anywhere, we are going to go through a more extensive vetting process for the safety of all Americans."

Etan: Well, if he would have said that, I don't think anybody would have had an issue.

Cuban: Right! That's my point. So on one hand, he was trying to do that, but on the other hand, he was proving to the people who voted for him, who showed up in masses, that he is exactly who they think he is.

Etan: He was using the dog whistles.

Cuban: Exactly, and of course everyone wants to be safe, but we want to be humane too. And reducing the refugees isn't going to change anything. It's not like President Obama didn't deport any refugees. But he communicated. Trump doesn't know how to communicate, even on an elementary level, and he loves to blow that dog whistle, like you mentioned earlier, just to get the people all riled up. And then Rudy Giuliani comes on and says how great the Muslim ban is and I'm just thinking, *They can't be serious here.* So one of the reasons I turned against him is that Donald Trump makes no effort to learn, really learn, not just read the footnotes but actually learn the issues. He hasn't read a book in thirty years. If you asked him about Obamacare, he couldn't detail for you what was wrong with it.

You saw that in the presidential debates. It wasn't even close as to who was more knowledgeable. He would say things like, "Obamacare is a death spiral." Really? Why, Donald? . . . He is just going to tell you what he has been told to say. And if you don't understand the issues, how are you going to understand the impact of immigration? How are you going to understand the impact of free trade or fair trade? How are you going to understand the impact of health care or human rights? You're not going to, and that's his problem. He's just not smart enough for the job.

Etan: So what do you think about the misogyny? I have daughters, you have daughters.

Cuban: You know, I have heard a lot in my lifetime, and if you wanna be a player, be a player, but abusing somebody and harming somebody, that's way past ridiculous. And I'm not going to name names, but I know some of the women, and it wasn't funny. It wasn't like he was just hitting on them, or even making questionable comments. It was like some crazy stuff, and it was wrong, period. And nobody cares who he is sleeping with—at least I don't—but if you are physically abusing people, that's a whole different issue.

Etan: I agree. Let's talk about the racism, especially during the elections. I mentioned the dog whistles, and we can see who he plays to in Texas, where you are from, and in Oklahoma, where I am from. There is a certain demographic that . . .

Cuban: Oh, you mean the rednecks.

Etan: I wasn't going to say that, but there is a certain demographic and it was troublesome to hear and see that demographic feel empowered because they felt he represented them. So they voted against their own interest, and he of course played to that, although he cares nothing about them.

Cuban: He knows exactly what he is doing in that respect. He may be ignorant and oblivious in certain areas—well, a lot of areas—but he knows exactly what he was doing here because it was an obvious strategy that proved to have worked. He knows the dog whistles, he knows he's inciting people, and I don't think he has a problem with it, and that's as scary as anything . . .

You know, I think resistance is a good thing. Especially in this case with Donald Trump . . . There's rarely fights, people aren't burning things; it's just people standing up and cheering and shouting what they think is right, and that's always a positive. I don't think he will last four years because he is so uneducated about governing that he'll screw up on something and not realize he did it and get impeached for something, because if you don't read, you don't know. If you don't know the rules of basketball, and you decide to just run with the ball without dribbling, it ain't gonna work. I want him to succeed, because the economy does well if the country does well. Even if you have someone that you hate at the top of the food chain, you can still do well. You don't always have to love your boss and you don't have to always like the people you work with.

Etan: Athletes are speaking out at a level that we really haven't seen since the sixties. Do you think that's a positive development, and do you encourage your players to speak their minds?

Cuban: Definitely. But in terms of the bigger picture, should athletes and coaches and CEOs, as you say . . . should they all speak out? Definitely when the Iraq War happened and we had Steve Nash who spoke out against it, and I was perfectly fine with that. Athletes should speak out. You're a citizen. It's your right to speak out. And if you don't take advantage of your rights as an American citizen, it's not about the game, it's not about the sport—it's about you. Of course, you don't have to do it. Everybody isn't politically outspoken or even has a political opinion. I avoided politics forever, but you should definitely have the freedom to do so if you choose.

Interview with Steve Kerr

My mother used to tell me how people would stop her in the grocery store, at the mall, at church, wherever, to warn her about various repercussions I could face from speaking out the way that I had ever since I found my voice in high school. People would warn her that no university was going to want to recruit a rabble-rouser. That proved to be incorrect, and although Coach Jim Boeheim and I may have had some strained relations over the course of my four years in college, he never once suggested that I should not be the outspoken person that I always was. From the day I was on the front page of the Syracuse paper protesting a policy that allowed campus security to use pepper spray on students, to when I was speaking out on the NCAA exploiting college athletes. Now, Coach Boeheim didn't agree with me and felt that it was perfectly okay for him to enjoy a lavish multimillion-dollar salary, his own radio show, TV deals, endorsements from Nike and various other companies, and that the "opportunity" given to college athletes was more than enough compensation for us. Still, he never attempted to silence me.

In fact, I just recently commended Coach Boeheim on using his platform to bring about change when he spoke out for the need for gun control after his nine hundredth win. He became the third coach in NCAA history to win that many games, and he seized that moment when he had the ear of all of college basketball to say: "If we in this country as Americans cannot get the people who represent us to do something about firearms, we are a sad, sad society. I'm a hunter. I've hunted. I'm not talking about rifles. That's fine. If one person in this world, the NRA president, anybody, can tell me why we need assault weapons with thirty shots in the thing. This is our fault. This is my fault and your fault. All of your faults . . . If we can't get this thing done, I don't know what kind of country we have."

Of course, not every situation is like the ones I have had. But from college with Jim Boeheim, to the pros with Mark Cuban, to Abe Pollin, to Coach Eddie Jordan who was also very supportive of my activism, to Sam Presti, to Scott Brooks who told me that he had read a few of my articles over the years and thought that I touched on a multitude of topics that were difficult but very necessary for people to discuss—I just didn't experience what I always heard people were afraid of. Now, there are definitely people who have experienced repercussions, such as Mahmoud Abdul-Rauf and Craig Hodges, but that was then and this is now. We are living in an age where for the most part athlete activism is being encouraged and met with praise. Again, you will always have people who will criticize, but it is unnecessary to have the same fear of repercussions as so many people once had, especially when you have so many coaches who themselves are using their platforms and their voices to speak out on different issues, such as Golden State Warriors head coach Steve Kerr.

After the 2016 elections, Kerr spoke passionately to the media about his thoughts on Donald Trump. He said that not only did he disapprove of the lack of respect that Trump had shown so many, but that he was outright disgusted. In his own words:

Maybe we should have seen it coming over the last ten years, you look at society, you look at what's popular, people are getting paid millions of dollars to go on TV and scream at each other, whether it's in sports, or politics, or entertainment, and I guess it was only a matter of time before it spilled into politics, but then all of a sudden, you're faced with a reality of the man who's going to lead you has routinely used racist, misogynistic, insulting words . . .

I hope he is a good president. I have no idea what kind of president he will be because he hasn't said anything about what he's going to do . . . But it's tough when you want there to be some respect and dignity, and there hasn't been any. And then you walk into a room with your daughter and your wife, who have basically been insulted by his comments, and they're distraught. Then you walk in and see the faces of your players, most of them who have been insulted directly as minorities. It's very shocking, it really is.

I was glad to be able to sit down with Coach Steve Kerr and ask him to go into this subject a little deeper.

Etan: What pushed you to speak out the way that you did and as strongly as you did?

Steve Kerr: I think just the injustice that I was seeing. There are a few issues that I am particularly passionate about, one being gun control. My father was murdered, so gun control is always something that I am very passionate about, and that was really the first issue that I brought up with the media about a year ago. So, that kind of opened up the door a little bit. Then the elections came and people started asking me for my opinion and reaction . . . In the past, the media didn't ask me about political or social issues. But between the Kaepernick situation and the elections, athletes were all of a sudden being asked more and more about these topics.

Etan: Did you have a conversation with your players after the election?

Kerr: Yes, we talked leading up to the elections, and we talked the very next day after the elections. I asked the guys how they felt the day after, and everyone was extremely upset, but we had a great discussion about it and it was great for us as a team. Everyone had a chance to vent, which was definitely needed for them and myself. It was a very intense discussion, but we needed it. I like to get the players' opinions and for them to have a voice and to think about things other than basketball all the time, and it was really productive for us to do that, especially at that moment after the elections.

Etan: Trump's misogyny: how did that affect you as a father and husband?

Kerr: My daughter and my wife were so disgusted when the tapes came out of Trump talking about grabbing women by the you-know-what. You start examining the totality of the situation and you start thinking that this man is in the most important leadership position in the world. Forget politics, forget policy, forget gun control or abortion or tax laws, forget all that—there are always going to be people on both sides of those issues—but dignity, human respect, those things are the most important things in a leadership position. And the only way to get through the issues that we argue over year after year is through genuine human connection and respect and communication, and those things have to start at the top. So when all of a sudden you see the guy who is going to be leading your country using these profane remarks and treating people like dirt, that's pretty upsetting.

Etan: Do you think that more coaches speaking out is a sign of the times and how drastic of a situation we are in with Trump?

Kerr: I think it's a couple of things. First of all, I think there's definitely a call to action right now that maybe didn't exist over the last twenty or thirty years . . . But you're right, coaches in the past have generally not been at the forefront, it's been mostly players. But I think the connection with Pop [Gregg Popovich] and Stan [Van Gundy] and myself is that number one, all three of us feel very comfortable in our own skin . . . We have had success so we have some job stability and security. But beyond that, I don't think that any of us really have any fear about being fired over saying something that is just, if that makes sense . . .

Etan: So you think the same pressures on players not to speak out are on coaches as well?

Kerr: Maybe even more so, because I think coaches are definitely representatives of the organization. Whereas players are viewed more as the labor force and coaches are more perceived as being on the management side. And I had that conversation with our owner, Joe Lacob, and I was very sensitive to the fact that I . . . was representing my views . . . I wanted to make that clear to Joe, and he and I had a really good discussion about this. He was very respectful of my right to speak and I was respectful of the idea that I needed to toe the line a little bit and make sure that people understand that these are *my* remarks and not the remarks of the Golden State Warriors organization.

Etan: How were your conversations with the team about the Kaepernick situation?

Kerr: Well, I asked them how they felt about it and I reassured them that they had the organization's blessings to do whatever they wanted and whatever they felt was right, but they also had a responsibility to let us know beforehand because it directly affects the perception of our franchise . . . and that we had to prepare for the best way for the organization to react to people's responses to that. But I reiterated that they were grown men and American citizens and they could do anything they want . . . I think with Kaepernick, we all saw his message become more refined as it went, and he did a great job of seeking counsel from people—for instance, going from sitting on the bench to kneeling, I thought that was a great step for him. It showed more of a respect for the flag.

Etan: It would be great to see more organizations and more coaches follow your lead and the Golden State Warriors' lead in how you give them the freedom to be who they are. Would you like to see that become more prevalent as well?

Kerr: For sure. I think that's just my coaching philosophy all around, whether dealing with politics or the game itself. I ask our players all the time: "How do you want to guard the pick-and-roll? You guys are the ones on the floor. This is what I suggest, but what do you think?" And I believe it empowers them and I think the same thing should be true with off-the-court issues. "You guys are grown men, what do you think? Your opinion matters. But understand that if you're going to speak out, make sure that you are informed on these matters." I think that's where some people can get in trouble: if they are not quite informed on a subject but they bring the subject up. It's easy to get cornered . . . so you better be prepared and ready to stand up for what you believe in and what you think is right.

Interview with Kenny Smith

When a coach like Steve Kerr has conversations with his team after Trump's election, and he can teach and learn at the same time—that's how it should be. He gave them the space to vent and air out that anger and talk about it as a team. That's how coaches should handle their players. Respect their opinions and give them a safe space to voice them while also being secure that what they say can't and won't be used against them. I can't stress how important that is. Not only from a standpoint of respecting their opinions, but from one of team unity. It brings guys together. As one unit. You are able to learn more about your teammates and what affects them and what they are passionate about.

On November 14, 2017, *Time* magazine published an article by Detroit Pistons head coach Stan Van Gundy in which he wrote the following:

> *After reading the book* Tears We Cannot Stop: A Sermon to White America, *I invited its author, the acclaimed scholar and expert on race Dr. Michael Eric Dyson, to come talk to our team. He discussed the difference between nationalism and patriotism, and it stuck with me. Nationalism, he said, is supporting your country no matter what, right or wrong. Patriotism, on the other hand, is caring so deeply about your country that you take it as your duty to hold it accountable to its highest values and to fight to make it the very best it can be. Under this definition, these athletes and coaches are role models of American patriotism.*

I wanted to ask *Inside the NBA*'s Kenny Smith how important it was for coaches to use their platforms, and he brought up a lot of good points. A former NBA player turned commentator, Smith talks about the effectiveness of having someone like San Antonio Spurs coach Gregg Popovich publicly speak on various social issues. How some people are simply going to hear it differently coming from Popovich or Coach Kerr. That's just a fact. I remember being floored by Pop discussing white privilege in an article. He was simply asked the question what Black History Month meant to him and his response was priceless: "It's a celebration of some of the good things that have happened and a reminder that there's a lot more work to do. But more than anything, I think if people take the time to think about it, I think it is our national sin."

He went on to say, "It always intrigues me when people come out with, 'I'm tired of talking about that,' or, 'Do we have to talk about race again?' The answer is, you're damn right we do. Because it's always there, and it's systemic in the sense of when you talk about opportunity, it's not about, well, if you lace up your shoes and work hard, you can have the American dream. That's a bunch of hogwash. If you were born white, you automatically have a monstrous advantage educationally, economically, culturally . . . We have huge problems in that regard that are very complicated, but take leadership, time, and real concern to try to solve. It's a tough one because people don't really want to face it. And it's in our national discourse."

But he didn't stop there. He continued, "We have a president of the United States who spent four or five years disparaging and trying to illegitimize our president, and we know that it was a big fake, but he still felt for some reason that it had to be done."

I remember seeing the clip of Pop saying that and being like, *Wow!!! I never would have imagined that he felt that way.* I remember seeing Coach Stan Van Gundy speak after Trump was elected and again was floored when he said: "I didn't vote for [George W.] Bush, but he was a good, honorable man with whom I had political differences, so I didn't vote for him. But for our country to be where we are now, who took a guy who—I don't care what anyone says, I'm sure they have other reasons and maybe good reasons for voting for Donald Trump—but I don't think anybody can deny this guy is openly and brazenly racist and misogynistic and ethnic-centric . . ."

Powerful, powerful statements. Never before have so many coaches in any sport used their positions and their platforms to speak about an election in this way. We are definitely living in a special time.

Etan: How significant is it for coaches and management to use their voices around social justice issues?

Kenny Smith: I think it is vitally important because, when you think of your coach, a lot of people relate that to a father figure . . . So, how could a coach, who is coaching Black players, and is seen as a father figure, not have some form of Black consciousness? . . . In addition, them having Black consciousness is a great awakening to the masses who they also touch. And that's why it's vital that Steve Kerr, Stan Van Gundy, Popovich, and Cuban are all a part of this activism. It will make them allies to further the cause. It wasn't important to the masses in the sixties until non–African Americans thought it was important.

Etan: They speak to an audience who is not going to be able to hear Colin Kaepernick.

Smith: Unfortunately, some of us have the mind frame that if it's not happening to *me*, then why should I be concerned about it? So those coaches saying, "No, it's not happening to me, but I am concerned and bothered and frustrated by it," that raises a different type of awareness that I don't think we could do on our own.

Etan: Who surprised you the most?

Smith: Steve Kerr and Van Gundy. Only because Steve Kerr has typically been very quiet and mild-mannered, and he spoke with so much intensity . . . And Stan Van Gundy just blew me away because of the passion behind it . . . as if he himself was experiencing this. Or that it happened to his brother or father . . .

Etan: Moving from the NBA ranks to the high school ranks, there were a lot of coaches who collectively with their team took a knee. What did you think about that?

Smith: I never understood the problem that people had with Kaepernick . . . If you think about this, how can we as a country not support that? He took a knee in order to make a statement, and he explained his reasoning and his logic very eloquently afterward, so whether you agree or disagree with what he was actually saying, how could we as a society not support his right to do so? I thought it was beautiful what he did. I thought it was beautiful what the college players and high school players did. I thought it was beautiful what the WNBA did. But for people to be upset with them to the level that they were upset just baffled me.

Etan: A lot of the young people are saying, "We protest, y'all are mad, we riot, y'all are mad, we speak out, y'all are mad, we take a knee, y'all are mad, and then we're killed by the police, and y'all are silent."

Smith: I have a little bit of a different viewpoint. I think that it's almost like they *want* you to be violent. When you riot, they expect that and they can accept that. And they know how to react to that. But when you . . . express your opinions and your viewpoints eloquently, as Kaepernick did, and as a lot of the high school and college athletes I saw did, that's more intimidating. They don't know how to handle that. The thought-provoking responses are met with more hostility. Intelligence is probably the sharpest weapon and intelligence is feared . . . You are mentally challenging me and I can't handle that, and it makes me even more angry. That's what we dealt with then, and that's what we deal with now.

Etan: I coach AAU and I know you do as well. How important is it for a coach to also be a mentor, specifically at the amateur age?

Smith: I have been blessed to have great coaches who were also great mentors . . . Basketball teaches lifelong lessons, and we should utilize sports as a vehicle to be able to instill those lessons into our young men. I think the educational value that sports can provide is severely underrated. People think that it's all about winning and getting buckets, and it's absolutely not. I have a kid on my team and I was talking to his parents, who were telling me that they felt their child should be playing more, and that they were considering moving him off the team because they were not happy with the amount of playing time that he was getting. So I told them, "Your son is going to go to the next team, and he is going to play about the same amount of minutes."

But on my team, he has a quality he's learning that is far beyond basketball. If Johnny says, "Let's all meet over here at ten," every single one of the players will be over there with Johnny. Some CEOs don't have that quality . . . And his parents were completely unaware that he had that potential inside of him, but I have been nurturing and encouraging that, and it will be invaluable to his character far beyond his basketball career, wherever that may take him. So you would be doing him a disservice by removing him for a situation that is nurturing a special quality in him.

Etan: How important is it for the *Inside the NBA* crew on TNT to use your forum to educate and lead in the same way we were talking about?

Smith: Well, it wasn't always that way, but I think as of late, it has become that. I think that Charles [Barkley] has a lot to do with that, honestly. Even though we may not like some of the things he says, his ability to bring unique ideas and nonbasketball vernacular to our show all started with him, and people have to recognize that. People look at us as the voice of basketball, and it's important for us to be able to tackle all types of issues, and to not shy away from anything if that's what's on the hearts and minds of the people. We are not the game, but we are the voice, for sure, and we have separated ourselves to be able to make that statement.

Interview with Adam Silver

Like Ted Leonsis, the commissioner of the NBA, Adam Silver, has said that he values and respects the opinions, thoughts, and beliefs of the players even when he doesn't necessarily agree with them. The NFL, obviously, with what we are seeing happen to Colin Kaepernick, may be quite different, but when I spoke with Silver, he expressed great pride about how he personally values activism.

Etan: What makes the NBA different from other leagues?

Adam Silver: I feel like I really only know *this* league, and I will say that, to me, I inherited a legacy of activism within this league. People like Bill Russell, who not only was an activist in terms of things that mattered in society, but also even on behalf of player rights. Bob Cousy, another person who I've gotten to know well over the years in the league, who is one of the founders of the Players Association along with Oscar Robertson. There was a precedent and a history here at the league of using the league and our players' voices on important issues that mattered far beyond the game of basketball . . . I like to think it would be no different at any other well-run company that has highly valued employees. It's critical in this day and age that your employees do feel that they have a vital voice about the direction of the company and about the conditions under which they work.

And so, when the Donald Sterling matter happened, my first instinct was to turn to our players, and at the time, Chris Paul not only was a member of the Clippers, of course, but he also was the president of the union . . . We quickly established a rapport in terms of how we were going to deal with this situation. A lot of credit goes to Kevin Johnson, former player . . . Kevin happened to be leading the search for a new executive director at the Players Association, so he was also someone that, in essence, I could partner with at the time . . . We could talk through the implications of Donald Sterling's statements and what made sense and how as a league we should react . . .

I will say, what is special about this league and something I've worked very hard at, is making sure that players feel safe having a voice on important societal matters, because I've heard from employees in other industries, other companies, athletes in other situations, where they have told me they have a strong point of view but they're concerned that it will have a direct impact on their employment . . . I think that because of the strength of the Players Association, players have felt comfortable and safe speaking out on issues that matter to them . . . In fact, we've made it a point to encourage players to be active participants in our system. To have a voice . . . They have a point of view about what's happening around them. I qualify it by saying "in a respectful way," but that's just me.

Etan: With the Donald Sterling situation, none of that happens if you don't listen to the players, you know what I mean? None of that happens if you don't make the decision to value what the players actually think and feel.

Silver: Right. Well, again, I'd say that we are a league that is roughly 75 percent African American. The speech in question here was, of course, directed at African Americans, and I felt that the players had life experiences that I, by definition, could not have had . . . I felt it was very important to understand from a player's point of view exactly how those words were impacting them. And to understand even from them what their expectation was in terms of the league reaction and also how it was affecting their ability to do their job. Because, remember at the time, it happened early on in the playoffs, but the Clippers were very much alive in the playoffs. Even in fairness to Chris, and others on the Clippers, who were being asked by some people to boycott games, to stage protests, that they also were focused very much on their game and basketball, understandably. In part, they were looking to me. They wanted to let me know how they felt but they were also looking for me to lead . . . I think for many of the players I spoke to, they were not in a position to even know the range of options that were available to them with the league.

The answer is yes, it was my job to bring all of those points of view together. Whether those be the players, whether it be other NBA owners, business partners of the NBA. So that then became my job: it meant that I had to be the ultimate decision maker. But again, having the support of all these various constituencies and the players' willingness to talk with me directly and share their feelings . . . was very impactful on me.

Etan: What you are saying, just so we are crystal clear, is that you have pretty much given them a safe space—as long as they speak respectfully, of course—to utilize their voices and follow in the tradition of Bill Russell, Kareem, and Oscar Robertson, without fear of repercussions.

Silver: We are not a political party, we're a business. But I also feel as a business in this day in age, especially when I think of our young fans, and we probably have the youngest fan base of all the major sports, that there is an expectation that we are going to stand for something . . . What I have tried to encourage among those players, and even among our fans, is to not become one-issue voters when it comes to the NBA. There is a type of person who can say to me, "Well, if that's your position, I'll never watch an NBA game again." I really made an effort with those people to say, "Well, all right, but just because we disagree on this issue, I would hope that ultimately you would respect us for having a point of view, and I'm very interested in understanding why it is you disagree with us . . ." I've had those same discussions with some of our players, and some of our owners for that matter as well. The Sterling issue seemed very straightforward; some of the others we've been involved in have not been as straightforward. There are genuine policy disagreements. But there I felt, once again, we have this platform and sometimes it's a platform just to encourage dialogue . . .

People have made the comparison of our arenas to modern-day town halls. You have people from different walks of life all coming together for a common purpose to cheer for a team or cheer against a team, and we should be mindful of that and encourage people that it is safe to express a point of view. It doesn't mean that they have to agree with you, but what I would like to encourage back is that people would respect the league. Respect our players' point of view.

Standing Up for Black Lives Matter Matters

On July 17, 2014, Eric Garner was choked to death by NYPD officer Daniel Pantaleo. It was videotaped and afterward shown on a continuous reel on every major news station. Although NYPD policy clearly prohibits the use of choke holds by its officers, that didn't stop Pantaleo from literally choking the life out of Eric Garner while arresting him. No weapon was found on Garner, nor was he suspected of any other crime outside of selling "loosies," a term for single cigarettes out of the package. To make matters worse, at the end of 2014, after hearing the case for two months, the grand jury decided on December 3 not to indict Pantaleo for the killing of Eric Garner.

A few months later, in February 2015, the NBA All-Star Weekend was held in New York City. The killing of Garner was fresh on everyone's mind, with the event in the very city where this tragedy took place. I wanted to do something meaningful. Something powerful for the New York City youth who were understandably upset about what had happened. So I decided to hold a Black Lives Matter event. I wanted to do it for all the young Black and Latino men and invite different NBA players to discuss Black Lives Matter, including the recent killings by the police and how the youth can survive in a system that is built for them to fail.

I connected with Canaan Baptist Church in Harlem and they were more than happy to host the event. I warned Pastor Thomas Johnson that the program might be met with some controversy and criticism—considering how this would be happening during the NBA All-Star Weekend, and just coming off of the Eric Garner murder. The pastor told me that his predecessors in the church always prided themselves on activism and community engagement.

I connected with Paul Forbes and his Expanded Success Initiative program, and with some administrators at New York City public schools, who were also extremely interested in their students taking part in this event. The church's capacity was a little over 2,500, and within a few days we had exactly 2,500 students confirmed to come. I reached out to Alonzo Mourning, Isiah Thomas, John Wallace, Chris Broussard, and Kevin Powell. BET connected me with actor Hosea Chanchez and we had our panel set.

As discussed earlier in the book, I then reached out to Emerald Snipes, daughter of Eric Garner, and invited her to participate. I told her she didn't have to speak if she didn't want to, but I wanted her to come if she felt up to it. She said she would be there.

Once word started spreading, there were a lot of people who didn't like what they were hearing and didn't want to see it happen. They attempted to pressure me and the church not to hold the event, or to water it down to the point that it resembled an NBA Cares program (no offense). Some NYPD officers said it sent the wrong message. Their key problem was with the term *Black Lives Matter.*

My family proudly wearing our Black Lives Matter shirts together.

Interview with Bomani Jones

I wanted to delve further into the misrepresentation and misinterpretation of the phrase *Black Lives Matter* with Bomani Jones, the sports journalist and ESPN cohost of *Highly Questionable* with Dan Le Batard. Naturally, he had many thoughts and opinions, as he has covered this topic multiple times.

Etan: I want to read a tweet of yours from a few years ago: "Why can't people just be honest and say, 'I really don't care if black people die'? The excuses sound every bit as racist. We're not fooled." I would love to hear you expound on that quote.

Bomani Jones: Well, when an unarmed Black man is killed by the police, we wind up playing these intellectual games where the attempt is made to justify the fact that somebody has been killed. No matter what happened. For instance, Officer Darren Wilson, who killed Mike Brown, got over half a million dollars raised for him on Facebook and GoFundMe with the title "Support Officer Darren Wilson." Half a million dollars!!

Etan: Well, Daniel Holtzclaw, the Oklahoma City police officer who was accused of sexually assaulting eight different African American women while on duty, raised seven thousand dollars in less than a week before GoFundMe was forced to take it down, but I'm sure his numbers would have ended up being comparable to Darren Wilson's had it remained on the site.

Jones: And that's just my point. That's absurd! And the only thing that people know about these cops is that Darren Wilson killed an unarmed Mike Brown, or Daniel Holtzclaw raped and sodomized a bunch of Black women, and they donated! They said, "You know what, I would like to support this person and give my hard-earned money to them."

So what winds up happening—if you start from that point, and think that's something that should be rewarded, to do that means you have to justify whatever the action is . . . And they end up stacking up all of these nonsensical reasons and it leaves the rest of us to wade through all of this "logic," because those people wind up getting the benefit of the doubt where we have to respect their perspective and disprove it before we get to any other discussion. And instead of dealing with the reality—that the value of the lives of Black people are placed lower than the value of the lives of everybody else in this country—we end up having to justify the forensic evidence and everything else and try to debate every ridiculous possibility that is raised as a justification for the police yet again killing this particular unarmed Black man . . . It would be a whole lot easier if people would just tell the truth. Just say, "Hey, we don't care about the lives of Black people."

Etan: And that's why the term *Black Lives Matter* then becomes a "controversial statement," which it really shouldn't be.

Jones: There isn't anything really bold about the statement *Black Lives Matter* . . . You would think that the response to that from more people would be, "Of course they matter, why wouldn't they?" We didn't even say that it matters a lot, just that it matters. They can't even give us that it matters *at all*? Not even a little bit? It has to be met with the opposition of, "No, all lives matter"? . . . Instead of them asking themselves, "Why would this subgroup feel the need to point out that their lives matter? What is going on in society to make this subgroup feel that their lives don't matter?"

Etan: Shortly after LeBron and D Wade and Chris Paul and Carmelo made their statements regarding Black Lives Matter before the ESPYs, you said that while you were glad they spoke out, you wanted to hear something from the white athletes who haven't by and large been very vocal on this topic.

Jones: Not only that they aren't speaking on it, but they aren't being asked to speak on it. They aren't even asked to pick a side, lend their voice, use their platform to "bring about change" like the Black athletes are consistently asked to do. The police are treated in the discussion as whiteness, right? It's Black people on one side, and we have the police on the other, which I believe is also telling . . . But nobody really asks white players to weigh in on this discussion in any way, shape, or form . . . And if we're going to be honest about this, mainstream America, if I may use your term, would be more apt to listen to a Peyton Manning or a Tom Brady or a Kevin Love if they had something to say on these matters. White athletes could have a tremendous effect on not only the psyche of the masses of mainstream America, but they could move the needle toward actual justice. There is tremendous unrealized potential and unused power . . . because white athletes are simply not asked or pushed to enter into the discussion, and that's really unfortunate.

Etan: There is this notion out there, with Black media especially, that if you do speak on this you will be punished. Would you agree?

Jones: I think generally speaking that people would prefer not to offend. I think no matter the topic we are discussing, people would generally not want to isolate people, or lose supporters, and overall not offend anyone. And I can't necessarily knock people for that because I can see where their point of origin is. Now, as far as the thought that you will be punished for saying certain things, you definitely run the risk of doing that . . . I do feel there are people who fear that those who are "on top" will punish them for stating what these views happen to be.

Etan: Do you think that some reporters and media personalities put the fear of offending mainstream America over the fear of offending the people in their own community?

Jones: *(Laughing)* Yes, people do put the fear of offending mainstream America over the fear of offending the Black community. I think people think that the community will understand their hustle and what it takes to get to the position they want to get to . . . I think it is far more harmful and far more toxic if someone is willing to come out and say something they don't believe just because.

Etan: Maybe they would get a pat on the head from the executives. Maybe they would be rewarded by being moved up the ladder past other people who don't always say what mainstream America wants to hear. So if someone wants to see them tap-dance, they bring their shoes nice and shined and ready, even if they don't like tap-dancing and it actually hurts their feet to do so. It's the price they pay.

Jones: Hmm, okay, I see what you did there *(laughing)*.

Etan: But do you disagree?

Jones: No, I don't. It happens.

Etan: I remember seeing you on *Mike & Mike* wearing the T-shirt that said, *Caucasians,* with a caricature of the Cleveland Indians logo. I live here in DC and we've been having our own battle with the racist name of our Washington NFL team. But you knew that by wearing that shirt, and drawing that connection to the topic of mascots and the level of offensiveness they possess, you were going to offend people in mainstream America. Take me through the reaction you received when you wore that shirt.

Jones: You know, the funny part about that was I am probably the only person in America who didn't see or realize how that was going to go over when I wore that shirt.

Etan: Really? How did you think it was going to go over? Did you think mainstream America was going to draw the conclusion that, "Yeah, I would be offended if a team had a mascot of my people like that," and see the error in having Native American caricatures for so many sports teams across the country?

Jones: Well, when you say it like that . . . *(laughing)*. But yeah, I thought that it was so transparent and so obvious. I mean, we have been having the mascot conversation nationally for some time now. This wasn't like a new discussion that I brought to the forefront or anything. The only thing about that shirt that turned out to be bold or anything was that I found out that a whole lot of white people were really offended and didn't like the notion of the word *Caucasians.* That was perhaps the most surprising thing about it . . . It's not like it said *Pale Faces* or anything like that. *Caucasians* was just about as technical of a term that we could have possibly used . . .

I thought that the logic was so clear and so transparent that if you tolerate and are comfortable with the notion of the Cleveland Indians, then you cannot have any issue with this shirt . . . But the hypocrisy of it all—that all you had to do was make a simple flip-flop with a nonoffensive image and they would be that irate—was just amazing to me. And the funny thing is, if you asked someone to logically break down why they were so upset and why they were so offended, they wouldn't be able to.

Etan: What was the reaction from the people at ESPN?

Jones: Well, I didn't have any disciplinary issues or anything like that, and I think part of it was, nobody was in any position to logically say what I had done wrong when they use that same image on *SportsCenter* when the teams play.

Etan: Do you think it would take something like flipping all of the cases of Black people being killed to them all being white in order for mainstream America to understand why we say Black Lives Matter?

Jones: That's a really good question. I honestly don't know the answer to that. I don't know if it would make those same people make the connection to Black folks, just like me wearing the shirt didn't make them see the connection to Native Americans like I thought they would. The ultimate issue is, there is a different set of rules when dealing with Black people than there is when dealing with white people. There is a different level of empathy when mainstream America hears that a Black man was killed versus when they hear that a white man was killed . . .

Etan: I was hoping it would make them open their eyes to say, "Oh, this is what Kaepernick was talking about, this is what John Carlos and Tommie Smith were talking about back in the 1968 Olympics, this is what Mahmoud Abdul-Rauf and Craig Hodges were talking about in the nineties."

Jones: But you know what? There are some people who do make the connection. I don't want to make it seem like nobody connects those dots, and hopefully, when people are reading this and hear us connecting those dots, it makes them think about this in a way that they never had before. But I think you will in fact find a lot of people who are more offended by a false accusation of racism than they are by any racism whatsoever, and I feel that they are defending their own self-esteem as much as anything else, because everybody wants to believe that they are good people . . . So Black Lives Matter in a lot of ways is about self-esteem, but in a totally understandable and justifiable way. Look, we matter, and we are going to reinforce the fact that we are fully human beings and that we should be treated like human beings. That is an assertion of one's self-worth.

Interview with Bradley Beal

After the back-to-back murders of Alton Sterling and Philando Castile, Washington Wizards guard Bradley Beal tweeted out the words *Black Lives Matter* around two a.m. on July 8, 2016. He was surprised to have been met with an onslaught of *All Lives Matter* responses as well as criticism about his timing, being that police officers were also killed in Dallas. One person wrote, *Lost respect for you,* while another wrote, *Disgraceful.* Beal did not issue a hurried response or a heartfelt apology to any of the *All Lives Matter* fans; instead, he offered a fervent statement on Instagram.

Beal is not someone who takes this topic lightly or simply gives a knee-jerk reaction. He is about doing the work. He attended one of President Barack Obama's town hall meetings on the topic. He went not only because he was a Black man, but also because he was a Black athlete. He felt that he needed to hear the firsthand accounts, the experiences, the tragedies, and process everything. He has attended Obama's speaking engagements before, and he has a desire to become more involved with My Brother's Keeper, an initiative that aims to couple young men of color with mentors to address racial inequality in America.

Beal doesn't believe that athlete activism is some type of a fad that will fade away and transition into something new. He believes that as long as injustice prevails, there will be athletes who feel a strong responsibility, and who step up to the plate to use their positions in ways that will push for change. He acknowledges that it may make some people uncomfortable, and may cause him to lose some of his own fans, but that's a price he is definitely willing to pay for standing up for what is right.

Bradley Beal took time after practice to talk to me about Black Lives Matter and his willingness to speak out despite any criticism that comes his way.

Etan: We interviewed Ted Leonsis, the CEO of the Wizards, and he was saying how proud he was of you when you stood up and spoke your mind after the deaths of Alton Sterling and Philando Castile. When I asked him whether athletes will be reprimanded if they speak out on certain issues or controversial topics, he said that that's not what they do here with the Wizards. Is that pretty much your experience here, that you have the freedom to speak on whatever it is that is on your heart?

Bradley Beal: Sure, because at the end of the day, we're still human beings, we're still a part of society. I think people sometimes get it misconstrued because they see us as athletes, they see us as role models, and they see us as celebrities, and that we are conformed to not speaking. And I will admit, some of us think that there is going to be too much backlash if they do decide to voice their opinion, so they remain silent and just stay out of it completely. But we live in a free country, and yes, our job description reads to play basketball. But at the same time, we are still citizens of the United States, and we are members of society, so why should we not be allowed to voice our opinion? Why should we not have a say in our everyday surroundings? About things that deeply affect our everyday lives?

If there is something that needs to be brought to light, professional athletes have one of the highest platforms to do so . . . What we say holds a lot of weight, so I feel that regardless of what backlash may come our way, or whatever people's opinions may be . . . you're voicing your opinion about something that needs to be brought to light as you personally see it . . . And when you say it, you have to stand on it. You can't be that person who straddles the fence when the criticism and pushback comes your way.

Etan: One of the things I saw after you spoke out was the criticism that immediately followed. And it was really harsh. And as you said, you didn't back off or retract your statement.

Beal: No, you can't do that.

Etan: Let me refresh everyone's memory to exactly what we are talking about before we go any further. After you received the criticism, your exact words were:

> *So b/c I say Black lives matter: 1. I don't think ALL LIVES MATTER 2. I'm in favor of cops being killed? Some people are ignorant af. The issue at hand regards my race and I have every right to speak on it! If you don't like it, it's a big ass UNFOLLOW button on the top of my page. Saying all lives matter is like saying we all need air to breathe! We all know that!!!! Killing a cop is no better than a cop taking a life! Innocent black lives are being taken by those sworn to protect and serve, not murder! When does it come to an end? And you wonder why people rage? We aren't getting justice, just more body counts! People are getting sick of this sh*t. So yes, Black Lives Matter!*

After I read this, I was applauding in my living room. Because it was so strong and to the point and answered all of the criticism you were receiving, all of the attempts to twist and contort the message of Black Lives Matter, all the ridiculous attempts to divert the issue. But let me ask you this: did the criticism surprise you?

Beal: Honestly, it was just something that I felt needed to be said. I couldn't just stay quiet and say nothing while I have this tremendous platform. But the criticism didn't surprise me at all, really. It saddened me to see where we are as a society. You would think that some of the tragedies—like these two with Philando Castile and Alton Sterling—were tragedies that happened decades ago back in the sixties and civil rights era. These are things that we are supposed to be reading about in our history books, not experiencing in this day. So it made me sad reading some of the mentions on Twitter and some of the criticisms, because this makes it clear that some of our mind states are still there, that we haven't progressed as far as we thought we have.

So in that aspect, you pay attention to it, but then again you don't, because it's about what's right. Regardless of who it may have been, it's simply not right. That's not how human beings should be treated, that's not how those sworn to protect and serve should do their job, and that's not the way someone should lose their life to never be able to be with their families again. People don't understand—these aren't just cases or hashtags, these are actual people with children and families. Little daughters who will never see their father again. If that doesn't bother you at least a little, then something is wrong with you.

Etan: Definitely agree. If we were talking about the Holocaust and we said the lives of the Jews mattered, I don't think people would answer back with, "No, no, no. Not just the Jews—all lives matter."

Beal: Yeah, it's ridiculous. When people heard me say that Black Lives Matter, they just immediately responded with . . . All Lives Matter. And you can't even begin to explain how heartless that comeback is. And I like that you made that comparison, because people need to see it in those terms. That would make people see how absolutely ridiculous the criticism is. Well, it *should* make them see it. And these killings by the police are on TV now, you see video clips of it, where you can see clear as day what happened. Why wouldn't we say anything, but even more so, why wouldn't the entire country be in an uproar? Why are you okay with what you have just seen? Why doesn't it affect you at all? Why does your heart not ache like mine does after seeing this? Why would you not feel the urge to do anything to help this situation? Why would you not feel sympathy for the people who are going through this, but attempt to use that moment to proclaim that your life, which is not being taken away, is just as important as the people's lives who are being taken away?

Etan: I do a lot of panel discussions and speaking to youth across the country, and I tell them that no matter what they are seeing in the media, with every police shooting, every not-guilty verdict, that their life does in fact matter. And a lot of the people who have those criticisms don't understand staring out into a sea of hundreds of young people's faces—Black young people's faces, girls and boys—and have them look at you like you're telling them something they've never heard before, or like they have a hard time believing their lives actually matter. Have you experienced that yourself?

Beal: Unfortunately, I know exactly what you are saying and have experienced that myself. That's why I tell people, and other athletes as well, when they ask, "Do you feel that it is an obligation to be involved, or to speak out to raise awareness, or to speak at schools to young people?" I wouldn't say it's an obligation, but you *should* do it. Granted, everybody made their own way to the NBA, and everybody has their own life to take care of, but at the end of the day, we are still role models to kids. Some kids will only hear that positive message that their life matters from *us*. Imagine that, having the power to be able to instill a personal pride in a young person who didn't have that before you spoke to them?

That's a great power and responsibility to have. Us as athletes, we have the biggest platforms, especially NBA players, because we don't have helmets on like the NFL players, so people know you, they know your face, they know your product, they know your brand, and they know your life. You can relate to them on a level that somebody else may not be able to. My mother used to always tell me that as a youngin. You don't listen to Mom all the time, but when somebody else tells you the exact same thing that your mom says, it kind of registers with you. So I tell players all the time, it's always good for them to hear it from someone else, especially in the position we are in, because what we say holds so much weight, it will stick with the kids. They will look and say, "Man, you had to deal with the same things that I am dealing with? You had people make you feel like your life isn't important too?"

Interview with Swin Cash

I got my nine-year-old daughter Imani involved in one of the Black Lives Matter panel discussions I moderated in November 2016. I wanted her to sing a song for the event's opening because I thought her beautiful voice would really set the tone, but I also wanted her to get a chance to hear panelists like Swin Cash, Ilyasah Shabazz, Emerald Snipes, and Erica Garner. Swin discussed how the entire WNBA responded to the deaths of Philando Castile and Alton Sterling, how the league took a stance together and decided that they were going to be agents for change. Imani was so inspired I can't even put it into words.

Now, I have brought Imani to hear me speak before, and I can tell when she is paying attention and when she isn't. This occasion, the entire time Swin Cash was speaking, Imani was locked in and engaged. She listened intensely as Swin explained how women were being subjected to crimes by the police just like men were, but that it wasn't being publicized as much. Imani heard the names Sandra Bland, Rekia Boyd, and Korryn Gaines, who I had discussed with her before. But she also learned some new names, like Symone Marshall, Gynnya McMillen, Darnesha Harris, Yvette Smith, and Malissa Williams.

At one point, Swin was asked how they were able to get all of the WNBA players to participate, both Black and white, in contrast to the NFL, which at the time barely had any players—definitely no white ones—supporting Kaepernick. Swin talked about how important it was to do things together and how the WNBA at first tried to break their unity by imposing fines. She talked about how much stronger they were together and how sometimes women can have issues working with each other. She mentioned mean girls that exist in every school across America, which Imani definitely related to. And Swin stressed that their lives mattered, no matter what they have been told by society, no matter what they have been shown on TV or heard on the radio. The WNBA was able to prove that when women come together, they can do something special and show everyone that they do in fact matter. Imani wasn't the only one hanging on her every word—every student in that audience, especially the females, were focused on everything Swin was saying. Hearing all of this from a woman made it even more powerful for them.

I was glad to be able to sit down with Swin Cash of the Detroit Shock to talk about these subjects.

Etan: Take me through how all of you came to the decision to collectively take the stand in the WNBA?

Swin Cash: It really came about as a result of everything that was going on in the country at the time. There were forty-eight hours that really had everyone in a state of shock. There were back-to-back murders of Alton Sterling and Philando Castile, and there was the video on Facebook Live that actually showed Philando Castile being killed and another video showing the police kill Alton Sterling, and at the time I think people were really numb and didn't know what to do. I know that Minnesota were working behind the scenes. I know their team really wanted to take a stance. I was actually on the executive committee of the union and we heard from other players, so everyone was wondering what they were going to do and it really was pretty much a forty-eight-hour turnaround where we had Minnesota who first publicly took a stand and two days after that we were in New York taking a stand and other teams were following suit . . . We understood that by making this stance, it wasn't going to be favorable with everyone, but at the same time we were so committed and we collectively felt that we needed to use our platform in that way.

Etan: What was your reaction to the police saying they were not going to do security for WNBA games?

Cash: Yeah, the officers decided that they were not going to remain on their posts during the game and do their duty as to what they were hired to do and they walked out of the arena. So not only were they refusing to acknowledge that we had a constitutional right to voice our opinion, but they were abandoning their responsibility as policemen to protect the players and fans alike . . . Minnesota had a press conference first and they verbalized how they felt and where they stood on all of the issues and the shirts displayed that as well. In New York, we took a different approach; immediately following the two shootings of Alton Sterling and Philando Castile you had the five Dallas police officers that lost their lives. So we had *Black Lives Matter* on the front of our shirts, but we also had *#ForTheDallasFive* out of respect for those officers, and there was a lot of debating and going back and forth. We really let every team decide what exactly it was that they wanted to stand for, because obviously the players in Dallas wanted to honor the Dallas Five but they still wanted to keep the focus on Black Lives Matter. It was . . . not a lot of sleeping, but a lot of conference calls talking to players from around the league and mobilizing in different markets.

Etan: WNBA president Lisa Borders fined the New York Liberty, Phoenix Mercury, and Indiana Fever five thousand dollars each and their players five hundred each, which was a very different way than the NBA handled a similar situation. But the fine didn't deter you; it actually seemed like it motivated you to take the entire protest to another level.

Cash: Yeah, we had a new WNBA president and she was trying to figure out how she would discipline or enforce the rules, and at the end of the day . . . We knew going in, especially after exploring everything with our legal team, that they could legally fine us because of this direct violation of the rules, but because the WNBA didn't fine Minnesota at the beginning, everyone was even more inclined to do it . . . And once you saw other teams joining the movement and it was spreading like wildfire across all the teams and the players, the league came down with a decision. We didn't back away from it. We knew the decision was going to happen because we were advised that it would happen . . . Collectively, we all said we were not going to back down just because of their fine that we all knew was an attempt to squash our movement . . . So we continued. And the next phase of that was the media blackout where in the postgame interviews, we would make a statement, then we would only answer questions about what was happening in our society and about Black Lives Matter. That was explained to the media and they understood our position, and that was that.

Etan: So what led them to rescind the fines?

Cash: You'll have to try to get a statement from the WNBA and ask them. After they saw that we weren't going to back down . . . we received a call from our union informing us that they were in fact going to rescind the fine and that they really liked that we were having a dialogue and that they wanted to discuss with us where we go from here and offered their support. That leadership came straight from Lisa Borders, so I really give her credit . . . You don't see people in that position admit that they were wrong and listen the way she did. So at that point . . . those conversations started happing right after the fines were rescinded.

Etan: I asked D Wade this same question, because after Miami Heat players wore *I Can't Breathe* shirts they faced some of the same criticism. He said that it wasn't about police, it was about *bad* police. Talk about that aspect of what Black Lives Matter actually means.

Cash: I definitely agree with Dwyane and we got the exact same pushback. Some of it was because some people were in fact uneducated and . . . believe everything they hear or are shown on television. And when you have people who go on television and use consistent negative descriptions of Black Lives Matter, and you make it seem like it's something that it's not, people will be more fearful of it and believe what they have been shown and told . . . Even in school they tell you if you don't know the answers, go do the research, and people don't do that today. Everybody has this microwave-popcorn society that says, "I don't want to look it up, just give me the answer right now." And of course we had so many females who had family that were police officers and we had people who served in the Marine Corps and the army and they understood perfectly that we weren't saying that it's all police or we weren't antipolice, but that we needed to pay attention to what was happening . . . We had to make sure that all of our women understood where their positions were, how they felt, and to only speak to what you felt. We continually stressed that just because you say that Black Lives Matter doesn't mean that all lives don't matter, but Black lives have to matter in order for all lives to matter.

Etan: Yeah, one of the main criticisms I've seen is: "Shouldn't all lives in fact matter, and not just the Black ones?"

Cash: I know for me personally, I always answer that in pointing out that, statistically, young Black men and women are being killed at an alarming rate by police officers—more than any other race—and looking at the justice system, receiving longer and harsher sentences for the same crimes as other races. We are getting profiled, we have family members who are constantly suffering. I could keep going and going. People think that just because I have a specific job or live in an affluent area that it somehow separates us from the struggle, but the reality is that if we are not training these officers, if we're not making sure that everyone has a fair opportunity, we're just basically being a part of the problem instead of trying to be part of the solution.

Etan: Why is that such a difficult concept for some people to grasp?

Cash: I think there are some people who want to live in their bubble, and when they are exposed to reality they push back because to them it is so un-fathomable and they just don't want to accept it as reality. Or they may care about it and hope that someday it changes, but it doesn't affect their day-to-day, and when you're living in a country now where people are talking about *my job, my health care,* they want to focus on other issues that are directly pertinent to them. "If I am not Black or brown, I don't have to walk around every day with this type of struggle. My experiences aren't the same, so basically it's not my problem." So it's different for people of color because . . . this is our reality. They can change the channel when they get tired of hearing about all the racial issues or the issues with the police, but *we* can't change any channel because we are living it every single day.

Etan: Talk about the power of solidarity.

Cash: First, you have to always keep in mind that whenever someone wants to accomplish something, the first order of business is to conquer and divide. You know what the enemy's mind-set is and what they are going to try to do, so you have to know how to combat that. There is always strength in num-bers, and there are going to be some people in your group who do not have as much strength as you . . . Right after the inauguration of Donald Trump, the very next day we had a women's march, not just in different cities but across the world. I was talking to players from other countries overseas and they were just so proud to see men and women and children who came out to support . . .

The march got a response from the president of the United States because he saw us and he saw us together, unified, in full support of each other. So many times, the first step is to make them see you, then after they see you you can verbalize what you want to be done, but you have to get their attention first and there is strength in numbers. I was proud of the WNBA players because for a lot of people, they finally saw us. A lot of people didn't want to acknowledge our game, our sport, or acknowledge *us*, because they didn't see us . . . And let me make this point: we had people in our locker room who were Republicans, Democrats, all different races and nationalities and beliefs, we have a lot of players from overseas, so it's not like we were all the same demographic or shared the same belief system. It simply came down to what's right and what's wrong.

Etan: How do you get white players to speak out?

Cash: It goes back to the locker room and a sisterhood . . . We understand the purpose of fighting for women's rights, whether it's fighting for equal pay or women's health; we have been taught from a very young age to stand together and support each other. The reason why there were so many not only white players but international players who stood with us was because, one, they saw the suffering from their teammates—not heard about it or read about it—but visibly saw it firsthand, whether it's seeing their teammates crying or seeing them angry or hurt and expressing themselves and explaining their frustration. And we had those dialogues with each other before we publicly made our statement . . . If we're going to really form a sisterhood, we can't tiptoe around issues that are deeply and emotionally affecting us to our core . . . We didn't force anyone to join us at all; we made it known that this was what a majority of us would like to do, but it's your choice. Either way, we are not going to judge you, but they all understood and all wanted to support, and we had players that really stood up. So I was really impressed by how together our women were and how we were willing to sacrifice for each other without hesitation.

Interview with Tamika Catchings

I can't say enough about how impressed I was with what the WNBA players were able to accomplish together. Before the July 2016 game against the Dallas Wings, the team captains for the Minnesota Lynx spoke to the media. One of them, Maya Moore, said, "If we take this time to see that this is a human issue and speak out together, we can greatly decrease fear and create change. Tonight, we will be wearing shirts to honor and mourn the losses of precious American citizens and to plead for a change in all of us."

Cheryl Reeve, the coach of the Minnesota Lynx (who happens to be white), tweeted, "To rebut BLM with 'All Lives Matter' implies that all lives are equally at risk, and they're not. #BlackLivesMatter doesn't mean your life isn't important if you aren't black—it means that Black lives, which are seen without value within White supremacy, are important."

The New York Liberty had the entire team wearing T-shirts with the words *#BlackLivesMatter* and *#Dallas5* on the front and a blank hashtag on the back. I interpreted the blank hashtag to symbolize the next unarmed Black man or woman to have their life snatched away by the police, the next one we unfortunately know is coming, though we don't know the victim's name. After the game, five players walked in formation into the media room to address the crowd of reporters waiting to hear an explanation. Swin Cash stated, "My husband is 6'6", 220 [pounds]. If my husband gets pulled over, when you look at him, does he make you scared? Is something going to happen to him? Those are things that go on in my head."

When the WNBA initially threatened to fine the players, Los Angeles Sparks standout Nneka Ogwumike was immediately vocal: "Everyone has their own opinion. But for me, at the end of the day, it's about the ethical nature of everything. The reason why we wanted to do this or why we wanted to come out and express ourselves, as a lot of other athletes do, is because of what's going on in our world. And a majority of our league is African American."

Reverend Al Sharpton said that his National Action Network would pay the fines, which he called "unacceptable." But as Swin Cash discusses above, that ultimately proved to be unnecessary. League president Lisa Borders announced in a statement, "While we expect players to comply with league rules and uniform guidelines, we also understand their desire to use their platform to address important societal issues."

Fever all-star Tamika Catchings, who was the president of the players union at that time, called the league's decision to rescind the fines a "huge win overall." I got a chance to meet with her to discuss what followed those initial protests.

Etan: During the playing of the national anthem on September 21, 2016, the entire Indiana Fever team knelt and locked arms against the Phoenix Mercury. Talk to me about what pushed you all to do this?

Tamika Catchings: It really started earlier in the season. Our team was watching everything that was going on and we all agreed that Black Lives Matter was really at the forefront after all of the police killings that were happening specifically to Black people. It really hurt our hearts seeing everything, we were really bothered as an entire team. And as a team we decided to use our platform to speak about it . . . So, we get to the playoffs, and talking to some of the members of the Phoenix team, and we told them that as a team, we were thinking about making this statement of kneeling during the national anthem.

And I posed it to our team that it's either all or nothing and that if anybody felt uncomfortable, we don't do it, and you know how it is with teams—you may get a response within twenty-four or forty-eight hours, and some may have different opinions or fears, but literally within ten, fifteen minutes max, everybody had said that this was definitely something that they wanted us to do together, and that includes our two Caucasian teammates.

Etan: What were the conversations like with those two white players?

Catchings: I think for them, being in the locker room, and hearing stories, and hearing us talking about how deeply we were affected by seeing people getting shot for no reason by the police, and beaten and brutalized by the police—it drew them into a deeper understanding. One of them just recently married an African American man, so for her it was like knowing what her husband has to go through, and gaining a better understanding of what everyday life is for him. And the other one, literally the conversation in the locker room opened her eyes to something she has never firsthand been exposed to. When you are drawn into a conversation and you don't really have much say because you can't speak from experience, but you also . . . know the difference between right and wrong, and you can visibly see your teammates hurting and literally in tears, you can't help but be drawn into what they are hurting about.

Etan: What did it mean to have the support of your coach?

Catchings: It was awesome . . . When we walked to the huddle before the game, Coach knelt down and said, "I'm really proud of you guys. Not just that you guys are standing up for something you believe in, but that you are doing it together." And even now when I think about it, I get some chills. You know, I think back to my dad, and I remember as a little girl sitting on my dad's lap, and he has this big scar on his leg, and I remember asking him, "What happened?" He proceeded to talk about being a part of Martin Luther King's marches, and he was a young kid with his dad taking him to the march, and . . . in all the chaos, they were running away and something happened and the police were arresting people, and my dad fell, and he has like a gash on the side of his leg where something was sticking out from a car and it punctured his leg . . . Now fast-forward forty years, and it's your daughter fighting for the same things that he was fighting for with his dad, so it's kind of putting things into perspective.

Etan: What was his conversation like with you after? I'm sure he had to be beaming with pride.

Catchings: Definitely . . . I remember him telling me how people were upset with them for protesting for their rights, and after we made our stance, I remember getting a call from the GM, and she was like, "The fans were terribly disappointed and we have had a couple of sponsors drop out because they don't want to support us." Then someone tweeted out my address, and was saying that they were going to form a massive protest in front of my house.

So, for a while, I had cops sitting in front of my house, posted twenty-four hours a day, and it just made me realize that there had to be some type of change in our world. For people to be so upset at us kneeling during the national anthem, and to be accused of being anti-American . . . Now, I've been an Olympian. I've represented my country, and me kneeling has nothing to do with the flag. I respect our military forces, our firefighters, our policemen, all the people who have fought for our country. But there are still some issues that need to be dealt with. We did a silent, peaceful protest. Which is what our military fought for us to have the right to be able to do . . . I'm not going to be deterred by them . . .

So, for example, one of the many things we have done since is we held a conversation here in Indianapolis—we had sixty-four youths that represented thirty different schools, we had twenty police officers, we had forty community leaders, and we discussed some of the issues that are happening in society. But more importantly, we discussed how we in our small group can bring about change here in Indianapolis. And we came up with solutions and plans in association with the police and the community activists and the youth. That's where my mission goes. I'm not kneeling just to kneel. I'm kneeling to start change, but realizing that the change has to also start with me too.

Etan: How important was it for the world to see all of the white players kneeling together in support of the Black players? For me, it was very important—like your coach said, it was bigger than basketball.

Catchings: You just hit it on the head. It showed the united part: "While I may not have to go through exactly what you are going through, I understand the need to proclaim to the world as a white person that yes, Black lives do matter, and I want to be a part of this change and do my part as a white person . . . I am going to join my Black sisters and do my part to create change. When we are talking about the *Black Lives Matter* shirts and blackout media protests earlier in the season as a league, one of the things that kept coming up was: "Be the change, change needs to happen, change starts with us." And it was awesome because when we were having this conversation . . . it was literally *all* of the players putting their voices in . . . So you saw all the teams who had many non-Black players, international players, and we did it together as a league. And when you have strong women who are all willing to stand for a cause that they believe in . . . we can't be pushed over and we want to be a part of that change.

I look at myself, and as a young girl, I was trying to find my own identity. And trying to figure out where they fit in—that's where our young girls are now . . . It's important for young girls to be told that this can be you, and the power and self-confidence and self-assuredness that you see us possess, this can also be you. It's inside of you, but you just have to be able to nurture it in the midst of a society that tells you the opposite and that your life doesn't matter. Every opportunity where we can . . . shower them with love, and show them positive examples of what a true woman looks like, and how we carry ourselves, and what we represent in this world. We are the majority. There are more women in this world than there are men. And we have to constantly show them how beautiful and special they are.

Etan: Sometimes in the conversations about police brutality and Black Lives Matter and murders by the police, women are left out of the conversation. There also need to be more panels and other public forums directed at young women.

Catchings: We definitely should, and it is unfortunate, and now we go to a whole 'nother thing, because we talk about Black Lives Matter, and we talk about Black people, and being a minority, and always being put to the side, so now you get to a whole 'nother element within the Black community and within the world, where women are still looked at as second-class citizens. I feel like in every single thing, women are pushed to the side . . . You get to the topics of the killings and you hear, "Oh, well, she is probably at the wrong place at the wrong time," or, "Her attitude wasn't what it should have been," which was an actual justification in the murders of both Sandra Bland and Korryn Gaines. Their attitude? That's like, "She got raped because of the outfit that she was wearing." So we as a society have to look at the misogyny that goes on in every single aspect, whether we are talking about the workforce, or professional sports, men and women being killed. That is a definite issue that needs to be brought to life.

Ignoring Critics and Haters Matters

After the racist comments by NBA CEO Donald Sterling became public, many throughout the media world and on various social networks took the Clippers players to task for what they called an "inadequate gesture" and "meaningless response." Vicious and uninformed attacks began to flood the Internet questioning the players' character, heart, overall commitment, and connection to their community, their race, and their history. Disparaging views about the players began popping up like dandelions in an open field.

Once again, the entire illustrious roster of Black athletes was being painted with a broad brush of ridicule.

The players handled the entire situation very intelligently. They were strategic in their demands and patient in their responses. This was a game of chess—it wasn't checkers. Unfortunately, many critics simply didn't understand that. It's always interesting when the Monday-morning quarterbacks discuss what they would do if they were in a certain situation.

What so many people were unaware of was that after Sterling's comments became exposed to the public, the Players Association—in particular the organization's president and Clippers player Chris Paul—decided to appoint Sacramento mayor Kevin Johnson to speak on their behalf since they were still in the process of finding a new executive director.

According to Mayor Johnson, they decided to have him meet with Commissioner Adam Silver to not only voice their disgust but to make a very clear demand: that Sterling receive the maximum possible punishment allowed under the bylaws and that this matter be handled swiftly. Commissioner Silver assured them that he was just as disgusted and appalled but asked the players to give him a few days for what he called "due process." It was wise for the Players Association to give the newly appointed commissioner a chance to make his decision while strategically preparing their next move—in the event that a proper punishment was not handed down.

Meanwhile, the Clippers had a game to play, and decided to wage a silent protest, refusing to publicly speak about the issue. They ran out of the tunnel wearing their usual warm-ups, then huddled together at midcourt and tossed the outer layer of their warm-ups to the ground, revealing that the team had turned their red practice jerseys inside out.

This was met with public ridicule, as if the players had done something wrong. Many people said that they should have instead boycotted, held a sit-in, marched, rallied, or set a life-size cardboard image of Sterling on fire and circled around it while it went up in flames. You heard every suggestion under the sun.

Then, three days after the racist recordings of Sterling were made public, Adam Silver handed down the harshest punishment allowed—exactly what the players had demanded. Players Association vice president Roger Mason Jr. told ESPN that he spoke to player representatives from each team and they had all been on board with a decision to boycott that Tuesday's games if they weren't satisfied with the commissioner's decision.

Frederick Douglass once said, "Power concedes nothing without a demand. It never did and it never will." Many of the players were aware of this.

Interview with Jamal Crawford

I played for a year in Atlanta with Jamal Crawford, who was a member of that Clippers team, and I developed a friendship with him. I wanted him to walk me through the process of everything that happened, including how hearing the criticism affected him and his family from a personal standpoint. I am so pleased that he agreed to go on record with this.

Etan: Take me back to 2014. The Donald Sterling incident happens and the entire Clippers team collectively decides to make a statement . . .

Jamal Crawford: We never really saw him but we always heard that he was kind of different . . . So when recorded tapes leaked out and we heard the things he was saying about Black people as a whole . . . a bunch of emotions started pouring in throughout the entire team. We couldn't even sleep. We were in the middle of a playoff battle against Golden State at the time, and we had no manual on how to handle this situation. If you want to be a better shooter, you get up more shots. If you want to be a better ball handler, you go through cone drills. There was no guide or pamphlet to say, *Hey, this is what you do in this type of a situation.*

Then you get calls from everyone you know or have known, and everyone has opinions . . . And we had to make a collective decision. We are a team, we're not an individual sport. Some guys wanted to do one thing and some guys wanted to handle it other ways. We had a lot of different opinions within our team of how to handle this situation. We met, everyone had the opportunity to voice their opinions . . . but whatever we were going to do, we emphasized that we were going to do it as a team. We didn't want anyone going by themselves and taking heat or criticism or taking it all on their shoulders. We wanted to take our stance as a team.

One of the best handles in the league, Jamal Crawford didn't hesitate to speak about the ousting of Donald Sterling.

Etan: How were the coaches and management during this process?

Crawford: The way we saw it, we weren't playing for Donald Sterling. It was about *us*, the brotherhood . . . Doc [Coach Doc Rivers] was very open and very supportive. He just kept emphasizing that whatever we do, we are going to do it as a unit . . . He told us that he was affected by this just as we were all affected by this . . . Not to sound cliché, but this entire thing brought us all even closer as a team because we were all in it together.

Etan: That's what prompted me to write an article for *Huffington Post* in May 2014 called "The Clippers Players Were Far from Cowards in Handling the Donald Sterling Situation." But isn't it interesting that so many people were doing so much criticizing afterward? What type of criticisms did you hear?

Crawford: Oh, we heard it all: "You guys are all cowards," like you said in your article, and thanks so much for writing that . . . But we heard, "You guys didn't stand for anything, you should have done it like this; the athletes of the sixties would've done this or that; this is your moment," etc. We heard it all. Sometimes you will be criticized either way. I am reminded of how tough everything was at that time because people thought they knew what was going on, but they really didn't. We went through a whole team process and came up with the most effective strategy in order to get the results we all wanted, which was to have him removed, and we did just that.

Etan: How did this entire ordeal effect y'all on the court? You struggled a little bit against Golden State that next game after everything came out.

Crawford: Struggled *a little*? We got blown out the next game . . . Our minds were not there. That's how heavily everything was weighing on us. We had made the decision to give Adam Silver his time to do his investigating and due diligence and go through the process . . . but we were fully prepared to take a different course if needed, and we expressed this to him . . . But kudos to Golden State. They told us, "If you don't want to play, we won't play, and we'll sit out with you." So that was really cool of them to have our backs like that and they talked about it publicly. I'm just glad our strategy worked out the way that it did, and he is no longer a part of the organization.

Etan: Isn't it interesting that some of the same people who criticize current players and say they are nothing like the players from the sixties . . . they still criticize, even when the players take action?

Crawford: It's definitely a damned-if-you-do, damned-if-you-don't situation, but you can't go into it thinking that you can please everybody . . . You'll always have people who criticize. Think about the job that President Barack Obama did for eight years in the White House, especially with what he walked into and the mess that was left by the president before him. And people never stopped criticizing him—even to this day, they are still criticizing him. So at the end of the day, we just had to do what was best for us in this situation to get the results that we wanted and not even think about trying to please everyone.

Interview with Dr. John Carlos

Right before I wrote the article for *Huffington Post* defending the Clippers players, I made a Facebook post that in effect read: "Attention all reporters: please refrain from inviting me onto your shows to bash my fellow players. It's not going to happen, so please stop trying."

In July 2015, I joined Dr. John Carlos and Adonal Foyle on a panel in Los Angeles for the Special Olympics. Once again, the discussion turned to the issue of athletes today, with Adonal and I defending them, while the moderator, Alan Kasujja, was hell-bent on casting a dark shadow over them.

Della Britton Baeza, president and CEO of the Jackie Robinson Foundation, echoed Kasujja's sentiments, and instead of simply giving honor and respect to Jackie Robinson, she took the opportunity to bash ALL current athletes. She proclaimed that modern-day athletes were not only failing to carry the torch set forth by Robinson, but that in general they outright refused to be proactive in using their influence and reputations to bring about social justice.

I was so relieved that Dr. John Carlos didn't share those sentiments, although they relentlessly attempted to get him to support what they were saying. He simply would not do it.

I sat down with Dr. Carlos to discuss social activism and athletes today. I wanted to speak with someone who I have admired and respected from the first time my mother taught me about him in middle school. Someone whose poster I've had on my wall in high school, college, and even now in my office at home.

With the great Dr. John Carlos. He is pointing to my T-shirt of Malcolm doing the Black Power salute. He really got a kick out of it.

Etan: When you look at Kaepernick and LeBron and Carmelo and the current athletes, do you feel that they are carrying on the tradition of you and Tommie Smith and Kareem and Bill Russell and all of the great athletes who used their positions as a platform to create change?

Dr. John Carlos: Yes, I definitely do, but let me say this: activism started a long time before the individuals that you just mentioned . . . We were not the originators, and I always want to make that point. We have to recognize athletes that I looked up to and that inspired me, like Jack Johnson, Paul

Robeson, Jackie Robinson, Jesse Owens. They are the athletes who laid the foundation for Peter Norman, Tommie Smith, and John Carlos to be able to take the stand we took during the 1968 Olympics. We're nowhere near the first. And those individuals, Kaepernick, LeBron, Carmelo, they are the fruit of our labor, but these bread crumbs were laid way before us. In our time we were able to take a stand on a tremendous stage for the world to see, and I love seeing young brothers like yourself who have always been aware and active and passionate . . . We are proud of the work you young brothers are doing and for us to be able to be involved in what you are doing.

It's one thing for me to read about what Jack Johnson did and admire and be inspired by what I am reading, but it's another thing for us to be able to interact with the current athletes and have you all pick our brains . . . We are now fighting this fight together and that's what it's all about. And these people who say that athletes only care about getting the big check and not worry about their community, that's not what I see . . . I see current athletes engaged, interested, knowledgeable about the history of athletes that came before them, studying and being aware, and they are bothered by the injustices toward their race . . .

Etan: How do you respond when people ask why you are "different" from other athletes who don't speak out?

Carlos: People like to talk a good game, but I don't see them speaking out at their place of employment, and they want to criticize athletes for having the same reservation that they have. You can't expect everyone in athletics to lead the same charge. Some people are wiser earlier and some people it takes a little longer for them. Some people it's just not their thing, and that's okay too . . . But the bottom line is, it builds courage when you see more individuals start to speak out and stand up, so then you see young superstars who were inspired by the courage that they saw and they come into the game with a totally different mind state.

Etan: It has to make you smile when you see a player from this generation like Kaepernick say your name.

Carlos: I'm always smiling to the point that my cheeks hurt when I see individuals have the courage to take on the world like Kaepernick did to take this stance . . . Of course that makes me smile. Makes me jump up and down and high-five my sons too, which is exactly what we did. That's a tremendously hard load to carry and put on your shoulders . . . It makes me think about Hercules, because that's the level of strength that you have to have. That makes me do nothing but smile.

Etan: You mention that it's worth remembering that not everyone spoke out.

Carlos: I don't remember what year it was but I was excited to meet Dr. King and I asked him a question. I said, "Why would you go back to Memphis if they threatened your life?" And he said, "John, I had to go back and stand for those that can't stand for themselves." So in essence what I'm saying is, there are now and were then athletes who may not have been saying anything for different reasons or doing anything for different reasons, but that doesn't mean they don't and didn't want the same justice and equality that I did. So I have to speak for them. And when I speak . . . they are encouraged by what I did—so encouraged that one day they may step out and speak out against the atrocities that people have to endure every day. All we are doing is lighting a fire under them.

Etan: What would be your advice to young athletes who want to speak out?

Carlos: You have to realize we as a people have always been criticized . . . But the question is, will you be defeated by this criticism or stand up against it? Three hundred and fifty years ago we were in bondage in slavery—that's the ultimate form of criticism. That says, "Don't even look at us as human beings." And just as we didn't fall to the criticism then, we can't fall to the criticism now . . . Was Trump concerned with criticism when he saying the things he was saying throughout the entire election process? . . . If he wasn't concerned, why would you be concerned with criticism, and you know you are going the right way? It's crucial for today's individuals to weigh these things in their minds.

Etan: Talk to me a little bit about the support from your peers.

Carlos: I remember Harry Edwards attempted to educate O.J. as to why it was an imperative that we as Black athletes come together and make a statement or do a boycott . . . O.J. may have been relatively interested from a heritage standpoint, but the economic factor and the fact that he didn't want to do anything that could in any way, shape, or form, even have the possibility of jeopardizing his economics, made him go the complete opposite way to where he made the proclamation, "I'm not Black, I'm O.J.". . . It would've been tremendous, magnificent, stupendous—any other description I can think of—if O.J. would've stood with us, because everybody loved O.J., and by everybody, I mean white folks. You know how big it would've been if O.J. would've said, "I support the Olympic boycott," and he articulated the reasons why? You understand what I'm saying? That's the power that O.J. had and it was all just squandered away as a missed opportunity.

Etan: So now I look toward LeBron James and Dwyane Wade, Kyrie Irving and Derrick Rose, Kevin Garnett, and the entire Phoenix Suns, Kobe and the entire Lakers team, including the white players, and Jeremy Lin, and even entire college teams and the entire WNBA—white and Black players stood together.

Carlos: That is the perfect example of what athletes can do when they stick together. Back in '68, if Tommie Smith had made the statement by himself, they would've run over Tommie Smith and said that this man is crazy . . . But the fact that we had an arc of unity, and not just the two of us there, and that strength caused Peter Norman to say, "I support what you guys are doing." You're stronger with numbers. And that's why they couldn't immediately squash this demonstration with the *I Can't Breathe* display of the NBA players, because it was too many of them collectively doing it. And like you said, white individuals step up and support the Black athletes . . . The nucleus of the NBA stepped up—and even if it wasn't everybody, they proclaimed to the world, "This is not right and it's time for a change."

Etan: When Trayvon Martin was murdered and all of the players on the Miami Heat posed in the iconic picture in hoodies, what went through your mind when you first saw that?

Carlos: It reminded me of the movie *Spartacus*. When the guy stood up and said, "Who's Spartacus?" and the one guy stood forward and said, "I'm Spartacus," and the real Spartacus stood up and before he could say, "I'm Spartacus," another guy said, "I'm Spartacus," then another . . . In essence, the Miami Heat players did the same thing in saying, "Oh, you murdered this young teenage Black man and took him off the face of this earth because he had a hoodie on?" So they made the statement to society, "No, I'm the thug, I got the hoodie . . . we all are wearing hoodies. The whole team. Black, white, or whoever. We all wear hoodies and we are all standing here telling you that you are wrong and we are standing against it." It was a powerful and important statement. And there is power in that just as we sent a message to the world back in the '68 Olympics.

Etan: When you hear critics say that current athletes have no connection to their own legacy and are not following in the footsteps of John Carlos or Muhammad Ali or Jackie Robinson, what is your reaction?

Carlos: I would tell them that they need to go back and study more and do their research more . . . The players I would even say now are more collective. We didn't have all the Black boxers come out and support Jack Johnson back in the day and say, "Yeah, he has a white wife and has the right to take this woman across the railroad tracks whether she is white or not." Now, of course, the circumstances were different back then, but still. Jesse Owens— the same thing when he was dealing with Hitler and the Germans in the Olympics and . . . disproved his myth that the Black athlete was inferior. For him to do that there and come home and be ridiculed—what athletes stood alongside with him? These were individuals.

But now from a collective standpoint, I actually see growth. I didn't just see LeBron standing there. I didn't see Kaepernick by himself taking a knee. I saw players across the NFL taking a knee, holding the Black Power salute; even the ones who didn't take a knee with him were publicly saying that they support him . . . They didn't just leave it at "We support Kaepernick"—they went into detail and listed what was wrong in society . . . So those individuals who want to sit back and point fingers, those are like the armchair quarterbacks. You ain't never been in the game or even came close to the game, but you wanna talk like you're the MVP quarterback. Let somebody tackle you a few times then you come back and tell me about what he or she did wrong.

Interview with Juwan Howard

Hate usually comes with the territory when you are an athlete. Those "brave" fans say some of the meanest, vilest, most repugnant things on Twitter and in online comments sections, which sometimes serve no purpose other than allowing certain people a platform to spew their hate.

I wasn't really surprised when former NBA forward Juwan Howard told me of the truckloads of hate mail he and his teammates received while at the University of Michigan during the Fab Five era—a period in which Michigan's basketball team dominated collegiate basketball thanks to five incredibly talented freshmen. It was enlightening to talk with Juwan about his experiences at Michigan.

Etan: Can you take me back to the controversy you were involved with at Michigan?

Juwan Howard: Being a young kid, coming from the inner city of Chicago, to be able to get a scholarship at a prestigious university like Michigan, I was completely elated. I was young, like my other Fab Five brothers. We were all teenagers and just enjoying the ride. Then we started to realize that here are these big-time shoe companies, and the one who was the sponsor of our school was Nike. They would send us a ton of shoes and apparel for us to wear on the court in order to give them the type of visibility they wished to achieve . . . They wanted their brand to specifically be associated with the University of Michigan. So, as we were becoming more mature and aware, we began to realize that this was a huge financial gain for the university and for the Nike company, but we weren't really benefiting from it. Myself, Chris Webber, Jalen Rose, Ray Jackson, and Jimmy King all barely had any money in our pockets to do anything . . .

We were noticing our jerseys being sold in every single sporting goods store in Detroit. Not just on Michigan's campus, but everywhere in the state people were buying jerseys with our numbers on them. And we would see the same thing when we traveled outside of the state of Michigan. We had become this global phenomenon, but we weren't seeing any money from it. And it's hard for people to understand how that feels unless you have been in that situation . . . So we wanted to take a stand and send the message that we weren't going to wear this product and allow ourselves to market your brand for you, to exploit us the way you were so comfortable in doing . . . And we had incredible backlash from that. We weren't even prepared for the level of backlash that we received, but we didn't care . . . We wanted to not only stand up for ourselves, but we were thinking of the many athletes that were to come after us.

Etan: Talk a bit more about the backlash you received.

Howard: We received so much backlash and it was really unexpected. And we didn't have social media back then. We didn't have outlets to voice our own opinion and speak to the public, unfiltered. If we had social media at that time? Man (*laughing*), it would have been crazy. Actually, maybe in some ways it was good that we didn't have Twitter accounts back then (*laughing*), but all we had were newspapers and media . . . to paint the picture of us the way they personally viewed us. That's all the public was able to get. And they were so against us and everything we were about even before we took our stance . . . They didn't like the fact that we were confident, which they considered cocky, and I still don't know how we got branded with that word.

We were a group of athletes who had confidence in ourselves and our skill set and we were confident enough to feel that every time we touched the floor that there was no team that could beat us. The media didn't like our appearance. They thought the bald heads were representative of a gang, or they looked at us as glorifying a gang image, which I also didn't understand. Then they would talk about the scowls on our faces. We would dunk on someone and scowl and they didn't like that . . . Then you talk about the black socks, they didn't like that either . . . But we wanted to do something different and we wanted to do things our way . . . We were told we were being like a group of militants like Black Panthers on the court, as if that was a bad thing, but there were all types of letters that were delivered to the university and to Coach Fisher.

A lot of them had a very racist and hateful tone to them. Many were latent with the N-word . . . It was like we were back in the sixties and trying to integrate an all-white school. But we were not going to allow anyone or anything to steal our joy. And we were determined to send a message with every game, every win, that it was okay that you hated us, but we were going to keep winning, and winning our way.

Etan: You represented so much more than just the Fab Five, you represented Black youth across the country.

Howard: Well, at that time, I can honestly say that I didn't know that we were representing the Black community and Black youth until after my freshman year and I went back home . . . I invited Jalen, and as we were walking around Grant Park and I was showing him my hometown [of Chicago], there were tons of people walking up to us, asking for our autographs and asking to take pictures. We could not walk anywhere. And it wasn't just the regular *We are taking pictures with a celebrity*, it was like we were getting hugs from young Black youth and they were saying things like, "Thanks for representing us," or, "Thanks for representing the hood and standing up for our community." Now remember, we are eighteen-year-old kids at this point. And looking back at it now, that entire experience was really so special.

Interview with Craig Hodges

Craig Hodges played in the NBA for ten seasons and led the league in three-point shooting three times. He won the NBA championship with the Chicago Bulls, and along with Larry Bird is one of only two players to win three consecutive three-point shooting contests at the NBA All-Star Weekend. When he visited the White House in 1992 for the ceremonial championship team visit, he wore a dashiki and delivered a handwritten letter to then-president George H.W. Bush critcizing the administration's policies regarding the poor and minorities. Craig also took a lot of heat for his public criticism of Bulls teammate Michael Jordan for not using his platform to shine a spotlight on injustice. In early 2017, he published a book titled, *Long Shot: The Triumphs and Struggles of an NBA Freedom Fighter.* There were so many subjects I wanted to talk to him about.

Etan: What are the main two questions that people ask you about your NBA career? I would imagine they revolve around the visit to the White House and the public critique of Michael Jordan.

Craig Hodges: There's a third one that people always ask me and that's what's it like to play with Michael. And that's the fun side, but then for me of course the conversation is many times much more serious . . . What they don't understand is this is a lifelong commitment for me . . . I am committed to our community and what we desire our communities to look like. People come up to me and say, "Hey, you went off on Michael and told him to do this and that." It wasn't about me telling Michael Jordan what he should or shouldn't do with his money at all, it was more about . . . to whom much is given, much is required . . . We have to love ourselves and support each other and uplift each other, and when we do that, the entire community benefits.

Now, back to M.J. specifically, he has done things to help the community and has spoken out on issues that greatly affect the community, like police brutality in particular . . . I think a lot of people took it out of perspective when I gave the interview back in the day. I wasn't going off on M.J.—this was bigger than M.J. This was actually a lot larger than all of us . . . We as a nation have to come to grips with the questions and answers that show how the exploitation of our people and all people of color, whether Black, red, brown, or yellow, has occurred in this country and is still happening today.

Etan: How important do you think it is to have these public discussions even if some people take them the wrong way and end up missing the entire point?

Hodges: Oh, I think it's very important . . . I felt like we as an organization could really get things done and help the people in the city of Chicago a great deal, and I think a lot of guys—not just Michael but the entire Bulls organization as a whole—didn't see the impact that we could have. And me being from here, I had more of an affinity for it and more of a connection to the community . . . We could've been heavily promoting nonviolence and education and employment, etc.

Etan: In 1992, William Rhoden wrote an article for the *New York Times* entitled, "Hodges Criticizes Jordan for His Silence on Issues." What was the overall reaction when this article came out?

Hodges: I really think people were just focused on the fact that we had won the championship, even to the point that the powers-that-be didn't want that to be the focal point at that point in time. They didn't want to look at the hurt of our people or the violence that was going on in the city . . . the fact that we were making all of this money for a franchise that could have been doing so much more to actually help the community. If you look at where the United Center is actually located, and the impact of the community around it once it was built, there were a lot of things we could do not only as individuals, not only as a team, but as a franchise.

We could've been an example for other teams of what they should do in their respective communities to actually have an impact . . . We, as current and former players, have made enough money for our teams and for the NBA as a whole that we have earned the right to speak and say, "Listen, if we are making this amount of money, then a certain amount should be targeted toward urban centers to create jobs and employment for the next generation of young people."

Etan: But saying that *publicly* helps push it along. There is a big difference between having a private locker room conversation and making a public declaration.

Hodges: Absolutely, and that's the part that was always frustrating to me. I have heard these guys discuss these issues in the locker room . . . I know they see it. And in this generation, especially with social media, everybody is up to date and fully aware of what is going on . . . I look at it from a different standpoint. I look at it like we should create a base so wide that there is nothing they can do but to give in to our demands . . . We have to tap into our power.

Etan: How did you have the courage to take a public stand? Especially in that era of lower salaries?

Hodges: I never made a million dollars in a year. That's why I respect you as well, because we weren't the highest-paid guys on the team. We weren't the ones getting all the endorsements and the ones making all the money on the team. So we were more expendable, when it came down to it, than the superstars. But that only made us have more power . . .

My granddad was a great sportsman so we watched all the sports and discussed the impact of a Jim Brown, of a Muhammad Ali, of a Curt Flood and George Foreman. And I was always directed to look at those athletes, the ones who stood for something . . . Black people are my first love, and then basketball. And basketball gave me opportunities and opened doors for me my entire life, but I wasn't going to have one without the other. That wasn't even a question. I had to study and be intelligent about life and maintain my connection to the Black community as a whole. And that was more important than any sport.

Etan: So how did you deal with people who criticized you for speaking publicly about these things?

Hodges: That's the part that is gratifying for me, the way things have come full circle, because back in the nineties, nobody wanted to publicly talk about what was goin' down . . . And a myriad of people—my friends, my family—said I was stupid for doing it. They said, "Why are you so committed to putting your neck on the line for Black people when most of them don't even care?" And I'm laughing because the goal is still attainable . . . I see it happening. We both have seen people in the locker room who shared our beliefs and felt exactly how we felt. But sometimes they simply were not educated and mentored on the importance of being able to speak truth to power, but also the amount of heart that is required to be able to do that . . . It takes heart to go to the White House and stand by yourself in a dashiki and your culture. There was no hesitation in me because I know who has my back. The elders who have gone and who have come before got my back.

Etan: Did it surprise you that so many of your peers and teammates didn't stand with you?

Hodges: It didn't surprise me at all . . . I have learned those lessons of history where many people stood by themselves. Muhammad Ali stood by himself. Jim Brown stood by himself for the most part . . . It's funny, because that's how bad it's become. They have so miseducated us that you can have a teammate who will run through a wall for you, take a charge from a big 250-pound mammoth of a human being, they will bust up their whole mouth and knees diving on the floor for a loose ball for you, and not think twice about it, but won't stand up for Black people. They're willing to take that pain, but won't withstand this little bit of blowback from standing up for Black people.

Etan: Is there anything you would change if you could go back in time?

Hodges: Not in my decisions, but I would've liked to have had social media back then. Bring that technology to me . . . I could've said whatever I wanted to say to millions of people whenever I wanted to just by pushing *send?* And we had just won the championship and I was winning back-to-back-to-back three-point contests . . . so all of Chicago would've been following me on social media. If I had that power that these young guys have now? Man! I wish. Wouldn't have had to worry about going through the media just so they could put their spin on what I want to say . . .

And that's why I wanted to do my book: so that I could publicly tell my own story. I was tired of seeing publications messing up my story. Many times, they didn't even have the facts correct, they were just creating a narrative that they thought was going to make them some money. Well, now I have my book, and I have my own soapbox to stand on and can speak to these issues that affect my people.

Etan: Talk about the need to be a public voice against commentators, particularly Black commentators, who condemn, ridicule, mock, or otherwise publicly chastise athletes when they make political statements.

Hodges: Well, they get guys to say these things because they know the people love them. It's an intentional tactic. See, I was birthed from a freedom fighter. So you can't buy me. I received this knowledge of self from birth. It is all about the public discourse. I see Charles [Barkley] doing what he does and the buffoonery aspect of it. You always have the ones who can be bought. I'm not even going to say they are selling out, I'm going to say they are selling themselves short. They don't understand that they are becoming the mouthpiece for a system that has no interest in us as a people . . . If they are going to continue to garner these high-priced salaries and yet turn a blind eye to racism . . . you may as well stay in your tap shoes. Look, we can't hoop anymore, we don't know how to transit the game on a level where it still maintains our dignity as Black men . . . We're taught, "Okay, you get this opportunity to brand yourself, now you exploit your people the same way that everybody else exploits your people."

Etan: And this is my issue—because they don't have to do that. They don't have to tap dance.

Hodges: Of course they don't have to. It's a choice. That's fear. You know that the only reason why you stop at a red light at four a.m. when nobody is around is because you have been conditioned to fear the consequences if you don't adhere to the rules. The assassination of our leadership bred fear into our generation. This current generation, the fear is pretty much bred out of them. You got the hip-hop, the style, the defiance, and I love it. But my generation, we had been taught that the powers-that-be will kill you over this matter, so keep your mouth shut. And I don't even mean kill you in the literal sense, although that is a fear too, but I mean kill you in terms of cutting off your economic lifeline that we control. So you're going to say what we want you to say, if you want this financial stream to continue.

Etan: There needs to be more people who call them out. For instance, why does Barkley get a pass? Or when Jim Brown went to meet with Donald Trump and came out saying he "fell in love" with him.

Hodges: You are absolutely right. I wanna know myself. Jim, what made you say that? You are my elder. You are one of my heroes. Talk to me. And I love you the same. You have the right to say whatever you wanna say, but tell me . . .

Going back to your original question with Michael Jordan, it wasn't about berating or calling out Michael Jordan . . . It was: we have all this going on in Chicago, you are the king of not only the city but the NBA, your words could immediately have an impact. If you say it, it will be done . . . The lessons of the past tell us everything we need to know. What is freedom and what is not freedom. What is justice and what is not justice. What is exploitation and what is not exploitation. You can't give me something, then think because you gave it to me, I have to think how you think. I gotta believe what you believe? . . . I can't be bought with my silence or my acquiescence through somebody paying. I think it was Karl Malone who said if you kiss enough you-know-what, you can have a job in the league for life, and unfortunately, too many brothers are kissing and tap-dancing their way to the top. So I say, keep calling them out.

Speaking Out in the Age of Trump Matters

The day after Trump was elected president was particularly difficult in the Thomas household.

The night of the election I started getting tired around my regular bedtime, which is shortly after the kids go to sleep. Watching the election results and the commentary had the same effect on me as the sound of ocean waves or a lullaby after some warm tea for me. I woke up in the middle of the night, rolled over to check my phone to see the updates, and I couldn't believe my eyes. Donald Trump had won the election. I must have gasped because I woke up my wife who had been sound asleep, and she asked what was wrong. I told her and she replied, "Stop playing, that's not even funny." But she turned on the TV and it was confirmed: Donald Trump would soon be sworn in as the next president of the United States of America. We couldn't move. I just couldn't believe what I was seeing. I had to be having a bad dream, a nightmare. So after it finally set in, my wife and I asked each other a question that kept us up for the rest of the night: what were we going to tell the kids?

The next morning, there was an eerie atmosphere. We sat eleven-year-old Malcolm, nine-year-old Imani, and six-year-old Baby Sierra down at the breakfast table and we told them the election results. They too were in denial for quite some time. Imani and Baby Sierra said they were ready to move to Grenada, where my family is from. Malcolm just sat there in disbelief; his little heart was broken. Like when a kid finds out that there is no Santa Claus, or no tooth fairy, or that wrestling is fake. It's like his whole entire world had turned upside down. He just kept repeating, "How could this happen, Daddy? There are that many racist people in the country? There are actually that many people who don't like women and who don't like Mexicans or Muslims or Black people? There are really that many people who agree with him and think that he would be a good president for us?" I told him apparently so.

Imani's mind was made up: she told me to call the prime minister of Grenada (as if I could just ring him on his cell phone or something) and explain that we were ready to come home. She said it wouldn't be safe for us here in the US. She had friends who were Latino—would it be safe for them here? Should they come to Grenada with us? Nichole was hugging them and trying to assure them that we were going to be okay, but her eyes betrayed her. I really couldn't come up with any words to say at all. I had nothing. I was still in shock myself.

Malcolm said he was scared and didn't feel safe, and that on the one hand he didn't want to live here anymore, but on the other—and he paused before asking—"Would Malcolm X, Martin Luther King, or any of the people I have learned about run away, or would they stay and fight? I don't want to give Trump this country, he doesn't deserve this country."

I told him that was a good point, then I said that Black people have survived much worse than Donald Trump, and we still made it. Malcolm said, "That's right." Nichole smiled and said she couldn't argue with that at all.

Later that day, I discovered there were protests all over the country, on social media, in DC, New York, Chicago, LA. All over the country people were letting their voices be heard. And athletes were tweeting their disapproval of the election results. It was almost as if Trump's victory was energizing everyone. Not long after, I asked ESPN commentator Michael Wilbon for his thoughts on athletes using their platforms to speak out against Trump.

Interview with Michael Wilbon

Etan: Right now, athletes are speaking out more than we've seen since the 1960s. Do you think this is a good thing, or do you think athletes should pretty much stay in the lane of sports and athletics?

Michael Wilbon: No, I don't ever believe in anybody staying in any type of a box. I think it's absolutely incredible what I am seeing from athletes. I think there are many reasons that have ignited this surge of athletes speaking out. Two of them are the election and the relationship, or the lack thereof, between police and specifically young Black men. And you're absolutely right—this is not new . . . But I think the difference is, there is less risk. I am old enough to have covered athletes when there was enormous risk. Where people would just shut you down completely, and I'm not talking about being at risk of losing your endorsement dollars, I mean being at risk of losing your career, your livelihood . . . We are blessed to live in a different world now. We are now in a time where we have more freedom, and I say "we" because I couldn't have my job in the 1960s if I had written some of the things I wrote in the 1980s, so there is less risk for me as well.

Etan: Now, with current players speaking out against Trump, and many NBA CEOs being conservative Republicans, I would think there would still be a great deal of risk in speaking out.

Wilbon: Well, you know why I don't think so is, for one, you have half the country speaking out against Trump, and in a case like Gregg Popovich, who is really in a place where few public figures in sports have dared to go, that's something that didn't happen thirty, fifty years ago . . . But it's a different time. We saw entire basketball teams speak out against police violence, even with the WNBA situation. They initially wanted to punish the players and silence them but they couldn't . . . The entire power dynamic is different now, and I'm sure that emboldens people.

Etan: Yeah, but it seems like sometimes you have the freedom to say it, but only as long as enough people agree with it. There are certain things that you still can and will be punished for.

Wilbon: Well, some protests are much more popular than others, there's no doubt about that. But there are others that have direct penalties and others that will allow you to only be unpopular, but won't cost you your job.

Etan: We have seen a surge in players speaking out about racism. Some players seem fearless: Jeremy Lin taking strong stances against racism and what he has been subjected to as an Asian American; Bradley Beal standing up for Black Lives Matter; Serena Williams taking a break in the middle of Wimbledon and tweeting, "In London I have to wake up to this. He was black, shot 4 times? When will something be done—no REALLY be done?!?!"

186 ⅋ WE MATTER

Wilbon: I am so glad that they are using their voices and I could do a complete section on each of the people you named. I was so happy to see Bradley Beal take the stance he took, especially me being here in DC and covering the Wizards. But let me talk about Serena. Look at the support she got from within the industry and outside of it—it was wildly effective. If Arthur Ashe did the same thing forty years ago in his heyday, would it have had the same effect? . . . There were other people who supported Serena in bringing that racism that she experienced to the forefront, and that was extremely important. Just as it was extremely important for Jeremy Lin to bring that racism to the forefront . . . When athletes like Lin and Serena take those stances, they are taking it for all of the people who don't have the power they have to bring racism to the forefront.

Interview with Chris Hayes

So many athletes did just what Michael Wilbon is referring to: they took to social media to show their disapproval of Donald Trump, especially when he signed an executive order to suspend the entire US refugee admissions system and implement a Muslim ban. The executive order targeted seven Muslim-majority countries and looked to prevent individuals from those countries from entering the United States for ninety days. It suspended the US refugee program for 120 days and put an indefinite halt to all refugee intake from Syria. It even prevented quite a few legal US residents who were en route to the United States when Trump signed the executive order from entering when they landed. Several of those travelers were detained and others were deported back to the countries that they had flown in from. Thousands of people flocked to airports across the country to protest.

After the signing of the order, a number of athletes utilized their social media platforms to voice their disapproval. Los Angeles Laker Luol Deng told reporters:

> *I would not be where I am today if it weren't for the opportunity to find refuge in a safe harbor. For the people of South Sudan, refugee resettlement has saved countless lives, just as it has for families all over the world escaping the depths of despair.*

It's important that we remember to humanize the experience of others. Refugees overcome immeasurable odds, relocate across the globe, and work hard to make the best of their newfound home. Refugees are productive members of society that want for their family just as you want for yours. I stand by all refugees and migrants, of all religions, just as I stand by the policies that have historically welcomed them.

Former NBA superstar Hakeem Olajuwon told reporters, "I'm a public figure. I'm a Muslim. We don't have too many public figures that can really speak up. If I don't, then I'm not taking my responsibility . . . We can't exclude some people or countries. He can say it's not against Islam, but really, indirectly, it is."

The Major League Soccer Players Union issued the following statement:

We are deeply concerned, both specifically for our players who may be impacted, and more broadly for all people who will suffer as a result of the travel ban . . . We are extremely disappointed by the ban and feel strongly that it runs counter to the values of inclusiveness that define us as a nation. We are very proud of the constructive and measured manner in which [US men's team captain] Michael Bradley expressed his feelings on the ban. It is our deepest hope that this type of strong and steady leadership will help to guide us through these difficult times.

I tried to show my son every time people were demonstrating or marching or protesting, and athletes were tweeting, and Malcolm's reply was always the same: "Good, I hope everyone who has a voice continues to use it."

I asked MSNBC's Chris Hayes, host of *The Chris Hayes Show*, for his thoughts.

Etan: You've been supportive of athletes using their voice as a political platform. How important do you think it is, right now, for athletes to speak out?

Chris Hayes: Well, I think it's always important, but I don't think it's any different from any other citizen. It's important because citizenship is important, and civic society is important, and athletes are citizens; they are human beings; they are fellow members of the American political system. It's particularly important, I think, because it's not just a massive platform, but access to audiences that might not find their perspective. That, to me, is why it is so important, but it is also a very loaded topic.

A professional athlete has an access to a set of people watching him or her that is not defined by politics. Whereas the rest of media is increasingly organized around political lines. So if you're LeBron or Dwyane Wade or Russell Westbrook or you're Colin Kaepernick, and you're giving a postgame press conference, the audience for that is not an audience defined by people's politics . . . That's actually what's both so powerful and so explosive about it. Because people are coming to it because they want to see how their fantasy football players did. And they're like, "Whoa, whoa, whoa . . ."

Etan: Right. So it's kind of invading their space.

Hayes: That's exactly right! Yeah, but that's productive. One thing I struggle with is that it's gotta go both ways also, in the sense of an athlete who's a Trump supporter has every right to express their ideas and thoughts and opinions as an athlete who is not. Because people are selective, where they'll be like, "Oh, I'm glad you're speaking out," when you agree with me, but it's like, "Oh, you're an athlete, why do I want to hear what you have to say?" when they don't agree. You can't do that. It has to go both ways.

Etan: Nobody is disagreeing with the athlete speaking out about domestic violence. But anytime you're dealing with a more divisive topic, whether it's Mike Brown or Trayvon Martin or Trump, that's where there's an issue. But from an athlete's perspective, you have to know that when you do speak out, some will agree with you, some will vehemently disagree with you, and that's okay.

Hayes: Oh no, that's fine. I just feel like people need to check themselves, myself included. If an athlete is speaking out in a way that you don't agree, there's that instinct to be like, "Well, what the hell do you know?" *(Laughter)* But if they speak about a thing you do agree on, there's an instinct to be like . . . *(clapping)*, but you gotta be consistent.

I do think there's a particularity around race. Because the racial dynamics of sports performance and fandom are so complex, and loaded, and now I think it's part of the other thing that's so profound and powerful, particularly around issues of race: that Black athletes have an access to a white audience to be able to talk to them about the experience of race that very few others will have or ever have . . .

I think the politics of sports are interesting, and sports is such a massive part of our public life . . . It's like Silicon Valley isn't "politics," but there's a lot of politics about what goes on in Silicon Valley. You can't understand Silicon Valley without understanding politics. Politics are what shapes the structure of those markets, the structure of how things get raised, the perception. The same thing is true with sports, and in some ways sports occupies even a bigger part of our mental landscape.

Me and Chris Hayes after an interview. He always enjoys talking sports and politics with me.

Etan: When the New England Patriots visited the White House on April 19, 2017, after winning the Super Bowl, many athletes chose not to attend. How strong of a message does that send, or do you think this is less about social justice and more about Trump himself?

Hayes: Yeah, I mean in some places, Trump is the polarizing thing. It's not just sports.

Etan: So it seems like you're forced to have an opinion about it even if you're not into politics.

Hayes: Totally, yes. Agreed. But now I'm going to go and walk on the other side and argue against myself.

Etan: Okay, go ahead.

Hayes: The country is increasingly polarized. That's a brute fact. This is diagnosed in a hundred different ways . . . Like what kind of restaurant you eat at. Like where you live, urban or rural. And the thing that I will say that I like about sports, I do like the fact that I find myself talking to someone who I don't share political views with, where we can discuss sports.

There's something amazing in a landscape of America in which people are so polarized. There is this pressure-valve thing . . . I can talk the playoffs or the Cubs or whatever, with anyone, across any political perspective.

And a really interesting moment in the culture right now is whether sports becomes something increasingly like other parts of culture. In terms of that polarization. And I'm not saying it's good or bad, I'm just saying that's a question right now . . . Can sports preserve that in the face of an increasingly polarized America?

Etan: Okay, let's say you have somebody who is an avid Trump supporter and you're talking to them about the playoffs. Are you saying that can provide some common ground? In hopes of moving toward some type of growth or something positive?

Hayes: Yeah. In fact, that's the power that particularly athletes hold: to have the ability to move people. And I'm actually more curious about what you think about this.

Etan: I'm supposed to be interviewing *you*, Chris *(laughing)*.

ETAN THOMAS ⚡ 191

Hayes: I know, but unfortunately, I don't get a chance to talk about this as much as I would like . . . but when you have really high-profile examples of athletes coming out on political issues, I feel like most of the coverage tends to focus on the backlash, right? . . . But I was wondering about the people who aren't being loudly backlashy. I always wonder if it's penetrating them. And you'll see these sort of interesting defenses from people . . . You'll see someone come and defend Colin Kaepernick and you'll be like, *I am absolutely shocked that you of all people would be a person to defend Colin Kaepernick.*

Etan: That's a good point. Because there was definitely some unexpected support that I saw, though it also worked the opposite way as well. Even with certain members of the Patriots choosing not to go to the White House because of Trump, you saw some people vehemently objecting to that, using words like *anti-American* and *anti-police.*

Hayes: So, Kaepernick took a stance that was this really admirably conscientious private gesture. And the response was, "Oh, you're an attention hog." And it's like . . . he was just doing this thing as his expression of conscience. But other people made it this big thing and then obviously it went from there. What's amazing about it is just the platform. And you were absolutely right when you said it's like you are invading people's safe space. You are forcing people, in a part of American life, where they're not thinking about politics, to think about politics.

Etan: As you know, I grew up in Tulsa, Oklahoma. I'm looking at some of the Trump rallies, and I'm looking at the same people who I went to school with on Facebook. And they are these avid Trump supporters. Or I think of fans who are filling up the arenas, going to the Oklahoma City Thunder games, then going to the Trump supporters' rally. So then there's this dynamic where you think, *Okay, it's not quite transferring. You see me and love me and cheer for me on the court, but as soon as the game is over, you put on your* Make America Great Again *hat and go talk about building a wall?*

Hayes: I think that's what's so powerful, right? I mean, the thing that you can't escape in all this is race and the centrality of it . . . But the racial dynamics of fandom are really complicated. Like the racial dynamics of white fandom. For many white people, the most intense focus and attention they have on a Black person is an athlete. For a lot of people, particularly for men of a certain age. Like if you're a fifty-five-year-old white man in Oklahoma and you're a Thunder fan, you're invested in Russell Westbrook in a way that's like really, fascinatingly, psychologically fraught.

Etan: No question. So you feel love and admiration toward Russell Westbrook, then Terence Crutcher is murdered in Tulsa and you feel nothing.

Hayes: But even when that happened to Thabo Sefolosha, no one did anything. That's what's so fascinating. I was surprised that moment wasn't bigger for that reason. Where I sort of feel like, even at the pure level of fandom, just apolitical fandom, you broke my dude's leg. He was going to play for us and you took him out of the playoffs. And I was surprised that was not a bigger thing.

Etan: Why do you think that is?

Hayes: I think because sports coverage is still conditioned to be resistant about letting those issues in. They don't know how to deal with it and it's like the police say, "Well, he was being unruly," or whatever they said about Thabo.

Etan: "Resisting arrest."

Hayes: "Resisting arrest," which is just like the first excuse or justification that is always given in any case . . . But it's like there's just this fear of wading into the thicket of that. Although that's changed a little, but it still has a long way to go as we saw with the coverage of Thabo Sefolosha.

Etan: It has a very, very long way to go, but the reason we are seeing any change at all is because of the athletes in particular. It's like they're forcing people to talk about it. So before, the CEO of Under Armour came out and supported Trump. Now Steph Curry, Misty Copeland, and the Rock—three of the most high-profile people sponsored by Under Armour—came out and said, "No, we do not support this." They were very clear about their position and then you saw the CEO completely backtrack on his statement. You know what I mean?

Hayes: That's power.

Etan: It's power. So the fact that more athletes, right now, are using that power, I don't know if we have ever seen this. We can go back to the sixties, but even then, it was a select few.

Hayes: Oh, it's more than I've ever seen in my lifetime . . . There is no question that athletes have been more outspoken, committed, and public on controversial political issues.

Etan: I just hope it continues to grow.

Hayes: Why do you think that's changed? Because I feel like when you were playing, you were like a real outlier in a way that if I put you on a team right now . . .

Etan: It would almost be the norm—almost.

Hayes: It wouldn't be the norm, but it would be closer to the norm than when you played. Because when you played it was like, "Whoooaaaa, he's talking about Iraq? He's talking about President Bush?" And not just lightly talking about it, but breaking it down to particulars and verbalizing those particulars in a way that I personally had never really heard an athlete do.

Etan: I think people are more aware now. I don't want to say things have gotten so much worse, but with Trump, you've got to say that people are more aware of how bad it is. A lot of that may have to do with social media as well. You had police brutality before, but now everybody is seeing it on video. Then they are seeing cops get away with it. So that is pushing guys to speak out who have never spoken out before. It's a beautiful thing to see so many young athletes using that power because it forces people to have conversations and deal with things that they don't want to deal with in their sports arena.

Hayes: Absolutely. That's 100 percent true.

Etan: So why do you think people don't want to deal with this so much in their sports arena?

Hayes: I think there's two reasons. One is it creates a weird, uncomfortable fan/athlete relationship. If a person's saying something that you don't agree with, it instantly complicates the emotional experience of fandom. So for me, my example of this is Jake Arrieta. Jake Arrieta is like stud star pitcher for the Cubs. I'm a huge Cubs fan, I am massively invested in Jake Arrieta's performance. I always sort of suspected his politics were conservative 'cause he's like a good ol' boy, he's from Texas . . . He tweeted after Trump was elected, "Time for Hollywood to pony up and head for the border #illhelpyoupack #beatit."

Etan: That ruined it for you.

Hayes: Right! Like all of a sudden, the emotional relationship that I had with this person, who's a complete stranger to me by the way . . . I just project, which is the experience of fandom, I project all this emotional investment and all of a sudden I was like, *Uhhhhhh, what a bummer.*

Etan: Right.

Hayes: It's like the experience of fandom is bizarre, irrational, childlike in its emotional simplicity . . . Then another part of it, particularly when the issues are front and center of race, which I think have been the most kinetic, explosive, dominant in this era . . . I think part of it is just like white resistance to talking about race and dealing with racial inequality and wanting and feeling like, *I don't want to hear about it,* or resistance or feeling like they are being attacked or they are being guilt-tripped for all these things, which shows up in other domains but is particularly intense in the very racially fraught experience of white fandom with Black athletes.

So I think it's those two things together. Which I think applies in different directions. Do I wish Arrieta had not tweeted that? Yes, and then I think there's a more profound kind of social justice point, the particular nature of white fandom and Black athletes and this sort of pretty messed-up kind of . . . thing that a lot of white fans want, which is like, "I want to root for you but I don't want to see the larger racial context of your life and your existence. Just shut up about that."

Etan: Interesting. I also interviewed Craig Hodges, who talked about his experience with the Chicago Bulls after he wrote the letter to the older Bush. A lot of fans turned on him. He was the three-time three-point champion. He had one of the highest three-point percentages in the NBA, but everybody looked at him differently now because they knew what he thought.

Hayes: Right. And in some ways . . . there's a certain undo-ability to that. Like I can never go back to the world in which I don't know that Jake Arrieta feels this way. It's like forever . . . But again, that's one hundred times more loaded in the context of "white fans, Black athletes" issues of racial justice.

Etan: Keep going with that. Say specifically what you mean by "loaded."

Hayes: It's loaded for the athletes in terms of the wrath that they can incur. It's loaded for the fans because they feel like some part of the edifice they built around their understanding of race is being challenged or they are being guilt-tripped.

Etan: Then you have someone like Trump, who is polarizing on racial issues, but in the opposite direction. That makes people uncomfortable too.

Hayes: Yes, it definitely does. I do think that Trump is definitely polarizing, but also so polarizing in sort of demographically predictable ways. When you're looking at the New York Knicks, what did Trump get of the share of die-hard New York Knicks folks? Not that much . . . What did he get of the die-hard Chicago Bulls fans? Not that much. Right? . . . I think in a weird way, because he's so polarizing and because that polarization has been forced into so many parts of life, it's made it safer for athletes to come out.

Etan: I agree.

Hayes: It's like, well, everyone's choosing sides and everyone's sort of out there about this thing and no one's going to pretend that this huge polarizing event didn't happen in American life. So I'm not going to pretend either. And then, also, if I happen to be in a market, I'm not saying that athletes are calculating, because I don't think they are, but I also think it's a case of, if you come out against Trump while you're a starter for the New York Knicks, I don't think you've really hurt yourself.

Etan: Okay, but then you have somebody like Gregg Popovich, who coaches in San Antonio, Texas. He hasn't really experienced a lot of backlash, but then there's a different racial dynamic since he's not Black.

Hayes: Yeah, I totally agree, although I also think it's like the same thing with Kerr. Like Kerr's a better example. Curry and Kerr, they're in the East Bay.

Etan: Right. They're different, but Popovich is in Texas and Cuban is in Texas and that's a little bit different, and they're also white men speaking out.

Hayes: Exactly, and they haven't gotten that same, "Why does anyone want to hear what you have to say?" Or the, "You're just an athlete so shut up and play basketball."

Etan: Let me ask you this, though. If they were both Black—if Popovich was a Black head coach and Mark Cuban was a Black CEO—would the reaction have been different?

Hayes: Hmm, good question. I think it would be. I think it always is . . . I do think the Popovich thing is a fascinating case study 'cause I was kind of blown away that he said that. I was like, *Whoa, dude.*

Etan: I was too, and I was waiting for the backlash.

Hayes: And I was waiting for the backlash too. I also sort of always assumed coaches are conservatives.

Etan: Especially in the NFL. The NFL is different than the NBA.

Hayes: I would be curious what you think. I also think there's just a huge difference, to me, in the politics of the leagues.

Etan: The NBA versus the NFL? Completely. Night and day. Not even close.

Hayes: The NBA appears to be a much more liberal league as a whole. There's a certain raw demographic nature of the fact that the NBA is a Black league. African Americans in America are more liberal than white people, on the whole, on average. Ergo, it's a more liberal league.

Etan: What are the percentages of Black people in the NFL, though? It's not a "Black league" but the percentage is pretty high.

Hayes: It's pretty high. The other thing to think about is that as leagues get less white, how do they manage the politics of that? Because my feeling about the NBA is so defined by these sort of . . . There was the Magic-Bird era, which is this perfect rivalry for the league to promote, both because they're incredible players but also one's white, one's Black.

Etan: And they're friends.

Hayes: They're friends. One's from, you know, one plays out west, one plays in the Northeast. It was so perfect. It was like this perfectly representative thing of what they wanted. Then you get the Jordan era and Jordan achieves this level of apolitical stardom because he chose to be apolitical—that's incredibly transcendent across racial lines because he chooses to sublimate anything that would threaten that, right?

Etan: Right.

Hayes: The point of politics in the league is the fight in Auburn Hills. The Pacers-Detroit fight.

Etan: Of course, the "Brawl in the Palace."

Hayes: Which is where all of the ugly subtext about white fandom comes out.

Etan: The fear.

Hayes: The fear. Thugs, all this stuff. The fact that they actually swung at fans. It was just like the worst nightmare from a management perspective. And that's the point where you see the league in its conception and projection, to me, take a kind of right-wing turn. Like that's when the dress code comes in . . . the idea of, we need to make these athletes less threatening from a marketing perspective. I remember you writing at length about this topic and you were spot on. There's also the Latrell Sprewell incident too, which was a Black man choking a white coach; that's when the league got into this very kind of reactionary Black-lash place, and then I think, for whatever reason, they started to come out of that in the last eight years . . . The league, to me, got less reactionary and more progressive over, say, the last eight years.

Etan: As far as what in particular?

Hayes: The messages it's sending, the tenor of its public service announcements, its relationship to American politics in terms of the outspokenness of its players . . . From 2004 to like 2011, there's this kind of reactionary turn. Three things happen in that era. There's [Allen Iverson] and the crazy challenge that A.I. is to the league's image because he's . . . so unapologetically Black. Everything about his game, the cornrows, the way he's perceived, he records a hip-hop album. The Latrell Sprewell coaching incident, the "Brawl in the Palace." That period . . . you can feel the league feeling a crisis about its management of how it's selling "Blackness" as nonthreatening to its white fans.
My question to *you* is, what happened?

Etan: So what I saw happen was, you had the Trayvon Martin murder. Then you had Eric Garner's murder. Then you had Michael Brown's murder. Then you had Trump elected. I think *that's* what happened.

Hayes: So you think it's just like society was driving consciousness among the athletes, who then pushed the league in a direction?

Etan: That's exactly what I think. What do you think?

Hayes: Yeah, I think that's right. I also wonder . . . I'm just curious about the demographics of the league's fandom . . . because the thing about basketball is it's all about economics, as is all sports. And the people that spend money on NBA league pass packages, jerseys, they're majority white but disproportionately Black. Right? So the league's fandom, the people it's marketing to, are a greater share of African Americans than the American populace. And I wonder how much of the "progressiveness" is simply because they recognize their fan base.

Etan: There's no question. Because you look at the difference in the NBA and NFL. The NFL is completely different—I don't think they would have embraced some of the activism we saw in the NBA. Can you imagine if all the NFL players wore *I Can't Breathe* jerseys?

Hayes: They'd go crazy. But you think that's also about the fan base?

Etan: I'm not sure if it's the fan base. I think the powers-that-be in the NFL are a lot more conservative. So it just kind of trickles down.

Hayes: Right.

Etan: So . . . there's a little bit of suppression of athletes speaking out in a way that you don't really see in the NBA.

Hayes: Yeah. That's definitely how it feels.

Etan: Because LeBron doesn't get the backlash that Kaepernick gets.

Hayes: No.

Etan: LeBron has done a lot and said a lot of the same things that Kaepernick has said, but the backlash is completely different. I think that's just the way it is.

Interview with Alonzo Mourning

Back in high school and college, if anybody asked me what type of player that I wanted to play like, I would immediately say Alonzo Mourning. When I saw him transform his body from his early years at Georgetown to his years with the Miami Heat, where he at times almost resembled an action figure, it made me get in the weight room. His power jump hook to the middle of the lane. His sweep to the middle, then spin to the baseline. The way he blocked shots, the physicality and intensity he played with, and how hard he worked on the court. In fact, one of the reasons I wore 33 at Syracuse was because of Alonzo Mourning.

Another thing I noticed about Alonzo Mourning was how much work he did in the community—his activism, and his willingness to take a stand on different issues. It was an honor to serve with him as a "surrogate" for President Obama during both terms. As a surrogate, I campaigned on the president's behalf: I woud appear at rallies performing spoken word or giving speeches; and I participated in debates and political discussions on MSN-BC and at various events in DC. Alonzo would engage in other types of activities, such as hosting campaign fund-raisers in Miami. I would support Alonzo's events and he would support mine. He has sat on a few of my panel discussions, including the Black Lives Matter program we did during All-Star Weekend 2015 in Harlem.

Alonzo is a great example of an athlete who took his education seriously, wasn't afraid to speak out, and has used basketball to open doors to change.

Me and President Obama shooting hoops at the Easter Egg Roll. It was an honor being a surrogate for the Obama administration, participating in his fatherhood initiative, and working with My Brother's Keeper.

Etan: What led to your decision to throw your full support behind President Obama?

Alonzo Mourning: When I saw the opportunity and the potential he had, and the overall way he communicated to the American people, that drew me to understand that this brother is going to need all of the support he can possibly get to become the commander in chief. So when I had the opportunity to support him, I jumped at that opportunity. He is a huge basketball fan as everybody knows, and through the up-close-and-personal interactions that we did have, we developed a brotherly type of relationship and it was genuine. We shot around on the court . . . We developed the type of relationship that allowed me to continue to support him on his journey and utilize that camaraderie to build bridges. He had a dedication to helping boys and young men of color, and by serving on his initiatives and boards like My Brother's Keeper and the President's Counsel on Fitness, Sports, and Nutrition, which was very near and dear to my heart . . . And as his term progressed, and he won the presidency and his responsibilities increased, it became more and more evident that there were forces who did not want to see him succeed, which made me want to support him even more.

Etan: You live in Florida, a state that often goes "red" in presidential elections. Did you ever fear the blowback for your support of President Obama?

Mourning: I wasn't concerned with anybody else's opinion in any way, shape, or form . . . I did what I thought was right and I chose to support a man who was on the right side of right. Yes, he was the first African American president . . . but if he wasn't on the right side of right, he wouldn't have received my support. I closely examined the candidates that he was up against . . . but there was a genuineness behind President Obama in his understanding and caring about the American people, and that's what set him apart. You could hear it in his speeches of how he laid out the plans for us to be a better nation . . . It wasn't about color; it was about service and doing the right thing for our country as a whole, inclusive of everybody. And I think during his terms he did a phenomenal job, especially considering what he inherited and the opposition he received throughout his entire presidency. No other presidency in history experienced the level of disrespect and opposition that he experienced. No one. But he never turned bitter. When they went low, he went high, like First Lady Michelle Obama said. And they represented themselves with nothing but grace and class.

Etan: There were probably more athletes who actively supported President Obama than any other president in history.

Mourning: That definitely didn't surprise me. The way he communicated to the American people and the way he articulated his message helped us understand the genuineness behind his purpose and reason in wanting to become the president of the United States. That drew athletes to want to support him.

Etan: Now, with the Trump administration, the opposite is happening. We are seeing an unprecedented number of athletes and management speaking out *against* the president.

Mourning: The one thing about our political system is that everyone has their own different values and different opinions of how they see our country. And based on those different perspectives, each elected official is put into those positions to make decisions to serve the public, and unfortunately, it is very apparent that not everybody has those intentions. Some people speak a certain rhetoric that encourages people to vote for them and to put them in that particular position, but when they get there, their words are simply not genuine and their hidden agendas become revealed. Hearing the messages from the Trump administration, it is quite disheartening. There are not a lot of facts that are being expressed; instead, there are a lot of untruths . . . So of course you will have a lot of people, not just athletes, who object to those messages and the rhetoric, the untruths.

Etan: You do a lot of work in the community, especially through the Mourning Family Foundation and the Overtown Youth Center. In this Trump era, what is your direct message to the youth?

Mourning: To first of all do your homework. We live in a world that is dominated by technology. You are able to find the truth. Don't just believe what you hear on television, or what you hear people say on social media, but actually do your homework and educate yourself about what is going on and the rules of the game. There is a reason why the current administration put a gag order on our environmental agencies. Because they speak the truth . . . Think about it right now: as we speak, our executive government is actually putting a gag order on our environmental agencies, and that's a problem. That's a huge red flag. That has never happened in the history of the United States. So that should send you the signal or raise your curiosity as to what they are hiding . . .

Etan: So you are basically telling them to arm themselves with knowledge to combat the hidden and many times not-so-hidden agendas of this current administration?

Mourning: The easiest way to control somebody is to keep them uneducated . . . They made it illegal for us to be educated during slavery. It was against the law . . . That's why we had to sneak in churches and act like we were just having Sunday-morning church service—because our ancestors knew the power of being educated. And just as it was crucial then, it is crucial now. Education is the only way for you to be an active participant; you have to educate yourself on what is going on. So, for instance, when you don't vote, that's a problem. Educate yourself on, first of all, why you have the right to vote, educate yourself on the sacrifices that other people have made way before you even existed . . . Then you will understand the reason behind your vote, and that's just one example.

Etan: What would be your advice to other athletes?

Mourning: When you think of the stage we have, the presence we have on social media and with the media in general, when an athlete says something, people hear it. Doesn't mean they agree with it, but they hear it. They are exposed to it . . . We live in a society where everyone wants to follow but people don't want to lead. The way you become a leader is you create a positive movement that everybody can attach themselves to with the goal of making a difference in other people's lives. When you do that, it will become infectious . . . We as athletes have to realize how much power we have.

Interview with Kareem Abdul-Jabbar

I remember my mother giving me a VHS cas about Kareem Abdul-Jabbar called, *Kareem: Reflections from Inside.* I must have watched it a million times. And my grandfather always had a tremendous amount of respect for Kareem, going back to his days at Kareem's Power Memorial Academy in New York City. My grandfather always said that the sky hook was a shot that more people should utilize, including myself, but he also always talked about Kareem's intelligence. Different books that he had written, and projects that he has been involved with.

When I took my grandfather to meet Kareem, he immediately began asking the legend about people from the playground back in the "Rucker Park heyday." He thanked Kareem for being a great example for his grandson to follow, in how he was never afraid to stand up for what he believed and how he valued his education and pursued his writing and all of his other talents. It was an honor to interview Kareem for this book, and an honor that he was eager to be a part of it.

Etan: You of course have been on the Mount Rushmore of athlete-activists since your days at UCLA, but in the contemporary matters of police shootings and President Trump, how crucial is it for athletes to continue to let their voices be heard?

Kareem Abdul-Jabbar: I think that anyone who is concerned with his/her community should be involved. It doesn't matter if you're an athlete or not . . . I understand the tremendous platform that athletes have, but sometimes regular everyday concerned citizens have a tendency to sit back and expect someone else to speak out or take a stand. We don't want to put it all on the shoulders of athletes and entertainers . . . This is America. The First Amendment gives you the right to speak out on issues that you feel are important, and you should not hesitate to do that. Now, back to your specific question: all athletes have that right, and their additional status as athletes will make their platform bigger and enable them to reach more people on their platform and gain more attention, and it is my belief that they should definitely continue to do so in a positive way.

Etan: How do you feel about the people who go out of their way to tell athletes to just shut up and play?

Abdul-Jabbar: Pay them absolutely no attention at all. Nobody has the right to tell you what you can or cannot or should not be involved in. Athletes are no different from any other person. If you are concerned about something and you have a platform, then use it. The reason why those people focus on athletes is because their additional status in their community, among their peers, fans, and the entire country, means they have power and can really influence people. And of course just think of it logically: if you have someone with that type of power and influence, pushing for something you don't agree with, of course they are going to try to do whatever they can to silence them, because they are a threat to them . . . But athletes should definitely never shy away from their power, but rather recognize and embrace their capabilities. Look at what happened at the University of Missouri. The football team made a statement and the people on campus had to listen. They had that much power. Now, they should always use that power wisely, but that power is there.

Etan: You recently expressed a "rage of betrayal" that you felt from the election results, which seemed to roll back progress for people of color in America. You also stated that the country will find it difficult to make this transition if society "embraces the leadership of a racist." How do you see us as a country surviving the Trump presidency?

Abdul-Jabbar: Well, that's a tough question. I can't predict what is going to happen. I definitely don't want people hanging on my words thinking that I have some answers that I don't have. But I will tell you this: unless we get together and organize politically, whatever answers we do come up with won't be listened to. I think that is the most important issue here. President Obama said it very clearly: "Don't boo, vote." That means you have to organize, you have to understand what the issues are and vote with the people who agree with you in how to achieve progress. One thing that everyone really woke up to when Mr. Trump was elected was there was too much apathy, too many people said, "Well, the people who vote will take care of it." Well, your vote was missing, and your vote would have made a difference in that election. So we have to change that.

Etan: What was your reaction when you heard about the Muslim ban?

Abdul-Jabbar: Well, anytime that one group is singled out, that's an alarm. Just think about this logically, and historically: if one group is being singled out, subjected to sanctions, pointed at as the cause of problems, or thought of to need extra vetting or to be an overall threat to the well-being of the larger society . . . it's only a matter of time before the finger will be pointed at your group as well. This is a slowly creeping situation. I am glad that the system of checks and balances stepped on Mr. Trump's toes and made that an impossibility. But we have to be careful here. We are starting to regress . . . and that's really what we have to avoid. We are looking at a blatant attempt to erode all of the progress we have made over these last eight years, and that's not to say that President Obama was perfect or all of his policies were perfect, but there was a lot that we accomplished as a whole under his two terms, and it's sad to see that so much of that is being undone with the swipe of a pen . . . This is a tragedy and we have to combat it with all of our ability and all of our strength. And we have to do this together: Black, white, Christian, Muslim, male, female. We all have a common problem, and we have to come together to fight against this common problem.

Etan: How would you advise young people to get involved?

Abdul-Jabbar: They should use whatever means they have to get people out to vote. The whole "Get Out the Vote" campaign—that takes money, you know. One thing that we are sadly lacking is the financial wherewithal to become active politically. When we do not vote, our voice is diminished. That's how we increase our voice. And we have to increase our organizational capacity so that we can go out and vote and make our political power known.

Trump's plan involves scaring voters with a constant barrage of lies and exaggerations. The fact that this propaganda is so effective is especially sad, because the nation that once stood up to bullies like Hitler, Castro, and Khrushchev is now falling into goose-step behind a homegrown bully who seems afraid of everything that isn't part of his entitled life, who responds to his irrational fears the way a child does.

There is a reason that the administration continuously attacks the news media—because if they can continuously create doubts in the minds of the average person who is too lazy to read and educate themselves on these issues, they'll be incorrectly informed . . . People have to get to the point where they are not gullible. But, of course, that may be wishful thinking.

Etan: Another aspect of the current administration that has brought many athletes out is Trump's misogyny. We saw a massive women's protest all across the country . . . Talk about the importance of not only female athletes but also male athletes continuing to speak out against the sexism coming from the Trump administration.

Abdul-Jabbar: It's an indication of how they view women and the status they want to keep. We have to educate people and the women have to organize. If you look at some of the polls, so many women actually voted for

Trump and helped put him in office, which I definitely had a hard time and I still have a hard time comprehending. They actually voted *against* their best interest. They are either naive or ignorant to exactly what his intentions were and what his history was. But I don't see how they could be ignorant to that fact, because it was broadcasted so much prior to the election, so I am just as befuddled on that one as anyone else. We have to inform people and inform voters. But it's not just women who voted against their own interest. Many people . . . are now getting a rude awakening as they discover who he is and the direction he is taking us. We all should be very, very concerned about that.

Etan: Were you as surprised as I was to see some Black faces in the sports world standing next to Trump, urging other people to support him?

Abdul-Jabbar: Nothing really surprised me, Etan. Anytime someone like that can win the nomination, you know that there is a lot more to it than meets the eye. There is a lot of nostalgia for the good ol' days, right after World War II and thereabouts, where the people who controlled everything politically and economically were very comfortable. And that's changed a lot since then, and Trump brings back a nostalgia for that . . . So we have to be fully aware of what's going on and do our due diligence before we support anyone or allow ourselves to be used in that manner. We can't be puppets. We have to be educated, informed, knowledgeable people who can in turn use our platform and our powers for good, not allow ourselves to be used or exploited or taken advantage of for a photo op and used for evil. I can't belabor the point enough that the vote counts, and is of the utmost importance. And we have to be very careful of who we align ourselves with.

Etan: How do you feel about seeing young athletes being as involved as they are these days?

Abdul-Jabbar: I know that the young athletes are noticing what has been going on and they are alarmed. And I'm glad to see that they are paying attention and they are doing something about it. Just the fact that they are calling attention to what the issues are is helping. When athletes speak out, it creates an immediate dialogue . . . When a prominent athletes takes a stand, he is going to shed light on that topic and people are going to start talking about it . . . You can't change people's minds if people don't discuss the issues. They may see something or hear a point of view that they never would have imagined. And sometimes they can't hear that from other political figures because the political line in the sand has been drawn . . .

But most, most important, and I know I have repeated this like a broken record, but I am going to end with this: we have to get out and vote and athletes have to use their platforms to urge the masses to get out and vote . . . We can't complain after the fact, and have voter turnouts as low as they are. Youth voter turnout is consistently lower than the older generation . . . And not just the presidential elections, but local elections—the elections that decide who the mayor will be, who the police chief will be, who the local officials will be that directly impact their everyday lives. We have to keep encouraging the masses to vote so that we don't allow a catastrophe like Mr. Trump to ever happen again.

9

Connecting with Activists Matters

I watched the five-episode documentary *O.J.: Made in America* with my son Malcolm and he had a lot of questions. The film explores O.J. Simpson's arrival at the University of Southern California as the unstoppable running back who ran his way into a Heisman Trophy and into the hearts of mainstream America. This is what O.J. had always dreamed of.

"As a kid growing up in the ghetto, one of the things I wanted most was not money—it was fame. I wanted to be known. I wanted people to say, 'Hey, there goes O.J.'"

Malcolm asked, "Why did he care so much what other people thought of him?" I told him to keep watching.

The documentary reveals how much O.J. was completely removed from and oblivious to everything that was going on around him as it pertained to the Black community. While O.J. was enjoying his newfound fame at USC, racial turmoil in neighborhoods near the campus gave rise to turbulent times. The documentary shows the great migration of African Americans to California, pursuing jobs and fleeing Jim Crow and the bigotry of the South. Many whites were not too happy with their new neighbors. The prevailing notion was that California was a utopia where prejudice and hate didn't exist; unfortunately, many of the Blacks who arrived found out that it was in fact far from a racially harmonious paradise.

When William H. Parker was appointed chief of police in 1950, LA's white population applauded and welcomed a new era of policing that boasted a military-like professionalism.

Yet the Black community faced increased incidents of police brutality and harassment—things that just didn't happen in the white communities.

Then there was the eventual tipping point of the Watts riots of 1965, when the entire city exploded amid growing tensions between the Black community and the police. Los Angeles went up in flames. Six days of looting and arson followed. The LAPD called in the support of thousands of members of the National Guard.

Malcolm watched the scene unfolding and said, "That looks just like Ferguson after Mike Brown or Baltimore after Freddie Gray." My wife glanced at me with sad eyes.

In the film, Dr. Harry Edwards discusses how athletes were looking to respond to the Watts riots and everything else that was going on. At a press conference to announce the Olympic Project for Human Rights—an organization formed to bring attention to racism and prejudice in sports—it was announced that the athletes were considering an Olympic boycott. When O.J. was asked about his position, he quickly distanced himself, saying that what the other athletes were doing was their own prerogative but he wasn't going to be involved. Dr. Harry Edwards offers his explanation: the athletes were tired of seeing our people being treated as second-class citizens, and if O.J., as one of the most popular athletes at that time, had joined them, it would have made a huge impact on the movement. That's when O.J. uttered the words that made Malcolm pause the TV: "I'm not Black, I'm O.J."

"What on earth did he mean by that?" asked Malcolm. He repeated it three times in disbelief.

I told him to keep watching and we'd talk after the episode. Malcolm saw the situation get worse and worse. He watched O.J.'s friends describe how he lost himself. How disappointed they were with some of his decisions and choices. After the episode's conclusion, Malcolm asked, "Why didn't some older people try to talk to O.J. or something? Mentor him? Give him some good advice? Why didn't his friends tell him he was tripping?" I said that I'd bet they tried but I wasn't sure he was listening to their advice.

So Malcolm said it again: "*I'm not Black, I'm O.J.*" He thought about it for a while and then put it all together. "So when he was at the table at the bar with the one guy—what was his name?"

"That was Joe Namath," I said.

"Yeah, him. Well, he was at the table at his bar and the white lady asked the old white man why O.J. was sitting there with all of those N-words, and the old white guy told O.J. what the lady said and was trying to apologize to O.J. and the dude was smiling and happy like, *No, it's great, this is exactly*

212 ☆ WE MATTER

what I've always wanted. They don't look at me as one of them. And he said that
he knew at that moment that O.J. was . . . screwed. He didn't say *screwed*,
but I can't say what he said." Malcolm continued, "Isn't that even worse for
an old white guy to be able to see that there was something wrong with that,
but O.J. couldn't?"

I told him yeah, it seemed pretty bad to me.

And then Malcolm said, "So, when all that bad stuff that was going on
with the police beating the Black people and hitting them with their batons
and snatching them up for no reason, and it was all happening right around
the corner from the school O.J. was going to, and all the Black athletes
wanted to do something major like boycott the Olympics and they tried to
get him on board with them, he said, 'I'm not Black, I'm O.J.,' because he
didn't want to make the white people mad at him and wanted to be in all
the commercials so he could be running through the airport and on TV and
movies and all of that. He cared more about that than standing up for the
Black community?"

"Well, it looks like you pieced it all together, Malcolm. If you want, you
can write your school report about this."

"Oh, this will be easy to write. This is not going to end well. Hope he
wakes up before it's too late. Did he eventually wake up? Did somebody talk
to him before it was too late?"

My wife and I looked at each other and shook our heads. I said, "We'll
just watch the rest of the episodes and I think you'll get your answer."

After watching the full documentary, I wanted to interview sociologist
and civil rights activist Dr. Harry Edwards. He currently works as a team
consultant for the San Francisco 49ers and has mentored Colin Kaepernick.
I wanted to ask him about the "I'm not Black, I'm O.J." statement, and
go a little deeper into the ramifications of athletes adopting that type of a
mentality. I also wanted to discuss the mentoring and nurturing he provided
for Kaepernick and how important it is for athletes to receive that kind of
guidance.

Interview with Dr. Harry Edwards

Etan: You have said that you believe Colin Kaepernick should be in the Smithsonian right next to Muhammad Ali and John Carlos and Tommie Smith.

Dr. Harry Edwards: I definitely feel that he should be in the Smithsonian and the National Museum of African American History and Culture right alongside Ali and Jim Brown and Bill Russell and Arthur Ashe and John Carlos and Tommie Smith and Curt Flood and Paul Robeson and some of these other great athlete-activists who have made such great contributions over the past decades in terms of the struggle for African American freedom, justice, and equality . . . Muhammad Ali was in one sense the godfather of the militant athlete-activist movement in the 1960s, beginning with his outspokenness . . . We have a whole generation of athletes who followed in that tradition of Ali and who in a sense broke with their fathers . . . that group that had come before in the post–World War II years into the 1960s.

Kaepernick provided that same function for this era of athletes. In speaking out—not after he was through playing and it was safe and he was away and nobody could say anything negatively about the team or the organization. He did it while he was an active athlete and, point of fact, while he was a backup, which did not detract from the courage and the sincerity of his message but magnified it . . . He ignited something that all of the congresspeople, all of the preachers and protesters and community organizers, including President Obama, had never been able to fully achieve. He got everybody from the president down to the people on the street talking about race, its meaning in this age, and how it is still contouring and influencing the quality and the caliber of life in American society . . . So I think it's appropriate that Colin Kaepernick's jersey, the *Time* cover that he was on, that all should be put in the Smithsonian right next to Muhammad Ali's gloves that he wore when he defeated Sonny Liston and the robe that he wore when he fought in the United States Olympic team in Rome.

Etan: You have spoken about how Malcolm X counseled Muhammad Ali. Were you able to be that counselor to Kaepernick, giving him guidance on how to handle the criticism that was sure to come?

Edwards: Absolutely. Everything from what he should be reading, such as *The Autobiography of Malcolm X*, various writings and articles by Muhammad Ali, right up to what to expect and how to handle the death threats that were inevitably going to come. I made it very clear that there is a price to pay for this type of a stance and he understood that and he was totally committed to doing all that he possibly could to educate and prepare himself for the stand he was taking.

I never tried to tell Kap what to do. That's not the job of a counselor . . . I've never counseled athletes about what to do. What I've counseled them about are what the options are and what the likely outcomes of those options will most likely be, and then I leave it to the athletes to make up their own minds about what they're going to do and how they are going to do it. I let Kap know unequivocally and absolutely I was always there for him, and if he had any questions or had any issues or if anything came up, I would be here to help as much as I possibly could . . . And of course, at the end of the season his teammates voted him the most prestigious award that the San Francisco 49ers organization gives to a player—the Len Eshmont Award for courage and strength—so that is indicative of the fact that Kap handled himself very well in terms of his teammates in the locker room.

Etan: I recently watched the ESPN documentary *O.J.: Made in America*. It shows what you tried to convince O.J. to do, and how he basically rejected taking any part in the type of thing Kaepernick is doing.

Edwards: Here is the conundrum in regards to this situation. When I approached O.J. about supporting the Olympic Project for Human Rights, he was very, very clear. When I said Black Athletes are looking to unite, he stopped me and said, "I'm not Black, I'm O.J.," and what he was saying wasn't that he felt he wasn't Black racially, he was saying that he wasn't Black in terms of the orthodoxy, that demands that there is a pattern that all Black people must subscribe to . . . And his point was well taken. I had to stop and pause, because what he was saying essentially was, "Larry Bird is not obligated . . . to stand up for all poor white people in French Lick, Indiana. So why should I be obligated to move away from everything I have worked for and be asked to make this tremendous sacrifice and stand up for all Black people in America?" That's a legitimate question.

Now, what's equally legitimate is, if you decide not to do that, there's a price to be paid for it. And Black people have every right to collect that price and that cost. So when somebody makes a statement like, "I'm not Black, I'm O.J.," they are telling you who and what they are. That is what they have chosen . . . There is a legitimate question as to the obligation of every athlete to do that. But you also pay for the choice that you make. So O.J., in doing what he did, made his choice.

And Black people have every right to collect that price and that cost. So when somebody makes a statement like, "I'm not Black, I'm O.J.," they are telling you who and what they are. That is what they have chosen.

Etan: Expound on that for me, if you could.

Edwards: It goes back to an old saying that has been passed around in the African American community. *What does a man gain who wins the world but loses his soul?* Something along those lines. Black folks know that. They feel that. And even though they cheered when O.J. beat the rap on those two murders, they weren't cheering for O.J. They were cheering for all of those Black people who had been abused and beaten and stomped down by the police and the justice system for generations and generations . . . So the question comes back up: is there an obligation for Black athletes or Black media to stand up for the Black community and speak on the behalf of the Black community? Because nobody puts that on Larry Bird.

And my answer to that is that white people are not in the same position as Black people here in America. So Larry Bird doesn't really have a dog in that fight. In America, there are people on death row for no other reason but that they are Black . . . There are people who are unemployed because they are Black. Little kids in school being suspended and expelled because they are Black. Little white kids doing the same thing are treated differently. There are people who are oppressed because they are Black. Murdered by the police because they are Black.

Etan: When Kaepernick took his stance during the national anthem, at first none of the other players really supported him. It looked like he was really out there by himself, and we know that throughout history, so many great people who stand for something are often standing alone. Did that affect Kaepernick?

Edwards: Well, first of all, my office at the San Francisco 49ers is the locker room . . . So anyone who thinks that Kaepernick didn't have any support in the locker room because he was the only one who took the knee has greatly misread the situation. The struggle for freedom, justice, and equality in the Black culture and community is so pervasive and so all-encompassing that even when people are not willing to necessarily stand with an individual, although they may not have physically joined the movement, it won't be long before they are still saying, "Amen" . . . He said things that most of us didn't have the position or the courage to say, and we not only supported him, but we loved him. And so even when Kap was sitting and kneeling by himself, when you talked to in particular the Black athletes, they said, "Yeah, we understand what the brother is saying. Am I ready to do it with him? No, but do I support him? Yes." So the idea of people around the league getting his message and people around the league supporting him and respecting him are two very different things. They got his message even though they didn't take a knee with him . . . I don't care if Kaepernick never does another thing in his life on the football field or off of it. That puts him in the same category as Ali in sports, as Rosa Parks in the nonviolent direct-action civil rights struggle.

A lot of times you can't see it until you're a long way away because history is like a mountain. And you can't see the mountain when you are right on top of it. You have to be a distance away from it before you can see it . . . So I insisted, I talked to the people at the Smithsonian, I talked to them about Kaepernick and his role in this situation, and their response was, "Absolutely." Even if people can't see it today, they will see it ten, twenty, thirty years from now, or like Ali, fifty years from now.

Interview with Ilyasah Shabazz

Every athlete needs a mentor. Someone to guide them, prepare them, encourage them. Someone who they can bounce ideas off of. I was blessed to always have mentors in my life. My grandfather; my AAU coach Reverend Potter; Louis Orr, my assistant coach at Syracuse; my current pastor, John K. Jenkins. You need people who will tell you the absolute truth and are not in the least bit worried about offending you, hurting your feelings, or damaging your relationship with them. Mentoring is often what athletes point to as one of the vital reasons for their success; or they might say that the absence of it contributed to their demise.

Everybody who knows me or has heard me speak is aware of the influence that Malcolm X has had on my life. I remember the day I picked up *The Autobiography of Malcolm X* in the seventh grade—it literally changed my entire life. It was as if I was walking around with blinders on and then someone took them off. Anyone who knew me back then saw the change. I started talking differently, told everyone to never use the N-word around me, started challenging teachers about what we were being taught. I was ordered by teachers and the principal to stop doing the Black Power salute during school assemblies (and of course I didn't stop). I could keep going, but my point is: at that moment I officially became WOKE, but I needed guidance and I needed mentoring, and I am just thankful that I had people at that time to help me through everything.

Dr. Edwards talks about Muhammad Ali being mentored by Malcolm X, and I wanted to delve a little deeper into this subject. Who better to speak with than one of Malcolm X's daughters? I have done several projects with Ilyasah Shabazz before, and she has participated in a few panel discussions I have organized. I wanted to ask her about the mentoring that her father provided for Muhammad Ali. Who knows what Ali's legacy would have been had he never received that nurturing? He may have just been another great boxer, and not the ultimate symbol of the athlete-activist who doesn't hesitate to stand firm on what he believes, even in the face of intense opposition.

Me and Malcolm with Ilyasah Shabazz. After the conversation Malcolm said to me, "Daddy, can you believe you just interviewed Malcolm X's daughter?"

Etan: How important do you think it is for athletes to link with activists the way that Muhammad Ali connected with Malcolm X?

Ilyasah Shabazz: My father played a pivotal role providing Muhammad Ali with a more accurate understanding of his self-worth, contrary to what was systemically taught about people of color—specifically of African ancestry. Muhammad Ali said had he not met my father, his epitaph would have simply read, *Here lies one of the greatest fighters.* But because of my father, he was so much more, and Malcolm helped him develop into the man he became . . . They developed a friendship and brotherhood. He was right there with him when he became the heavyweight champion of the world at the age of twenty-two. My father recruited Muhammad Ali into the Nation of Islam. He was right beside him on the day a young Cassius Clay announced that his new name was Muhammad Ali, when he became the heavyweight champion of the world and he had all eyes on him.

Etan: So without that nurturing from Malcolm X, Ali would have remained Cassius Clay—not only in name but in consciousness.

Shabazz: Exactly! He wouldn't have known his higher being, his potential and power as a man . . . Once you have an identity, understand your rich heritage, and you know your power and your capability, it's like someone turns on the lights when most of your life you have been sitting in a dark room . . . If nobody points out that something is wrong, you won't know that something is wrong. If nobody points out injustice, you'll think that everything is just. All that has to be cultivated; you have to be taught and then you can go about making a change in the world, and that's what we are all called to do . . . And so in history, we see why it is extremely important for scholars, activists, teachers—everyone who is in any position to mentor—to do so with the younger generation as a whole, and in speaking specifically about athletes, entertainers, musicians, actors who are able to move the needle and gain the attention of the masses because they have the eyes and ears of the world.

When Ali became the champion of the world, and he had all eyes on him, his message reverberated throughout the entire world because of that celebrated platform. My father spoke to him regarding his responsibility to others. So if Muhammad Ali, like many others, never knew of the power or the will he possessed, that in itself would have been a tragedy. And there are so many athletes now who don't know their potential and their power and responsibility, which is why I agreed to talk with you, Etan, and support your work.

Etan: What are some other things your father taught Ali?

Shabazz: Well, he taught him how not to be deterred by or fear the media, to use that attention to his advantage and make a stand for what he knew was right for all human beings . . . My father was fearless because he believed that God was the only judge, and he passed down that sentiment to Muhammad Ali.

Etan: How important do you think that level of mentorship is in today's world?

Shabazz: Again, this speaks to the importance of mentoring, especially having intergenerational discussions—especially for young men without fathers . . . We are missing the intergenerational connection our ancestors once instilled in their young. I mean, they went through an entire process of preparation. Lots of athletes have an emptiness and don't know that they are already an authentic jewel just as they are . . . Just think if some of our great athletes were told how great and powerful they really are *as they are*. If they were told of their potential and what they could really become. But they have to be taught . . . They also have to be forewarned of the many forces that will come to tear them down, which come in many, many forms.

Etan: Why don't we see more of an emphasis on mentoring?

Shabazz: Well, there are a lot of reasons why many of us are reluctant to mentor . . . We still have divisions within our culture that have been plaguing our people since slavery . . . One thing I learned from my parents is: when you understand history in its accuracy and totality, you understand your self-worth and you understand that no one is going to fix your personal or societal challenges. We have to do these things ourselves. And many celebrities really have stepped up to the plate. They understand the African proverb that it takes a village to raise a child. It's the only way.

Interview with Shaun King

When it comes to activism, social justice, and police brutality, one of the few reporters who I consider a fellow activist and who is making sure injustice is exposed is Shaun King.

King has written a great deal about the Black Lives Matter movement. His coverage of the Mike Brown murder and the following rebellion in Ferguson was groundbreaking. His contributions to the liberal website the *Daily Kos* centered on civil rights issues and violence against Black people. In August 2015, he started Justice Together, an organization focused on reducing police brutality.

King was a journalist for the *New York Daily News* until August 2017, producing an article just about every day that challenged injustice. He left the *Daily News* to become a writer-in-residence at Harvard University's Fair Punishment Project. He has also mentored several athletes, which is something that I was eager to discuss with him. He gave great exposure and coverage to Kaepernick's Know Your Rights Camp, at a time when many were suggesting that Kaepernick was all talk and not actually doing things in the community. King is an ally who many athlete-activists today should connect with. Not only for mentoring, but for covering their stories, their work, and properly presenting their messages. As Malcolm X said, "The media's the most powerful entity on earth. They have the power to make the innocent guilty and to make the guilty innocent, and that's power. Because they control the minds of the masses."

Etan: How important do you feel it is for athletes to connect with activists?

Shaun King: It was in my role as a journalist that I first started really connecting with a lot of athletes. It was almost two years ago that Colin Kaepernick first reached out to me . . . I'd seen that he was posting what I thought was some conscious, awakened stuff, and I could tell that he was growing and changing and he just started asking me questions like, "Hey, explain this to me"; "Hey, what do you think about this case of police brutality?" He just wanted insight. That's how our friendship started. He was playing in the league and he was disturbed about police brutality and was looking for somebody to give him some additional insight and perspective. I appreciated that. I had come to know many athletes and, as you know, a lot of guys are really isolated and insulated. Some of them, for a lot of different reasons, aren't reading the news on a daily basis . . .

What I saw in Colin was somebody who was saying, "Hey, for most of my life, sports has dominated every decision I've made." I saw somebody who was saying, "I'm trying to grow in wisdom and understanding about it."

Etan: He educated himself.

King: Yeah, you could put a mic in front of his face at any given point in time. When I first started hearing him speak about it publicly, he wasn't just parroting what I told him, he had developed these understandings of the issues . . . Everyone found out real quick that, not only was he a brilliant guy, but that he knew exactly what he was talking about and exactly what he was doing . . . I've had some of the top guys in the NBA, NFL call me and write me and . . . they're trying to understand like many of the guys. There's police brutality in the city that they're living in . . . People are asking them to speak out about something, and because of my own visibility, athletes come to me and ask, "Can you help me understand this issue?" Or they'll even run some of their own thoughts by me . . . A few times athletes speak out on issues before they are really ready, and they can really make a fool of themselves.

Etan: Or the media makes fools of them because they are not prepared to defend their position.

King: Right. I've seen a few guys do it and they meant well, completely, but they just didn't know what they were talking about . . . You can tell the difference between the guys who spent the time thinking about it, talking to people, or even taking the next step, doing work . . . When those guys speak, it's night-and-day difference. Some of it is just that the guys are twenty-two years old. Many have one year of really crappy formal education, where pretty much they are just there to play ball, and all of a sudden they are expected to speak on complex issues and they just struggle out of the gate doing it. Before Colin ever spoke up and said a word, he'd been in the league for a number of years. So we are talking about a guy who took a long time to understand, to come around, and it makes a big difference. Also, when you form these relationships with activists, they'll have your back . . .

Etan: Who are some of the other players you have written about and supported?

King: Cam Newton is probably one of the best examples. Cam has a really huge heart and he's a really good guy and he grew up in Atlanta, in the city. He and his dad both have been connected to people in life—not in sports, in everyday life—and experienced police brutality; they both have dealt with discrimination, but for some reason he has gotten the impression of the guy who doesn't care about the issue . . . There was a terrible incident of police brutality right there in Charlotte where there was a brother who was shot and killed. It was during the season and what most everyday people don't understand is, particularly during the NFL season, a lot of these guys are not looking at trending topics on Twitter. They're not watching local news, national news. Some of these guys are living and breathing football, they're dealing with injuries and struggles. They're dealing with the pressure of the team.

So people were asking him what he thought about this particular incident and he was trying his best to kind of articulate thoughts, and some activists saw it like, "Awww, man," and calling him names and thought he was a sellout. I was like, listen, you know I was working with his team, working directly with him and people around him to try to help him understand the issue. Here was the struggle with Cam. Cam had made up in his mind that he had a limited amount of influence, but he was going to use his influence to work directly with kids in Charlotte and around the country . . . He made the decision: "You know what, I'm just going to directly work to impact and influence kids to make a difference in their lives and that's going to be my thing." I respect that. But a lot of people saw it and were like, "I don't know why this guy isn't doing anything."

But if his thing is going to be children's education, children's mentoring, in Charlotte and around the country, let that be his thing. If Colin's thing is going to be police brutality, then let's also not expect his thing to be, you know, childhood obesity . . .

I saw the same thing with Damian Lillard. Damian wrote a couple of tweets basically saying, "There's so many things that we can't control, I wish we'd just focus on the things we could control in our own communities." What he was trying to say was very similar to what Cam was saying . . . This is a brother who was born and raised in the Bay Area, who grew up in Oakland. What he was really saying is, "Damn it, I just want to know what I can do to help my community of people in Oakland." It just didn't come out that way.

Etan: Did you ever talk to Richard Sherman after he criticized certain aspects of Black Lives Matter?

King: I didn't, man . . . I think most of what he said, I agree with. Some of it is how he said it. It's the same thing that jammed up Damian Lillard, same thing that kind of jammed up Cam. I think their heart's in the right place and I think they're doing the right stuff. I love Richard Sherman. I think he's one of the smartest, most brilliant guys in the league. He's brilliant period. But because he doesn't have deep relationships with activists, when he says something, it comes out in a way that I don't think represents his heart very well. That's what I tried to work with both Cam and Damian Lillard on: "I don't think what you're saying is a good representation of how you feel." Because what Damian was telling me was some superconscious, pro-Black, procommunity stuff. What he didn't know was, he was sounding like the talking points of some people who don't have our best interest in mind.

Etan: I want you to tell me what you did with Colin Kaepernick in covering the Know Your Rights Camp and how important that was, because people didn't know about that actual work that he was doing. Everybody was just saying, "He's talking about all of this, but where's the actual work?" And you showed it.

King: My ten-year-old son did the camp. He wanted to do it—my son is a huge fan—and so when I went out to cover it, it was a few things that I noticed right away. First was, this was something Colin had thought about and considered deeply . . . He brought experts to talk about Black history. He brought in financial experts to teach the kids about financial literacy. The kids showed up for Colin and they got Colin. He took pictures, he gave them wonderful gifts including membership to Ancestry.com. He shared with the kids how he was adopted and grew up with white parents, but that taking the ancestry test gave him deep roots to where he came from and who he was. There were so many things that touched me . . . He hadn't hired some PR firm. As a matter of fact, he asked me to sign a confidentiality agreement because he didn't even want any media there. He wanted it to just be for the kids. He was like, "Please don't tell anybody that you're coming. I don't want cameras there. I don't want the media there."

He went on to do that same thing in New York; he just did Chicago, and around the same time he also pledged to donate a million dollars from his endorsements and salary to charities all around the country. Colin wrote me and he said, "Listen, I want you to help us build a list of the best organizations all around the country," and he gave me a list of twenty cities . . . "We want to know the people that are on the ground." And like literally the next month he started giving away the money. In thinking about that in retrospect, Etan, this was a guy whose future was not even promised in the league. I think he understood that even then. We don't know if he's ever going to make millions of dollars playing professional sports again, and he's continued month after month to give away hundreds of thousands of dollars and to keep his promise. I've interacted with him even over these last few weeks. He's deeply fulfilled by it. He loves making a difference. He loves impacting the lives of these kids . . .

Colin is saying, "Well, damn, I'm going to speak out on police brutality, but I'm just going to go straight to the kids, I'm going straight to the community, and I'm going to impact them directly." And so Colin has an A-plus rating among every activist in America. And he's going to keep that for the rest of his life . . . So you're starting to see some other guys doing the same thing. You look at the Bennett brothers in the NFL. Those guys are doing the hard work behind the scenes, low-key. Activists love those guys because, behind the scenes, they are working with people, understanding it, and it makes all the difference.

Having "The Talk" with Young Male Athletes Matters

I coach my son's AAU team, the Dynamic Disciples. We were coming back from the nationals tournament in Virginia Beach. Driving past the Confederate tributes still on display makes me sick to my stomach. Robert E. Lee Highway, the stretch of Jefferson Davis Highway through Alexandria, the Confederate memorial statue in Old Town. Monument Avenue in Richmond features monuments of five Confederate leaders. Leesburg is named after Robert E. Lee. Gallows Road in Fairfax, Virginia, which runs from Tysons Corner to Annandale, is rumored to be named after the execution device, and who exactly do you think they were executing? Needless to say, I'm not a very big fan of Virginia.

We stopped at a convenience store so the guys could use the restroom and get some snacks. As soon as we walked in, I saw the clerks immediately perk up and they began to watch all of us very closely. I myself went to the restroom, then quickly came out and stood next to the front door facing the store. I said to all of the players, "Stop playing and joking, get what you need and let's go. Make sure you get a receipt for whatever you purchase." Their fun and laughing quickly disappeared when they heard my tone change. After they got what they needed, we walked out and saw the father of our center, Big Chris, speaking with a policeman near our van. I heard our team captain Riley literally gasp. I immediately grew concerned. As we approached the van, we saw Chris's dad telling the policeman that we were an AAU team and that we were coming from nationals, etc.

Once on the bus, Riley sat down next to me and said that he got nervous when he saw the policeman talking to Chris's dad. I confessed to him that I was nervous too. Some of the other guys heard us and kind of gathered around. I reassured Riley that not all police are bad, and then I asked Dar-

226 ☼ WE MATTER

rien, one of our shooting guards, if he understood why I got so serious back in the store. He said, "Not really, I just figured you didn't want us playing around in the store." I told him yes, but that wasn't the main reason. I explained how from the moment we walked into the store, the clerk and the other workers were watching our every move. They weren't paying any attention to the other customers. Why were they paying so much attention to us? The boys all started shaking their heads and Malcolm said, "Just because we are Black they started watching us? That's not right. We weren't doing anything wrong." I explained to the players that they will come across plenty of unfair situations and that they need to be aware that there are different rules for us sometimes, and that's just how it is. They are not going to be able to get away with some of the things they may see their white friends getting away with.

I asked them if they watched the 2016 Olympics and if they'd seen the story about the disgraced Olympic swimmer Ryan Lochte. A few guys knew the story and a few didn't, so I gave them the quick rundown: he was a twelve-time Olympic medalist who lied about being robbed and held at gunpoint with three other swimmers during the Rio Olympics. According to Brazilian authorities, the group tore up a gas station bathroom, urinated in public, threw punches at the security guards. But Ryan Lochte made up this big story about him being robbed at gunpoint and how he had to heroically escape. And do you know what happened to them? The International Olympic Committee (IOC) spokesman Mario Andrada released a statement on the situation that said: "I do not expect any apologies from [Lochte] or other athletes are needed. They were trying to have fun . . . Let's give these kids a break. They made a mistake. It's part of life. Life goes on."

Kids!!!! Ryan Lochte is in his thirties, but they said, "Oh, he's just a kid."

Riley shook his head and said, "That's just not fair. Why are we held to a different standard?" Others joined in shaking their heads.

I said, "I got another example for you: Brock Turner."

Brock Turner was a Stanford University swimmer who happened to be white. Long story short, he was caught raping a woman behind a dumpster who was passed out, intoxicated. Although he was indicted on five charges—two for rape, two for felony sexual assault, and one for attempted rape—he ended up only actually serving three months. Now, compare that to some of the guys I work with in DC prisons with Free Minds Book Club, a nonprofit group that helps youth offenders. Some of them are locked up for possession of a teaspoon of weed. For being at the wrong place at the wrong time. For getting into a fight.

I told the boys all about Turner and about my own situation with a substitute teacher in my high school Spanish class. I had been sick all day. In the middle of an uncontrollable coughing spell, I asked to go get a drink of water. To my surprise she replied, "No, you can't, now go sit down and stop disturbing the class." I asked again and she again she refused my request. Now, what I should have done was collect myself and calmly ask her if I could go to the nurse since I wasn't feeling well, because she couldn't legally deny me the right to go to the nurse. But I didn't do that. I allowed my emotions to take over and I said in an elevated voice, "Look, lady, I don't know what the devil your problem is, but I need to get a drink of water and I'ma get my drink of water."

Ms. Kimrey began to put together a report on me, adding every offense she could possibly think of. She said she felt threatened, that I was disruptive and even made an aggressive advance toward her. She used the word "terrified" somewhere in there. As a result, I was suspended for two days.

Was this fair? Of course not. Was it blown way out of proportion? Yes, it definitely was. But did I put myself in a position where they could throw the book at me because of my rash decision-making and failure to control my emotions? Yes, I definitely did. I was focused on winning the battle instead of winning the greater war. Was this the last time I was in a situation where I should focus on the war over the battle? No. I told the players that they have to understand that we simply can't do what other people do. "If you follow some of your stupid classmates into doing some sort of petty crime, you will go to jail, period," I told them. "You won't get a slap on the wrist." The system is not set up to be fair to us, and the quicker they learned that, the clearer they'd be that we are held to different standards. And again, it's not how it should be, it's just the way it is.

We discussed the killing of twelve-year-old Tamir Rice in Cleveland, Ohio, how even though police dispatchers were made aware that the "pistol" the boy was waving was probably fake—which it in fact was—Officer Timothy Loehmann, within moments of arriving on the scene, fired shots at Rice. He didn't yell at Rice to drop the gun or anything. I kept saying to the boys that it was a TOY GUN. Now look at Dylann Roof, a young white man who murdered nine Black people in a church—but guess what, the police took him alive. Of course this isn't fair, and yes, there are people like myself who protested vigorously.

Cleveland Browns wide receiver Andrew Hawkins wore a *Justice for Tamir Rice* shirt on the football field. I told the boys how the Cleveland police got upset at Hawkins because in their eyes, the policemen did nothing wrong. No policemen were charged with any crime for killing Tamir. I explained that the point of me telling them all this is that we can't do what other people do, and that the first objective is always personal safety. I also wanted to show them how athletes can use their voices to speak out about the injustice that happens.

They all dropped their heads and were soaking in everything I was telling them.

My proud AAU team the Dynamic Disciples after we won a tournament.

Later that summer, I brought the entire team to a panel discussion. They got to hear specific steps they should take when encountering the police. We had Raphael Grant, the deputy chief of police for Prince George's County there to speak to them. I have been skeptical in the past of having policemen at these panel discussions because, depending on the officer, the entire event can quickly go south. However, Officer Grant was very honest, open, and direct. He said that he would never attempt to justify what another policeman did if he didn't think that they were in the right. The problem is, you don't have any control over which policeman you encounter, so you have to always remember that the number-one goal is to get home safely. Unfortunately, even when you do everything right, a situation can still end in tragedy. Like the case of Philando Castile.

Interview with Valerie Castile
(Mother of Philando Castile)

Etan: You are doing a lot more speaking to youth these days. What are some of the messages you are telling them?

Valerie Castile: Well, Governor [Mark] Dayton spoke the truth after my son was killed . . . If my son was white, he wouldn't have been killed. He talked about the apparent racial bias that exists in the world today. He also said that it was a violation of state law that anyone is treated differently because of their race or the color of their skin. He said it was a violation of what he stood for and said that he would do everything he possibly can to put an end to that, and I appreciate him for saying that because he was absolutely right. My son would still be here if he was white. Same scenario, same situation, same everything . . . It's always a difference in how the police treat Black people and how they treat white people, and young people have to know that going in so that they are not under some false, fairy-tale assumption that they will be treated the same. They have to do things differently.

Etan: That's such a difficult pill for so much of mainstream America to swallow because they can't fathom that there is a difference in how we are treated. They actually think that we are playing by the same rules.

Castile: No, we definitely are not. Let me tell you about my son, Philando, and the type of person he was. What happened to him was so devastating to his friends, my family, me, because of the way that he was. You never, ever would have thought that he would be killed by a person that was supposed to protect and serve our citizens.

Etan: Can you talk a bit more about who he was?

Castile: Philando was such a wonderful human being. And I'm not just saying that because I am his mother, you can ask the people who knew him. I never had to defend his character or defend his behavior. I never had to go to school because of something he did . . . He didn't bother anyone, he hasn't so much as had a fight. You barely have heard him raise his voice. He went about things the right way. He wanted to carry a gun, so he purchased it legally . . . He started working when he was thirteen years old when Michael Jordan became popular. He said he wanted a pair of the Jordans and I said, "There is no way on earth I am gonna spend that much money on some shoes," and he said, "No, I . . . I would work for them." That's the kind of person he always was . . .

Right after he graduated, he filled out an application for St. Paul public schools, and they hired him, and he worked as a nutrition aid. And he loved what he was doing. He started doing that at nineteen and kept doing that for the next thirteen years. He became a supervisor and was liked by everyone. My son was the man of the house. We were a single-parent home, and he took on responsibilities that he probably shouldn't have had to take on at a young age. But he understood the principles and the importance of having the character of being a man, and he took that role very seriously. He understood the importance of your good name, and that's why he didn't do things that would ruin his good name or the family's good name. He was very, very principled . . . He maintained a level of respect from the people around him, even the people who weren't doing all the rights things. *Everybody* respected him.

There were a lot of things that I didn't know about my son. I didn't know the extent of how great and wonderful he really was. He was always great and wonderful to me, but after he was killed, I found out how much he meant to the community and how much he really did for those kids he worked with. He didn't brag about all the stuff he did so I didn't know about it. For instance . . . he had over five hundred different kids that he worked with and he knew each one of their names and their allergies. He knew who couldn't have milk, who couldn't eat gluten, who couldn't have peanuts. Five hundred different kids—he memorized all of their allergies because he cared about them and it was important to him. He wasn't doing this job just to pick up a check; he cared for these kids. He would wait on the kids who had disabilities and help them off the bus.

Etan: I remember seeing all of the people at the school rallying for him. In the school district's statement, an unnamed coworker said your son was smart and "overqualified" for his position, yet still took his job seriously. He said, "Kids loved him . . . He was quiet, respectful, and kind. I knew him as warm and funny." He wore a shirt and tie to his supervisor interview and said his goal was to one day "sit on the other side of this table."

Castile: Yeah, I saw so many accounts and people speaking that way about my son. It really made me proud as a mother. I always was proud of my son, but it made me even prouder . . . It was like, *Look what I raised.*

Etan: When you go and speak to young people at different places, what are some of your other messages to them?

Castile: I tell kids that they need to take their education seriously because that's your ticket out. In whatever you want to do in life, you have to get your education. People will take advantage of people who don't know. The police will take advantage of people who don't know their rights. You're in sports—agents will take advantage of people who don't know or understand how to read their contracts . . .

That's why young people have to be careful and be educated and take their education seriously. It's not cool to not know. Knowing could save your life. You gotta know that this system is set up for you to fail . . . And once you are under that rule of thumb, and in the system, everything just becomes ten times as hard . . . You will be treated differently than white people, and my son is a prime example of that different treatment.

Etan: Do you think we have enough role models out there for young people?

Castile: Of course we have enough, but too many of our young people want to listen to the negativity. There are plenty of positive athletes like yourself doing the right thing, out there doing great things with their foundations and speaking on different things in the media and being a good example for young people to follow, but they wanna pay attention to the foolishness . . . I have always told my kids that the thought is the cause of it all. The things that are planted in your head—if you feed that into your spirit, you will grow up to be just that . . . Look, my son, who was a good person, was killed by a cop and everyone from the governor on down to all the white people from my son's school are being vocal about how the cop overreacted when my son didn't do anything wrong . . .

Now, I told you the facts of what happened. The governor agrees it was wrong, congressmen and politicians have all come out publicly and said it was wrong, newspapers and columnists have said it was wrong, public figures like the Minnesota Lynx WNBA players all publicly said it was wrong—all of these people agree that what happened to my son was wrong. But is the cop charged with murder? No, he is charged with second-degree manslaughter. So he may go to jail, he may not. I spoke with the Department of Justice, the BCA, and ABC, I talked to everyone, and they all told me that even though you know it was a murder . . . it's almost nearly impossible to get a murder conviction for a police officer.

This is not a system for us. And my son didn't do anything wrong. My son did everything right. He trusted his mother—I told him to tell them people that he had the gun, and that's exactly what got my son murdered. He didn't say it in an aggressive manner or making a threat . . . When he got his license, they give you instructions on what to do if you get stopped by the police—to let them know you have a registered weapon. But it didn't matter . . . My son would never do anything to jeopardize that woman and that baby. He loved them both with all of his heart, they were his everything.

So, you ask me what I tell young people. If they will kill my son and he did nothing wrong, you can't afford to even try to do anything even remotely wrong and think you are going to get away with your life. Not get away with it, but get away with your *life*. We have different rules. We can't do what they do. So keep doing your panels and keep using athletes to try to influence these kids, because they need to be told the truth and be educated on how this system works.

Interview with Chris Webber

One weekend, we had a team car-wash fund-raiser at an ExxonMobil gas station. It was a great event, especially for some of our new players. I am old school, I don't believe in giving young people anything. I believe they will appreciate it more when they work for it.

Everything was going well until a man who happened to be white came up to Nichole and said that these kids were not supposed to be there and he was going to call the police. A little while later, the owner of the Exxon called me and told me the guy actually did call the police to report us.

This man saw a bunch of Black kids doing something positive and assumed they were, what, up to no good? Illegally there? Harassing people? It's sad that an AAU team can't even do a fund-raising event without being confronted with the harsh reality that they live in a society that will always suspect them of some type of wrongdoing, but it was an important lesson for them about how they will be treated and looked upon for the rest of their lives.

Another lesson for the guys came one day after practice. I was driving Malcolm and his teammate Camar home when we saw flashing lights behind us, followed by a siren. I saw their eyes grow wide with fear and told them to relax, take a deep breath, and sit back. I pulled over and turned off the music. I put my phone on record and set it in my cup holder facing the window. I took my wallet out of my pocket and put it on the console. I rolled down all the windows and put my hands on the steering wheel. As one policeman walked up to my window, his partner shined his flashlight from the opposite side of the car into Camar's face and then around the inside of the car. The first police officer said to me, "License and registration."

I replied in a very clear voice, "My registration is in my glove compartment, is it okay if I get it?"

He said yes and I slowly reached toward my glove compartment as his partner shined his light on my hand the entire time.

I then said, "My license is on my console, is it okay if I reach for it and take it out of my wallet?"

He said yes, and I slowly moved my hands toward the console and retrieved my license.

The officer took the information and went back to his car. I could see so many different emotions in Malcolm's face. Confusion, fear, concern. I looked back at Camar and saw the same. I asked them if they were all right and they both nodded their heads. I again told them to take a deep breath, to relax, and that everything was going to be okay.

After about ten minutes, the policemen returned. He gave me my license and registration and informed me that I had a taillight that was out and handed me a piece of paper and said I had ten days to get it fixed. Then he said, "Have a good night," and left.

I immediately recognized that this was a teachable moment. I asked Malcolm and Camar if they noticed everything I did before the policeman approached my window. Malcolm said, "Yes, you turned off the music, rolled down the windows, and put your hands on the steering wheel," and Camar said, "You took your wallet out before he could ask you."

I said, "Correct."

Malcolm said, "I understand why you did all that, but you shouldn't have to do all that. You didn't do anything wrong. All that for a broken taillight? Did they even have to pull you over like that and create that intense scene? Couldn't they have just taken a picture of your license with their special police cameras and mail you a ticket or something?" He was getting himself worked up.

I told him, "Okay, let's break this whole thing down. One: I turned down my music to avoid an atmosphere of aggression. We were listening to hip-hop, which is something that comes across aggressive to a lot of foreign ears—but it's just a good idea in general to turn off the music when you are stopped.

"Two: I rolled down all of the windows, even the back windows, because my windows are tinted and I didn't want the police to have any visibility issues when they approached my car. The first thing they did was shine the light inside. They shined it in Camar's face in the back, they shined it on the floor, in the third seat, they shined it all over.

"Three: I put both of my hands on the steering wheel so they could see my hands.

"Four: I didn't make any sudden movements. Even when they told me to get my license and registration. I didn't just go get it quickly. I asked very loudly and clearly if it was okay for me to go into my glove compartment and get the registration. And I moved slowly. Very slowly. And they still shined their lights on my hands to watch me carefully."

Malcolm said, "You shouldn't have to do all that, though. I get it, but we didn't do anything wrong and he's treating us like criminals. So, what, we gotta prove to him that we are not criminals? That's not fair."

I explained to Malcolm that fair ain't got nothin' to do with this. The number one goal is to get home safely, period. But nine times out of ten, they are afraid when they approach a car with Black people in it. That's just the way it is. Is it the way it *should* be? No, of course not. But it's the way it is. They have all the power, all the guns, the authority, but they're the ones who are scared. And when you know someone is terrified of you and has all the power and is in a position of authority, you have to be wise with your actions. It's about getting home safely. That's all that matters. It's reality and it does nobody any good for any of us to be dead in order to prove the point that this isn't fair. Because that's what this is—a matter of life and death. The difference between going home and discussing it like we are doing now, or becoming a hashtag and getting your name on a T-shirt. That's not what I want. I'm tired of seeing that. We have to understand the difference between winning the battle and winning the war.

Now, I was preparing to win the war. I put my phone in the cup holder, I verbally showed that I was in full compliance. And if anything went wrong, I had the evidence. I could sue them like Thabo Sefolosha and James Blake did. You have to make sure you do everything right in order to build your case.

I wanted to talk to someone who had their own encounter with the police while they were a professional NBA player, so I reached out to five-time NBA all-star, former rookie of the year, Fab Five Michigan legend, and former Washington Wizard—Chris Webber. Over the years, we have developed a mutual respect for each other and I was glad that he opened up to discuss his incident while stressing the importance of making wise choices. If we don't prepare young athletes to make wise choices, we may very well lose some potential athlete-activists before they ever get a chance to spread their wings.

Etan: I've heard you say you were one party away from being dead or in jail. What did you mean by that?

Chris Webber: If you live in certain communities or zip codes . . . you still want to have the same lifestyle as any other kid growing up. So, whether I am in the city or the suburbs or the country, at sixteen I'm going to a bonfire or a club or a party, period. The neighborhood I grew up in unfortunately was a lot more violent than others. Today they talk about Chicago—well, when I was growing up in Detroit, the numbers were far worse than the numbers commonly discussed regarding present-day Chicago. It was a really violent time . . . Some of the neighborhoods were ravaged by drugs and things of that sort and I was just aware of what was going on and the way the community was changing.

For example, I remember a ritual was that you had to have your front lawn cut, and slowly you started to see one lawn not cut, then another, and I remember that decline in the neighborhood . . . I've been at parties where people have been shot and where friends have been murdered, and it was just by the grace of God that I wasn't there at that time . . . So that's what I mean when I say I was a party away from being dead or in jail.

Let me also add this, because this really bothers me every time I hear it: everyone always redirects the conversation to Black-on-Black crime and police crime. They have nothing to do with each other.

Etan: I agree, but some people always link them together, for whatever reason.

Webber: I want to make sure I make this point and that I preface this first. I believe in helping your community, I believe in helping your brother, I believe in working together, I believe we have a special calling to be able to do that, but I don't believe that's anybody's job, but it's a policeman's job specifically to service the community. That's his job. So when people say, "You talk about police brutality, but you never speak about Black-on-Black crime," my first question is, "What other citizens are asked to police their own neighborhoods?" And to put that community that has been trivialized, and under a system that helps perpetuate some of the things that happen in the community, it's almost laughable to put that onus and that responsibility on the community itself . . .

You're not really looking to fix the problem, just point blame away from yourselves when your system created and is responsible for the problem. I just hate that argument. The same Black people in those neighborhoods who are getting harassed by the police are scared of those individuals who happen to be of the same color who are doing crime in their neighborhood. They make it like, "Hey, that's your brother doing the crime," or, "That's your cousin, why don't you just tell him to stop?" As if we all know each other and hang out together or something. *Everyone* is scared of criminals, and to put it on the community as if they should do something about it, that's not our job, that's *your* job. That's why we pay taxes, that's why we have policemen.

Etan: That's a great point.

Webber: One of the worst cases of demonizing the victim to me was Trayvon Martin. That's why I hope when we have these discussions that the young kids really look into law, which really changes everything. But when you look at Trayvon Martin's case in particular, he was targeted because of how he looked . . . He was targeted, assaulted, he protected himself, and once he protected himself, someone had the right to kill him. And the demoralizing and demonizing of the victim, we really have to all not fall emotionally for that and stick to what happened and how it happened. Just stick to the relevant facts only. We all have done something in our past somewhere that someone can throw into an argument in order to make the person look like a bad person.

Why do they do that? Because it works. Now . . . when we talk about police brutality, we always recognize the brave job of what they are doing, and I respect that and honor that, but it's still a service that is their job. Nobody is forcing them to do their job. And anytime you demonize the victim, anytime you demoralize an entire group of people . . . I don't think you can do as good of a job, and major problems arise . . . I think it's all based on fear, and that's why they use the words that they use. That's why they use the dog whistles that they use.

Etan: I've noticed that the media often finds a Black face to echo these sentiments. Does that frustrate you as much as it frustrates me?

Webber: I can't even tell you how frustrating it is to see that, and it happens so often, and yes, it's purposely done. They want to only present one side of the argument. And the Black face, as you referred to, knows that, and in order to get the face time, they take that side of the argument. So yes, it infuriates me because I know what they are doing.

Etan: In dealing with young people—and I want to be able to give young people hope in this situation—what would be your advice, not if but *when* they encounter the police?

Webber: If I was talking with young Black boys, Latino boys, Native American boys specifically, anyone who is not white and couldn't pass for white, I would tell them first and foremost, "Realize that you are viewed as Black. The world looks at you as Black. Society looks at you as Black. I don't care if you're mixed, if you're Spanish, to them you're Black. So you have to not only recognize that, but you have to fully understand the history of that, meaning you are going to more likely be treated unfairly by the system, and the system was not made for you to succeed." I tell my nephews, I tell family members, "Just be aware that you're Black."

And that doesn't mean that you don't look a man in his eyes. That means that when you are pulled over, you need to show the police officer respect because you are a respectful man anyway, and you deserve respect because they are servicing you . . . So when you assume that and you are respectful, I think it's easier to detect when something is not right. Then you don't have to go back and say, "Well, did I have an attitude, was it my fault? Did I exhibit defiance or create an issue?" So one, you should always be respectful. Two, make sure you always have your ID. Three, I think you should always turn your phone on record and sit it on the dashboard . . . Four, and I've done this before, I was stopped in DC when I was with the Wizards, this was years before you got there—

Etan: No, I remember.

Webber: Well, I was speeding, and I didn't have my license. Let me say that first of all, I was wrong on both accounts, but I told him that the car wasn't stolen and that's when things went wrong, because I laughed in his face like, "The car was paid for in cash, why are you telling me that the car was stolen?" That's a lie, just a bold-faced lie. And what I did was I had the old-school Mercedes-Benz that had the phone on the dashboard, so I called my lawyer and told him to tape this conversation. That helped me out tremendously down the road from a legal perspective. When you are aware, you know that the police are going to be believed before you. And so you need to be respectful, have your things in order, and know the law. Specifically in your state, and know your rights . . . So I would say really be aware. You have to be aware that people are dying out here for no reason. For reaching for their license in a glove box after the police told them to give them their license. I am thankful for the job that the good policemen do, but I'm more scared than ever to be a Black man in this country, and that's after growing up in Detroit, where like I said, the present-day crime rate and murders in Chicago don't surpass what was going on in Detroit in the eighties.

Etan: I've heard you talk about how growing up, your father offered you a lot of advice and gave you "The Talk."

Webber: I thank him more and more every day now that I'm older, because I don't know when I finally got it. My father was a disciplinarian. It was his way or the highway . . . I can't speak for anyone else, but for me, if I did not have my father at home, I don't know what it would've been like . . . I needed that discipline. My father was eleven years old when his mom passed away and he was actually picking cotton on a plantation. A lot of people may hear these stories or read about them, but I grew up having a direct connection to slavery through my father, and he instilled in me hard work, and if you get knocked down or beaten down and you have to cry and you're hurting, let's cry and have that release, then get your behind up and get back to work.

So I always wanted to be the man he was, and I always asked myself, *Could I have made it through what he was able to make it through?* . . . He would take me back in the summers when I was younger and show me . . . why their hands were calloused and bruised, and show me my great-aunt, who was less than a hundred pounds but had to pick a hundred pounds of cotton. So I grew up with an appreciation for what Black people went through, but even more what specifically my father went through. He may not have had the schooling or the education, but he is the wisest man I know. And my mother took a different route through education, so I definitely had a balance of the two, but my father really guided me in a way that was crucial for me . . . His whole thing was, "You gotta be a man," and he made it fun to be a man and he made it challenging to be a man, and I honestly don't know where I would be without him.

Interview with Joakim Noah & Derrick Rose

As previously discussed, one of the questions we consistently hear, whether we like it or not, is: *What about Black-on-Black crime?* I wanted to talk to Joakim Noah and Derrick Rose in particular about this topic. They both have been extremely vocal on different issues in the past. Derrick Rose was the first player to wear the *I Can't Breathe* shirt after Eric Garner's murder. He did it without hesitation and without knowing what the reaction was going to be. Joakim Noah elected to skip a New York Knicks team dinner with a group of army cadets that included a speech from a retired colonel, citing his stance against war and gun violence. Noah also said he felt "uncomfortable" that the Knicks were "conducting training camp for the third straight year at West Point, where the United States Military Academy is based."

Joakim Noah told the *New York Post*, "It's hard for me . . . I have a lot of respect for the kids here fighting—but it's hard for me to understand why we go to war and why kids have to kill kids all around the world . . . I have mixed feelings about being here. I'm very proud of this country. I love America. I don't understand kids killing kids around the world."

The *Post* further reported: "Noah said his decision to skip the dinner and speech was not intended as a form of protest. 'It's not my way of saying anything—I was not comfortable,'" Joakim explained. "Not surprisingly, the US Military Academy called the move 'inappropriate.'"

Joakim and Derrick have been involved in a lot of activism, but what I want to focus on here is how they have both been fighting against gun violence. It's no secret that gun violence and gangbanging in the poor areas of Chicago are out of control. Donald Trump couldn't stop mentioning this during the presidential debates, saying things such as, "Restore law and order," when asked how he would improve the relationship between the Black community and the police. Everyone in the country knew exactly what that meant.

As I was interviewing Joakim, I heard the passion in his voice, and how much it genuinely hurt him to see everything that was going on in Chicago. I asked him about Trump's threat of martial law, and I asked him for his thoughts on what could be done to curtail the violence.

I remember seeing a public service announcement he did in Chicago titled "Stand Up Chicago." In it, Noah, Derrick Rose, and others explain what they stand for—the city, the youth, peace, and reducing violence.

Noah and Derrick have both been committed to addressing the violence that has been afflicting the city of Chicago for far too long. I was glad they agreed to sit down with me and address their willingness to speak out and examine the roots of the violence, the systemic problems that feed into it.

Etan: Derrick, you were one of the first people to wear the *I Can't Breathe* shirts—you really started the whole thing. Tell me your reasons for wearing the shirt.

Derrick Rose: At the time, I was really fed up. Being in Chicago and growing up in the neighborhoods I grew up in, and seeing everything that was going on in particular with the police, and the killings, and the violence, I just felt that I needed to say something. I am blessed to have this platform that I have playing in the NBA, and I am able to really get a message out to a lot of people relatively easily, because the media and fans pay attention to every move that we make. When we say something or do something, it gets noticed and people pay attention, and I felt some light needed to be shined on this problem that was going on. And watching Eric Garner's murder over and over again, seeing the police choke him to death over and over again, and hearing him saying over and over again that he couldn't breathe, and all of the police standing around watching him be choked to death and nobody had the decency to stop it and say, "That's enough, he's down, he's not resisting, you're going to kill him," I just felt something needed to be said about that because that was just not okay and it was not right.

Etan: That was a really strong statement to make, stepping out there by yourself at the time and being the first one. Other players from all around the league joined you after that, but in the beginning, you were alone. Were you at all worried about the backlash that could come with that?

Rose: I really didn't care about the backlash at all—that was the last thing I was worried about. I called my friend and told him to get the shirt made, and I knew that in the NBA there was probably going to be some type of a fine involved, because usually the first thing they go for is your money, and I knew it was a violation of the pregame team-issued warm-ups with all the NBA logos and everything on it, but I didn't care. This was bigger than a fine. I felt like I was speaking for millions of people who are suffering and who feel no hope. I mean, how could you feel hope after seeing on tape a crowd of policemen kill this man and choke him to death and nobody even feels any remorse about it? It didn't even seem like it fazed them. Like he wasn't even human. They would have had way more of a reaction if they

242 ☆ WE MATTER

would've seen a dog being killed than this human being. So yeah, the last thing I was worried about was a fine or some criticism.

Etan: What was the team's reaction to you wearing the shirt? Did they reprimand you or tell you to stop?

Rose: No. Honestly, all of it went under the radar. Nobody even questioned me about it in Chicago. Honestly, there was a lot going on there at the time, and I was kind of feuding with the media and they were trying to throw everything against me in Chicago, so I don't know if that diverted their attention or what, but I get that question all the time: "What did the Bulls say to you?" But honestly, they didn't say anything at all.

Etan: Joakim, from your perspective, what was the team's reaction to Derrick wearing the *I Can't Breathe* shirt?

Joakim Noah: I was really proud of him. That was really a very strong and powerful and courageous statement. A lot of other players followed in his footsteps, but he was the first one to do it, and that took a lot of courage. It's not easy to take a stand like that in public, and with all of the scrutiny and the public pressure of playing basketball and staying focused on the game and having to deal with real serious issues on a day-to-day basis.

Etan: Definitely. And what do you think we can do to help this situation, help the community as a whole?

Noah: To me, it's just investment. There's gotta be more investment in the community, because society has failed our youth. We need more programs, drug programs, investment in education, I could keep going. And the deeper you get into it and examine the situation and the problem . . . the more unreal it got, because you could see how a lot of these kids are also being used. A lot of people are exploiting them in order to big-up themselves. And that's really hard to see . . . That hurts because a lot of these kids are hopeless.

Etan: What was your response when you heard Donald Trump threaten that he would send the feds to Chicago?

Noah: I think that before we start talking about sending the feds to Chicago, we need to start talking about these gun laws. We have to really reflect and say, "Are we as a country doing everything we can to stop these kids killing kids?" Because that's what it is: it's kids killing kids. Are we putting in the proper investment in trying to stop this before we send in the feds? Because it is, at the end of the day, a war zone.

Etan: Do you think these kids' lives matter at all to most politicians and decision makers?

Noah: Clearly not. People are making decisions without having any inclination as to what these kids are actually going through. When you talk about ways to stop the violence, it's not just punishing everyone, or sending in a tank. There are so many other things you can do. Investing in these community centers will help stop the violence. Investing in programs for these kids will stop the violence. Keeping these kids active and keeping them on a positive route and creating jobs so that these kids don't feel hopeless. Some kids are hooked on drugs and self-medicating themselves to numb the pain of the situation they are in . . . And they know that's what's happening. Honestly, the more I started doing with my foundation and with the kids, the more depressing it got. Kids you talk to and work with one day, and the next day they've been killed, murdered, sometimes by the police, sometimes by another kid. That's the madness that's going on in Chicago and something has got to change.

Rose: They closed like 150 schools, and a lot of schools they are turning into charter schools, and they are combining schools, they are purposely creating a friction in the school by putting rival gangs in the same school together after they decided to close the schools they were going to. There is no other way to describe it but as a setup, because there is no way that they don't know exactly what they are doing. As far as the martial law that Trump is talking about, there is no way that they should even be thinking about doing that. The people need opportunities to get jobs. They need centers for kids to go to after school.

In Chicago, we don't have opportunities. Unless you play ball like me

244 ⚜ WE MATTER

or rap, your opportunities are really limited, so if you don't give someone an opportunity, what do you expect them to do? How are they supposed to eat and feed their children and live and survive? They *created* the situation that Chicago is in today. They took away opportunities and closed schools and created this environment where people don't have any hope. What do you think they are going to do if they have no hope? Then, after you created that environment, you wanna talk about sending in the *feds* to, what, finish the job of the situation you created? You know how they are going to react to that. You know what's going to happen. They not gonna take that lying down. And of course y'all got bigger guns, they got a lot of guns, it's literally a war zone, but they don't have tanks and missiles and drones. I couldn't imagine what that would look like if they decided to send in the feds—that's just not the answer to solve this problem you created.

Etan: I definitely agree. Joakim, can you tell me about the work you do with your foundation?

Noah: Noah's Ark Foundation. Giving kids an outlet—our programs are about expressing yourself through arts and sport. We have basketball tournaments we call the "peace tournaments," bring kids from different neighborhoods, mix up the teams, have them actually playing on the same team with people who are supposed to be their sworn enemy. Having to pass to them and celebrate a victory with them. We have some of the OGs come and talk to them and spend time with them. It's not just about the basketball or the tournament, but a way to teach, inspire, and show them the right way. Show them the way that will save their lives, and letting them know how important their lives are.

Etan: Talk about your movement to stop the violence.

Noah: You look at the police brutality—it's depressing. I feel horrible about it just like anyone who has seen the Eric Garner video should also feel terrible. Nobody should go out like that. Nobody! I think for me, the work can't stop, the effort can't stop. Does it seem like we are losing the fight? Yes, it definitely does. But we can't give up. These are kids, we really have to keep that in mind, and a lot of them are really going through some of the most horrific things imaginable. You talk to some of the kids, and you can see it in their eyes. It's like they have post-traumatic stress disorder.

Etan: How do you convince those kids that their lives matter?

Noah: My youth coach, Tyrone Green, is the one who changed my life. He wasn't a celebrity who came there to speak to me. He actually showed me love and showed me that he cared and took the time to guide me and nurture me. Without him, I wouldn't even be here right now. He was like my other father. He always told me I shouldn't go back to France or travel in the summer, that I should stay with him in the hood. He molded me . . . and that's what changed my life. I'm telling you, if it weren't for him, I don't know where I would be.

What I realized with a lot of the kids who are going through these issues in the neighborhood—it's not about a message. These kids get preached on and preached on and preached on. They don't need anyone telling them they need to do this and they need to do that, and they definitely don't need any fake people coming to speak to them to make themselves look good . . . They are going to see right through you in a matter of seconds and be able to tell if you're genuine . . . or just trying to make yourself look good. That's how they feel loved—not so much by words but by actions, and so that's what I try to do for them: show them that they are important and that their lives matter. And then I encourage them to look after the younger kids, and to show them that they matter. Again, not just tell them, but to *show* them that someone cares whether you live or die and is willing to invest time and energy and resources into you, because that's how important your life is.

What you doin' with your son's AAU team, keep doin' that, man. That stuff makes a difference. Believe me. It really could mean the difference between someone making it in life and someone ending up dead or in jail . . . Keep it all the way real with them. Don't sugarcoat nothing. So much can be changed when people know that someone cares.

Having "The Talk" with Young Female Athletes Matters

I have always had a passion for speaking to young men. It started when my mother used to have me speak to the students in her class. I would share my experiences playing ball at Syracuse, and they would listen solely for the reason that I was an athlete at a major university. That was my introduction to the power that athletes have to influence the youth. I continued speaking all through college and during my career in the NBA. I would speak at schools, prisons, community centers, churches. I wrote my book *Fatherhood: Rising to the Ultimate Challenge*, I was appointed to President Obama's "Fatherhood and Mentoring Initiative," I worked with My Brother's Keeper, and I began appearing on celebrity panels for young men across the country in an effort to inspire, encourage, teach, prepare, and educate. It became something I did nonstop.

But then my daughters Imani and Baby Sierra started getting older and asking questions, just as my son Malcolm did when he was younger. Imani, at nine years old, heard people talking about Sandra Bland and Korryn Gaines at school, and she started to have questions. And just as I had with Malcolm, I now had to have "the talk" with my daughter. I still just wanted them to be playing with their dolls and watching cartoons. In many ways, I naturally felt like I needed to shelter and protect my daughters while I was preparing and teaching my son. That was the absolute wrong approach, and I'm glad my wife kept reminding me of the importance of preparing my daughters the same way I was preparing my son.

I took my daughter to a Black Lives Matter panel discussion, where she heard Swin Cash, Emerald Snipes, and Erica Garner, along with John Starks, Shaun King, Tiny Archibald, and Jerome "JYD" Williams. All of the speakers were fantastic, but it was the female speakers that my daughter connected with most. When Emerald and Erica told their stories of dealing with the death of their father, Imani listened intensely, locked into everything that was going on. I could actually see her being empowered. She listened to Swin talk about Black Lives Matter, and about Philando Castile and Alton Sterling, and then Swin talked about all of the Black women who have lost their lives to the police and may have not gotten the coverage the men have received. She told the audience about Sandra Bland and detailed the story in a way that showed what young Black girls in particular were going to have to deal with growing up, as far as their *attitude* being a threat. This hit home for so many of the young Black girls there, I am suspecting for the same reason that it hit home for Imani, and that is because she has an attitude. She is quick-witted. Imani is so much like me, sometimes it's almost scary.

Imani likes to be heard. She likes to be able to get her point across before she is disciplined. And as long as she can say what she needs to get off her chest, she is okay with dealing with whatever punishment comes her way. I am able to reason with Imani and the entire process works for her. The problem is, nobody on earth other than me is going to do that with her. Not her teachers, definitely not her grandmothers on both sides (ha ha), but also not her mother, not her aunts, not her Sunday school teachers at church— nobody. So when she heard the story of Sandra Bland, it resonated with her.

"Young Black girls are being looked at as a threat because of their attitudes. You have to prepare to win the war and not be focused on the immediate battle that you are NOT going to win." Swin brilliantly let those words hang in the air for a long time. She said we have to think strategically, fully evaluate the situation, and prepare for the bigger war. Now, coming from Swin, these girls heard the message. Coming from a man, it probably would have been offensive. I can say that to young men, but I'm not so sure I can convey that same message to young women. But it's the same message: they can't do what they see white women do. I have seen white women cuss the police out, tell them they will have their badge—but we simply cannot do that. The main objective, again, is for them to get home safely.

After that, Swin proceeded to explain what the WNBA does collectively to show their Black Girl Magic. She talked about how they were fed up with the killings by the police and how they wanted to do something about it. She explained how the players looked after each other. How after the WNBA said it was going to fine them for waging their protest, the veterans told the younger players that they would pay their fines and not to worry about the financial part. And every young woman in that audience, my daughter included, was inspired.

A few months later, I took Imani back to Canaan Baptist Church, where I was hosting a panel that included Chamique Holdsclaw, a former WNBA rookie of the year who has played with the Los Angeles Sparks and the Atlanta Dream. My daughter heard Chamique talk about peer pressure and what it means to be self-confident and self-assured no matter what anyone else says about you. Chamique spoke about how proud she was to see the WNBA as a league stand up for Alton Sterling and Philando Castile. Once again, my daughter was completely inspired. As were all of the other young women in the audience, and they were inspired in a way that just wouldn't have happened if it were a man speaking, no matter who he was. It was amazing to see girls raising their hands during the question-and-answer session, sharing intimate details about struggles they were going through. They talked about being bullied, being picked on, but then Chamique started talking about mental health. She related her own struggles—she told the entire story of everything she had gone through. She discussed her depression, her shame, putting up the facade that she had it all together; she talked about what it was like to see the media turn on you, to go from receiving all of the praise and glory to becoming a villain.

I watched the young women look on in amazement, because of course almost all young girls feel peer pressure. I told the audience that the NBA has finally instituted programs dealing with mental health, and that Chamique wrote a powerful book called *Breaking Through: Beating the Odds Shot After Shot*. In addition, there is an amazing documentary called *Mind/Game: The Unquiet Journey of Chamique Holdsclaw*, in which she tells her story to the world, because she knew that there were other people who were dealing with the exact same thing and she didn't want anyone to feel alone in that. She wanted to use her situation and her experience to inspire, and she has done just that.

I explained how in athletics, including the NBA, there is still a long way to go in the area of mental health. In most sports, it's thought that you are supposed to be mentally tough. I told them that Chamique had the courage to be able to come forward and be a catalyst for change. Many teams have now created programs that address mental health. I personally met the psychiatrist recently hired by the Oklahoma City Thunder; her sole purpose is to deal with the mental health of the athletes. Various players, including Metta World Peace, Michael Sweetney, Serena Williams, Terry Bradshaw, Jerry West, and Ronda Rousey, are now talking about their depression and their mental health issues—all of this started with Chamique. She has become an activist and advocate for others, highlighting the routine discrimination of people dealing with mental health challenges—the shame, the ridicule, the bullying, the stigma. She has changed the way so many people now look at mental health, and I applaud her for having the courage to do so.

Chamique Holdsclaw is such an inspiration in so many ways. Her willingness to be an activist for mental health is really courageous.

Interview with Chamique Holdsclaw

Etan: What gave you the courage to be able to come forward about your mental health issues and struggles?

Chamique Holdsclaw: I thought about the fact that this was something that I really struggled with for a long time. Something that was debilitating. I was faced with a situation where I thought about taking my life and I just felt that it was time to stand up. For so long I worried about what other people thought, and in the sports culture you're taught to be mentally tough and mentally unbreakable and I didn't want anyone to think that I was weak. That's like the ultimate knock on an athlete to say that they are mentally weak. So I hid it. And that just made me sicker and sicker, and of course one thing led to another, but as soon as I opened my mouth, I realized that a lot of other people were dealing with the same thing. I was really proud that I eventually became brave enough to take those steps, because people started sharing their stories with me and in a sense it helped me heal.

Etan: My mother used to always tell me that when you overcome something, it's not for you; it's for somebody else and it becomes your testimony.

Holdsclaw: Definitely, and it's healing . . . As I have grown into an adult, I see that the greatest gift I have been given is a talent, and that talent has allowed me to get people to pay attention. It's just a tool, basketball is a tool. And now with the platform . . . what was I going to do with it? I decided to be open and to be honest and to be a positive light on these kids.

Etan: You sat on a panel in Harlem with me at Canaan Baptist Church and I saw firsthand the way all of the young ladies in the audience identified with you.

Holdsclaw: It makes me feel really good, to be honest, because you see what your purpose is. It's like I have an out-of-body experience while I am talking to them . . . I'm talking to them physically, but I'm really talking to me, if that makes sense. And I'm telling them the things that I wish somebody would have told me. I know how being a young girl . . . at times we put on this mask and this brave face, but we are very fragile and very sensitive creatures. So I just try to pull back those layers. I know when I was younger, and things weren't going right, I pretended. I said, "No, I'm okay, I'm good," and eventually that catches up with you and everything just explodes. So it's always important to address that and really be honest with young people and give them a safe environment to express how they are feeling.

Etan: One of the things I always hear young people saying at these events and panels is that they don't want to open up about something they are dealing with or struggling with because they are afraid of people teasing them. Talk about how you were able to overcome the haters.

Holdsclaw: I remember when I went to live with my grandmother and lived in the projects, but I went to private school. I moved to a new neighborhood and I didn't go to school with any of the kids in the neighborhood. They would tease me all the time. "Catholic school girl, private school girl, what, you think you better than us? Oh, we're not worthy of the private school girl who is so high and mighty and better than all us lowly ghetto kids." I would be like, "I don't think I'm better than anyone. I have no choice in this. My grandmother is making me go to that school, so you're gonna make fun of me?" Then, like you said, it was about my feet: "Oh, you got big feet, you got bigger feet than all the boys . . ."

I was having a pretty tough time there for a little while. I remember coming home telling my grandmother they won't stop teasing me, and she told me, "Don't worry about them, you just stay focused." She just poured into me nonstop. And I was really focused as a kid because of her. I remember her telling me that I didn't have to be a product of my environment and telling me that it's okay to be different and I didn't have to be like everybody else . . . And I remember my grandmother telling me that one day the same people who once laughed at me and made fun of me were going to be singing a completely different tune, and her words definitely came true. It was like she could see the future . . . I am so thankful I had my grandmother to guide me through that process.

Etan: You were a media darling, you were the female Jordan, and then you saw the media turn on you. Talk about how you were able to use your platform to speak about mental health issues.

Holdsclaw: It was really hard because I was always seen in a positive light in the media, then all of a sudden there was story after story and people didn't know what was going on with me because I didn't really speak about it. So what I learned during those types of situations was: if you don't speak about something, people are going to start creating things. And that's exactly what happened . . . It really started to dig at me until finally I spoke up and explained in detail what really happened, and I saw an immediate shift.

252 ⚔ WE MATTER

As soon as I started to stand on my own and live in my truth, it was amazing how quickly things changed. I had media people coming up to me apologizing, saying that their moms or wives or husbands have struggled with this also, and they were sorry for how they covered my story and ran with rumors and speculations, and I really saw how the current media culture really works. They build you up, and as soon as something happens, it's almost like a resentfulness, like, "You let us down." So I tell young people, especially young athletes, to always remain balanced and know who you are and don't be afraid ever to speak about your truth . . . Own your own truth and stand up on your own story.

Etan: It's interesting that when athletes speak out about different causes, oftentimes they are standing alone and they don't necessarily get support from their peers.

Holdsclaw: Oh, definitely . . . My expectation was that I was the only athlete dealing with something like this . . . so I started speaking about it and teammates started coming to me in private and thanking me for having the courage to come forward with what I was dealing with, and saying that they themselves have been dealing with the same thing or something similar. And that kept happening. Even today I have athletes from all sports—football, basketball, tennis, soccer—who . . . want to pick my brain about it, because it's something they personally are dealing with, and we have become our own community, so to speak. We help each other and encourage each other.

Etan: I saw you participate in a panel with Metta World Peace, formerly Ron Artest, and he talked about how he was encouraged by you and influenced by you to speak about his own mental health struggles.

Holdsclaw: I watched Ron growing up, and I knew him and the things that he struggled with as a kid, but I always knew the core of who he was. And he was always a really good person and a really giving person. And even when he went through this tough time, to see people attack—they just want to attack; they have no idea. And it was tough to see because I feel like I want to protect him, you know? . . . But looking at him grow into the person that he is today, and the work that he's doing, to advocate for mental health and just being open . . . It's really courageous once you find that power in your voice and understand the power and influence that you can have.

Etan: There is this stigma with male athletes—female athletes as well, but especially male athletes—that if you say anything about mental health, it's like you become a leper. That's one of the things you mentioned that has to change.

Holdsclaw: The culture has to change. It hurts my heart hearing about all of those stories and hearing how all of these guys were not properly treated and how so many of them ended in tragedy . . . We have to keep putting the message out there and hopefully over time it will change, and we can't be afraid to stand up to the establishment and the institution. There have been so many situations where I have been on panels with really esteemed people in sports, and I'll be getting so frustrated because they're telling me how I should feel and I'm looking at them sideways like, *Have you had mental health issues? Have you experienced a manic attack? Have you personally experienced the emotions and feelings of having suicidal thoughts? You've studied it and I respect you for studying it because that's needed, but allow me or the person who has actually gone through this and experienced this to express how we feel . . .*

I think that a lot of times people who are professional doctors and educators and PhDs in this field, they just need to listen sometimes. People don't want to always hear about statistics and things like that, they want to hear about real-life experiences . . . That's why we like to read autobiographies and see how people overcame and what they had to go through to get where they are. It inspires and empowers us; we just have to allow and encourage people to share more. It's so important to build a community of support . . . because you really need all the support you can get.

Etan: Talk about *Mind/Game: The Unquiet Journey of Chamique Holdsclaw* and the public's response to the documentary.

Holdsclaw: We are screening the documentary at various colleges and universities, youth programs, to really just allow the public to put a face with mental health . . . It gives people a lot of hope because a lot of people in this country are experiencing some form of mental health issue. People think it's not that many people, but it really is. I will be at a random place and people will come up to me and say, "Hey, I saw your documentary and was so touched and this is what I was dealing with." In fact, I was driving from the airport this morning, and the driver asked me what I was here for, and I told him I was speaking at a mental health seminar, and he said, "I thought that was you, Chamique. You have been such an inspiration for me because I am diagnosed bipolar and I didn't want to tell anyone because of the ridicule and the stigma that comes along with it." You just never know who you touch, and really, a lot more people are dealing with mental health issues than people think.

Interview with Soledad O'Brien

Chamique Holdsclaw is shining a spotlight on a topic that many people are simply uncomfortable speaking about. And not just in sports, but all across America. According to statistics, there are almost forty-three million adults under the age of eighteen in the United States who are suffering from some type of mental illness. But there's still a stigma behind it. So people are forced to keep quiet, living in shame and in silence.

During the question-and-answer session of the Harlem program that Chamique participated in, one of the young women raised her hand and said that anybody who is different at her school is ridiculed, and that she wanted to get all of the girls together and fight against the bullying. Another young lady also shared that she got ridiculed. And one by one, Chamique responded to all of their questions and comments, often with personal anecdotes.

But then another girl raised her hand and asked a question that was really difficult for me as a father to hear. She said that a lot of the boys at her school feel that they can sexually harass females and get away with it. I saw Imani look at me in shock. I saw a teacher's mouth drop wide open. The girl went on to explain how as a result, a lot of the girls at her school wear baggy clothes and sweatpants. The fact that they felt this was a solution—rather than addressing the boys' offensive behavior—touched on an issue at the heart of a much bigger problem. I had a very disturbing discussion with CNN host and acclaimed journalist Soledad O'Brien on this topic. It was difficult for me to hear some of the things that Soledad said, but she raised vital issues that I needed to address with my daughters.

Etan: What is your primary message to young women in these troubling times?

Soledad O'Brien: Remember when you were on a panel at my event at Stony Brook a few years ago, and you told the story about your son and how he was already baffled, at the age of nine, about some of the things that he was seeing and beginning to understand in society? It's pretty much the same exact way with young women. On one hand, you hate the idea that you get to be the bearer of bad news and you want them to walk through life a little unaware, believing everybody's good . . . and everyone loves you, and everyone wants to see you succeed. Then all of a sudden something happens, invariably, and you sort of have to have this conversation. Basically, we have to inform young women that a lot of times, life is simply unfair. And some of the stuff that's unfair is unfair for really, really terrible reasons that connect to our nation's history; that we are probably never really going to solve . . . You really have to have these conversations with young people early.

Etan: And sometimes you don't even know where to start.

O'Brien: I think, again, that's just a continuum of the messaging that girls get all the time in their lives, right? Which is, "We don't want to hear from you. Make sure you're likable. Don't have an attitude . . . And make sure that you're selling what you think is pleasant and likable about yourself, ALL THE TIME."

I don't think for any young women watching that terrible Sandra Bland video, that was the first time that they heard the word "mouthy," and especially not for a Black woman. The message is, "These are the things that make me uncomfortable about you, and if you don't watch it . . . I'm going to take it out on you; and if you're a police officer, obviously that means one thing; and if you're a teacher, that can mean something else; and if you're a person in the community, that can mean something else." And I think that message is sent to girls all the time: "This about you makes me uncomfortable."

I think that a lot of people have a very hard time with young women feeling a little bit powerful, and feeling a little bit strong, and having a voice . . . so they go out of their way and that translates into, "Don't be mouthy, keep your mouth shut, I don't want to hear from you, you need to do this."

There's another subtle part of it that is, "Nobody likes somebody like that. Nobody wants to hear from you."

When Sheryl Sandberg started with the whole idea of, you know, "Don't use the word 'bossy.'" And I'm like, "Well, why not? What's wrong with being bossy? I'm the boss here. This is my company. I have nine people who work for me. I literally pay nine people, right? I am the boss, so yes, on occasion I am bossy because that is my job." But, you know, the idea is that nobody likes a little girl who's bossy.

Etan: Right, that's true. They don't say that about young boys.

O'Brien: Never, exactly! . . . So I just think girls get these messages all the time, and then as you get older, it gets translated into your work life. Your interactions with law enforcement officials or just other sort of official people in your life. It never ends, and so I do believe you have to figure out how to have conversations with young women pretty early on about how they have to advocate for themselves. And how they are responsible for their own story and their own versions and kind of fighting back for themselves.

Etan: My family was watching the coverage of the presidential election and my nine-year-old daughter heard the vulgar comments Trump made to Billy Bush, and she asked, "Wait, he said he wanted to grab her *where*? What? What did he say he wanted to do? Why would he say that?" There was so much inappropriate behavior, and you also see what just happened with Bill O'Reilly and his history of sexual harassment, and how it's been basically tolerated for so long.

When you said that we have to teach girls to stand up for themselves, and yet we see the actions of people in power like Trump and O'Reilly and their patterns of sexual harassment, how do we prepare our girls for what they are about to face?

O'Brien: They hear it and I think that no matter who's president, you have to say, "This is the way you need to think about life and yourself." Television news was a hotbed of people being groped. I remember thinking, *Well, what exactly is considered sexual harassment?* Because all of this stuff that's going on could definitely and should definitely fall into that category. There was a big sexual harassment case, Anita Hill and Clarence Thomas, and I remember everyone talking like this was a big new phenomenon. And I remember thinking, *Stuff like this happens all the time.* When I first started, the number of female editors who would . . . just talk about how their male colleagues or the anchormen they were working with would stand behind them and rub their shoulders and grope them. I mean, it was crazy!

I was at a journalism dinner and there was a guy there who everybody knew by name. I was wearing a strapless dress . . . and every time he talked to me, and I did not know him well, he would massage my back. He would literally *massage my back.* And I was mortified. This man could be my grandfather, and what do you do? Do you stand up and freak out? Of course not! You're at a dinner and it's an event and it's a journalism award, so you don't. And you turn so you can politely and subtly make it so it's physically difficult for them to grab you . . . and then you dodge and you say, "Oh, I'm going to go get a drink." And you do what women do, right? You maneuver and you dodge and you duck. And I was a grown person by then, I must've been thirty-five years old, maybe older. I had four children by then and I was like, *I cannot believe this person is really trying to grope me as if this were okay and a normal thing.*

Etan: So what's the solution?

O'Brien: Unfortunately, it happens all the time and, again, I think what people who've spoken out against it . . . don't really understand—first of all, I think there is tremendous shame. The first thing you do is start blaming yourself and questioning yourself . . . *Was I flirting with them? Was I wearing inappropriate clothing? Did I smile too much at him? Was this my fault?*

Etan: That's really messed up. There was one time at my high school with a young girl, and I won't say her name, but as you were talking I was picturing her and seeing her crying at her locker, and then I was consoling her, and she was saying that something terrible had happened to her but nobody believed her, and I didn't know how I could help her. I am kicking myself because as an athlete, I could have gotten everybody on the team together and we could have supported this girl. I could have gone to the papers. This was before I really found my voice. I didn't know how much power I had. I wish I knew then what I know now.

O'Brien: Well, hindsight is of course 20/20. And you were what, sixteen, seventeen years old? But from the young girl's perspective, you think, *Well, what I really need to do is just remove myself from this.* Then you think, *Obviously I'm not going to tell anybody, because it'll only hurt me.*

Etan: But then you have a situation like the one with Bill O'Reilly, who's had a continuous pattern of sexual harassment for many years and . . .

O'Brien: Well, because it's supported, right? I mean, to some degree, you have a culture, right? . . . If you have a culture where everybody's like *wink, wink,* you know, no one's going to go to HR because . . . HR, we all know, is really a way to protect a company. So typically, if you go to HR, it's probably the first step to you losing your job. For a lot of people, you simply do the math. *Is it possible for me to navigate this space where I both keep my job and don't have to sleep with this guy?* . . . That's the navigation that you do. I do think it's a really challenging thing.

Etan: So what can we say to young girls about something like this?

O'Brien: Well, I think it's all about finding your voice . . . Start strategically, building your case. Getting witnesses who can, if need be, speak on your behalf and support your claims . . .

You have to tell young women that they need to have a gut. And they need to trust their gut. Because what happens is, we actually make young women squelch that uncomfortable feeling. So you have to be able to say, "You know what? If something feels icky, it probably is. Your gut is probably right. Just like when you walk down a dark alley and you're like, *Eeeewwwww, this does not feel safe,* it probably is not. You have to be able to trust that."

Etan: According to the criminal justice statistics, only 344 out of every thousand sexual assaults are reported to the police. That means nearly two out of every three go unreported. According to the National Sexual Violence Resource (NSVRC), one in five women are sexually assaulted on college campuses. More than 90 percent of sexual assault victims on college campuses do not report the assault. Those are alarming statistics.

O'Brien: I think people feel like it's not necessarily clear. So a lot of young women will begin putting themselves on trial, and say things like, "Well, I was drinking." And they need someone to say to them, "Yeah, you're right, but still, someone doesn't get to rape you." I'll tell you, I've interviewed a ton of young women who were sexually assaulted and raped. And they'll give you the long list of things that they did that makes them feel like they're not a good witness or not a good person to bring a complaint . . .

Look at the young woman who accused the Stanford swimmer and look at the headlines in that case, right? "Stanford Swimmer" was how he was referred to. Even when he was convicted. They didn't say, "Convicted Rapist." They said, "Stanford Swimmer Ends Up Having to Go to Jail."

Etan: Brock Turner, of course. He actually blamed the entire thing on drinking, his environment, peer pressure, and promiscuity. And he added that he regretted drinking too much and that he made a bad decision. A bad decision? No, you sexually assaulted an unconscious woman.

We really have to tell girls that their lives matter and they matter enough not to accept this as the norm. And we have to tell them to be careful always because there are so many bad people out there. We have to keep giving young girls these messages.

O'Brien: Yeah, well, you know, sometimes you do have to just hear it often and hear it a lot.

Interview with Jemele Hill & Michael Smith

I have so much admiration for US Olympic gymnasts Dominique Moceanu, Jamie Dantzscher, Jeanette Antolin, and Jessica Howard, for having the courage to speak out about the horrors that they themselves witnessed and experienced. All four athletes bravely spoke out about the rampant sexual abuse in the world of gymnastics, including a culture of ignoring victims and their claims. The courage of these young women is going to help prevent this from happening again; it will put so many people on alert and make them ask their children questions that they wouldn't have thought to ask. I saw an interview with Dominique Moceanu in which she said that

USA Gymnastics president Steve Penny basically dismissed most of what she had come forward about. Moceanu was ostracized by the organization as a whole, though she has decided to continue talking about it because, in her words, "There's abuse going on in our culture that needs to be addressed, and we could have saved so many more children had we addressed these things more seriously when people spoke up. There were pioneers before me that tried to speak up but I was one of the first to come out in my book and talk seriously about the Károlyis and the mistreatments that occurred."

Dr. Larry Nassar, former doctor for the USA Gymnastics national team and alleged abuser of multiple gymnasts, is currently in jail after pleading guilty to federal charges of possession of child pornography. He also faces at least thirty-three counts of sexual assault charges in Michigan. If it weren't for the bravery of these athletes, he may have continued to harm even more young girls.

I don't want to teach my daughters that they have to learn how to navigate through a situation where they are being abused; if there is anything they are uncomfortable with, in any situation, no job or team is so important that it's not worth saying something. Athletes possess the power to bring about justice in a way that more should exercise. I had the power to support the young girl who I mentioned to Soledad who accused a faculty member at our high school of sexually abusing her. I could have used my position, my celebrity, to bring that to light and support her. I stayed quiet, and that is something I have regretted ever since I found out—that she transferred schools, that everybody turned on her, that nobody believed her, and that she was basically forced to recant a statement she had made.

One of the people my daughter Baby Sierra gets a kick out of watching is Jemele Hill. I think it's Hill's animation and the way she and Michael Smith go back and forth on different topics on *SportsCenter*. Baby Sierra says things like, "They're funny, I like them." But one segment on *His & Hers* that caught both of my daughters' attention wasn't funny at all. They watched intently as Hill and Smith discussed the body-shaming and slandering that Serena Williams continues to be bombarded with, even though she may be the greatest tennis player of all time. Imani listened to Jemele Hill discuss media reports that addressed Serena's body image—another tennis player said she was too manly; a coach said he didn't want his players to look like Serena; someone else said her butt was too big; and yet another said she simply didn't have the right body type for tennis and therefore technically shouldn't be winning. Imani had a frown on her face and her eyes grew pensive. She said, "Why do they keep talking about Serena like that? Why are they so worried about her body, and what's wrong with her body anyway? She's the one winning and beating everybody, so obviously they should try to have their bodies be like Serena, right? And didn't Serena beat that Sharapova girl like twenty straight times already, and they still keep talking about her like she's actually her big rival? If I beat you twenty straight times, you are not on my level. Man, they better leave Serena alone."

Then Imani heard Hill say that despite the fact that Serena had beaten Maria Sharapova seventeen times in a row, Sharapova had made a lot more money in endorsements than Serena. Imani was irate. She said, "Well, that's not fair. They're gonna talk bad about her and pay her less even though she is winning? How is that fair?" Imani was glad to hear Hill using her platform to point out the unfair treatment of Serena.

I wanted to go into a little more depth about this subject with Jemele Hill and Michael Smith, for all the Black girls who hear the criticism of Serena Williams, the body-shaming, the racial prejudice.

Etan: You have both used your platforms to speak on behalf of women in many different situations. What is that like for you in this world of sports journalism?

Jemele Hill: There are difficult things that you have to deal with. One of course being double standards. There is a different kind of scrutiny of what you say, how you say it, and that's not just in sports; that's with women in general. Women are treated differently, especially when you have forceful opinions. You're made more aware of the way you are coming off to people. You can easily be stereotyped as overly aggressive, especially if you are a woman of color, and even more specifically a Black woman. You're not allowed to be passionate like men are because you will be considered "irrational"; you will hear criticism of lacking a certain femininity and grace. You are accused of being "angry" or the "angry Black woman." So you are constantly combating these stereotypes, and despite the advancements and the change that has happened in the industry, women have to constantly prove that we belong in that space.

Etan: What's interesting is seeing that in the coverage of Serena Williams.

Michael Smith: Well, first you have the traditional and historic disrespect, devalue, and degradation of the Black woman from a physical standpoint, but when you have a Black woman dominating a sport that is reserved for white women, they are going to find some way to discredit her. It wasn't enough that there's these two young Black women in Venus and Serena from Compton, actual sisters who shared a bedroom growing up, defying all odds and becoming the greatest in Serena and one of the top three to five of all time in Venus. I mean, this has to be one of the greatest American sports stories of all time, but instead of embracing the beautiful story, they try to find a way to discredit what they are doing.

Hill: There is so much coded language with Serena to unpack . . . But let's examine a few examples. People go out of their way to overcompliment her power and to do it in a way that purposely tries to deny her a level of delicacy. One of the most difficult stereotypes that Black women face is that we are not considered delicate. Whenever white women are talked about, you hear words like "fragile." Most of the times when people characterize Black women, it's as someone who needs to be handled or suppressed or in some cases physically dominated. I think in Serena's case in particular, because she is such a powerful player, a lot of times they are so overcomplimentary to that power that they are proclaiming that the only reason why she is winning is because she is stronger and bigger than everybody else, when in fact, there is a beauty and grace to her game. But they go out of their way to deny her an even basic femininity and a feminine grace.

So I look at some of the pictures, and we have been guilty of posting this on ESPN.com—there is always a picture of Serena looking angry and powerful and almost predatory, as opposed to pictures of, say, Maria Sharapova or other white female tennis players looking more feminine and more graceful. I know some people may think that I am making too much of it, but people have to understand that much of the way that Serena is shown and discussed is an outright attack on the core of who Black women are.

Etan: In the beginning she was criticized for having the wrong body type, and now the criticism has morphed into suggesting she is only winning because she has a certain body type.

Smith: She went through so much early, so much criticism, that as she got older it appeared to have made her stronger. So now, when she speaks, she can speak through a place of unfiltered authenticity, because what else can they really say about her? They tried to rob her of her femininity, they tried to rob her of her youth, her innocence at the time, all of the mainstream always had something to say about her. And this was as recently as, what, two years ago? She has been a wonderful activist in her own right. Long before there was a phrase for the culture, that's what Serena was. She handles her business on and off the court. And she has to deal with the world media—we're used to the US media, but the world media just has such a different approach. The representation she has to carry, being a Black woman in that sport and being the best in that sport.

Etan: I definitely agree, and having two daughters, I see the inspiration as so desperately needed for our young girls.

Smith: I have two daughters as well, and Serena is showing Black girls that you have to be confident in yourself because the world is not going to be confident in you or support your Black Girl Magic or your Black beauty, just like they didn't support Serena's. In fact, you will have hurdles that you have to overcome, and Serena will be looked at as the activist who defiantly stood up to that criticism and took it head-on. She won Wimbledon and Crip-walked after; she was balancing the plate on her head, the beads, the outfits, all of that was her defiance, saying something like, "I'm not going to conform to who you want me to be, I am going to still speak my mind, be me, call out racism like when I was booed and called racial slurs at the Indian Wells Masters tournament, and dominate a sport you think is reserved only for you."

And even more than that—the skin, body type—young girls can look at her and see themselves. And what I love most about her is that no matter how much anyone has tried to body-shame her, her confidence never ceased. Her posting pictures in a bathing suit, tight dresses, whatever, that shows off the body that they spend so much time shaming her for—it's a message to Black girls that you are beautiful just the way you are. So she is an activist for Black beauty, and the fact that this is something that she even needs to be an activist for is tragic in itself. But necessary, especially for young Black

264 ✕ WE MATTER

girls to see, so they can build up enough self-confidence for the inevitable attacks on their hair, their lips, their noses, their skin tones, their bodies, all of the different things the establishment is going to criticize them for because they are not a skinny white girl with blue eyes, just as they told Serena. And we can show them this Black woman who looks like them, had to withstand this criticism, is proud, beautiful, successful, and the best. She's as important a person—especially for young Black girls, and grown Black women—as we have.

Hill: There is always going to be a certain conversation around her to delegitimize who she is and what she has accomplished. And she realizes that . . . How they have body-shamed Serena has definitely had an impact on how Black women view ourselves . . . There are definitely a lot of positives and a lot of inspiration to be drawn from the success and dominance of Serena and Venus.

But here's the other side of it—this can also be a roadblock. It almost makes us seem that we are incapable or not allowed to be vulnerable. So while I draw a lot of inspiration from watching and seeing Serena be so unapologetic, there is also a part of me that is saddened by it as well, because Serena has vulnerabilities much like all Black women do. She is complex, she is layered . . . so this idea that Black women are able to weather anything and defeat anything and are the backbone and strength of the community and of our entire race as a whole, and while that may be true throughout history, it also denies us humanity at the same time.

Etan: That is a great point. Now, pivoting from Serena and hearing similar criticism come up when Sandra Bland was murdered . . . Explanations were given that she was being too aggressive, too sassy, wasn't docile enough. This formed a lot of the justification for her murder.

Hill: I have this image cemented in my head of the police officer in Texas and . . . there are all of these Black teenagers in bathing suits, and he is seen literally grabbing a girl in a two-piece bathing suit by her hair and throwing her to the ground, waving his gun at the other teenagers that try to come to her assistance. And he sits on her back while she is handcuffed. While she didn't lose her life, like the other horrendous cases you mentioned, it spoke to the basic lack of humanity, and the vulnerability that we are often denied. And I guess this is why, to some degree, I struggle with the concept of the "strong Black woman," because it has been used in a way to justify outright assault on our bodies. Even if we are an unarmed teenage girl in a bathing suit at a pool party . . . Black women are a lot of times not seen as women. And if you look at somebody like Serena Williams, that all ties in. Yes, she is strong. Yes, she is powerful. But she is also a woman, and people struggle to combine those three . . . So when you have people who interact with us in everyday life, and we are seen as too aggressive, too sassy, too bold, those can be very dangerous stereotypes.

Etan: So what would be your advice to young Black women on how to interact with the police, knowing that that fear is going to be there?

Hill: We deserve humanity. It's not something that we have to earn. It's not something that we have to apply for. It's just a basic right. And I think it's unfortunate, but Black people in general are always told the message that we have to do something in order to gain your respect, as opposed to automatically having it. So you don't have to earn it, it's yours, because you are here . . . And whether it be interacting with the police, whether it be at work or at school or in dealing with a boy, you have the deep and abiding sense that you are worth something to yourself and to many others.

Interview with Laila Ali & Curtis Conway

"Treat other people with respect while accepting nothing less in return." Those were the words of Laila Ali when I asked her and her husband Curtis Conway how important was it to them to instill in their daughters the importance of standing up for their rights, standing up for themselves, and standing up for what they believe in. Who better to ask about teaching young women self-confidence, self-worth, and self-love than the daughter of Muhammad Ali? A man who was the epitome of the athlete-activist. A man who risked everything for standing up for what he believed and standing firm in the face of adversity and criticism.

Laila Ali is a former boxer who, like her father, was considered "The Greatest." She retired undefeated, after competing from 1999 to 2007, but not before winning the WBC, WIBA, IWBF, and IBA female super mid-dleweight titles, and the IWBF light heavyweight title. Ali has a passion for inspiring young people through her own experiences, and she is the author of the book *Reach! Finding Strength, Spirit, and Personal Power.* Curtis Con-way is a former wide receiver in the NFL. After being drafted by the Chicago Bears in the first round in 1993, Conway went on to play for the San Diego Chargers, the New York Jets, and the San Francisco 49ers.

"Treat other people with respect while accepting nothing less in re-turn." I repeated those words to my daughter Imani and asked her what she thought of them. She answered, "That's a good philosophy to have—whose words were those?" When I told her, she said, "Wow, I would like to know more of what she says. How she raises her kids. How she deals with being Muhammad Ali's daughter. If she faces any pressure to be 'The Greatest?'" I showed Imani pictures of Laila Ali and she said she looks a lot like her father and that she wanted to read more about her.

Laila Ali and Curtis Conway are a beautiful couple and a blended family, and neither is afraid nor hesitant to speak their minds and use their platform to help others.

Etan: What are some of the main principles you want your daughters to grow up with?

Laila Ali: Children learn by watching the actions of those who raise them, so we must always make sure we are modeling the behavior we intend for them to adopt in their own lives. When it comes to my daughter Sydney, I'm rais-ing her to be confident in herself and her abilities. I want her to believe that she has everything within her that's needed to achieve anything she puts her mind to. I encourage her to be a leader and not a follower, even when every-one else is going a different direction. At the young age of six, I'm explaining to her that she must have the courage to stand alone when necessary and do what she knows is right. Spirituality plays a big role in my life and I am instilling it in my daughter as well, so that she is in touch with her intuition, has a relationship with God, and knows that we are all connected and a part of something much greater than we can see with our eyes.

If I can instill self-confidence, strong leadership qualities, and spirituality into my daughter, I can rest knowing that she will be able to navigate life successfully. I teach my girls that God created all humans equally. "We are all special in our own way, but not better than the next person." It is so important that they know this because they will treat others with respect while accepting nothing less than the same treatment in return.

Etan: What is your advice to young women who might be patterning their actions and lives after what they see on TV?

Ali: Most of the reality TV shows that are being produced today depict women in a negative way. Sadly, young girls tune in and begin to emulate the women they are watching . . . You must understand that most of what you see on reality TV is not "real." When it comes to role models, look to women who consistently command respect no matter where they go in the world, such as First Lady Michelle Obama. Aim high!

Etan: Curtis, do you think athletes have a responsibility to be a positive light in all of this darkness? Or is it unfair to put that on them?

Curtis Conway: I do my best to be a positive example to both adults and kids. With that being said, I don't think athletes should automatically have the responsibility to be role models to kids, because we all have a right to decide how we want to live our lives and what image we want to portray. Just because you perform your profession in the public eye doesn't mean you should have to feel pressure to change who you really are to fit the public's opinion . . . There are a lot of athletes who haven chosen to be responsible with the platform they have, living positive lifestyles, and in some cases giving back to their communities. The media should start giving more coverage to those athletes.

Etan: How important is it for girls to stand up for their rights and beliefs?

Conway: As a father, I raise my girls to be strong, independent, and to stand for what they believe in. The only time I may not want them to take a stand is when it could physically hurt them. I'm just being real. That's the father in me, being protective of my girls, because I feel as men, we need to protect our girls and women.

Fighting for Your Rights Matters

Kareem Abdul-Jabbar brilliantly described the exploitation of college athletes in a July 2014 *Time* magazine article:

> *The irony is that the NCAA and other supporters claim paying athletes would sully the purity of college sports—desecrating our image of a youthful clash of school rivalries that always ends at the malt shop with school songs being sung and innocent flirting between boys in letterman jackets and girls with pert ponytails and chastity rings. In reality, what makes college sports such a powerful symbol in our culture is that it represents our attempt to impose fairness on an otherwise unfair world. Fair play, sportsmanship and good-natured rivalry are lofty goals to live by. By treating the athletes like indentured servants, we're tarnishing that symbol and reducing college sports to just another exploitation of workers, no better than a sweatshop.*

The popularity of the NCAA bowl games and March Madness continues to skyrocket, and so do the astronomical television deals and overall profits that come with that growth. While this raises the eyebrows of some, it simultaneously causes universities to clench their Scrooge McDuck empires even tighter. College players don't share in the spoils, yet the more money universities make, the more greedy they become.

Let's look at the facts, as laid out by Abdul-Jabbar in that article:

- College athletic programs are a $6 billion-a-year industry. Yes, that's billion with a "B."
- The NCAA president makes nearly $2 million a year. A salary that is steadily rising annually.

- CBS and TBS split $1 billion per year off of March Madness alone.
- The NCAA's top ten basketball coaches earn salaries that range from $2.2 million to $9.7 million per year.
- The average annual pay for coaches in the NCAA tournament field is $1.77 million. That's based on sixty-two of sixty-eight schools in the field for which *USA Today* was able to obtain compensation figures.

Yet the NCAA continues to oppose paying college athletes, and in polls, a slim majority supports this—but it's hypocritical. These are young athletes who play every single game, risk permanent career-ending injury, and get only scholarship money as their compensation. Case in point: my wife Nichole Thomas.

Some are naive enough to believe that the NCAA doesn't want to pay college athletes because they are 100 percent committed to educational and intellectual enlightenment. Some are actually convinced that if the athletes were paid, the very fiber of our institutions of higher learning would be compromised and the focus of scholastic achievement would quickly dissipate.

Kareem Abdul-Jabbar continues to let his voice be heard and utilize his influence and power as an athlete–activist.

Many do not realize that if you have a career-ending injury, you're no longer of any use to the university and can be sold up the river—or, in modern terms, lose your scholarship. I know this firsthand because it almost happened to my wife (then girlfriend), who, like me, played basketball for Syracuse University.

After Nichole's third knee surgery, the Syracuse specialist, Dr. Irving Raphael, told her that if she wanted to be able to walk without a cane and play with her kids in the future, she had to stop playing basketball. She was devastated, but after much convincing from the people who cared about her, Nichole made the right decision.

Then–head coach Marianna Freeman, assistant coach Felisha Legette, and the rest of the Syracuse women's program began a crusade to take Nichole's scholarship away, because, after all, if you can no longer play, what good are you to them? Nichole actually threatened to sue the athletic director, Jake Crouthamel, and the university itself, in order to keep her scholarship during her senior year.

If their main concern was education, this wouldn't have happened. The bottom line is that it's a business. When you play Division I sports, you're there for two simple reasons: to play, and to earn money for the university.

But naysayers will tell you things along the lines of:

"Universities are dedicated to inundating capital into each and every student-athlete's academic development."

"Paying college athletes would devalue the universities as a whole and discredit the student-athletes as scholars. It would diminish their overall academic growth and therefore be doing them a disservice."

"It wouldn't be fair to the other students who are bogged down with student loans, work-study, and financial aid programs, so we just wouldn't want to hurt their feelings."

If you believe any of that, I have some magic beans that you'd probably be interested in buying as well.

Amid a lawsuit brought by former football and men's basketball players in 2014, NCAA president Mark Emmert testified that paying college athletes a share of the revenue from commercial use of their names and images would alienate fans, damage competition, and ultimately harm the athletes. Emmert, who has led the association of 1,100 college sports programs since October 2010, said any such compensation would erase the boundary between college and professional sports. He has argued, "To convert college sports into professional sports would be tantamount to converting it into minor league sports," with a much lower fan base.

ESPN analyst Jay Bilas has continuously pointed out the ridiculousness of the entire argument. "It's laughable, but it's not funny. They pay the scholarship, which is the amount the school pays to itself. They're not out a nickel. The athletics department pays the school. Then they claim that they're poor. Then they pay themselves these outrageous salaries that are market-based, but they say they don't have any money to give to the players, but they have $8 million to give to a football or basketball coach and $1 million to give a baseball coach."

If we are all waiting for the NCAA to feel remorse for the way they have exploited athletes for decades, we are fooling ourselves.

Pulitzer Prize–winning author Taylor Branch looked at the state of affairs in college sports and could come to only one conclusion: "For all the outrage, the real scandal is . . . that two of the noble principles on which the NCAA justifies its existence—'amateurism' and the 'student-athlete'—are cynical hoaxes, legalistic confections propagated by the universities so they can exploit the skills and fame of young athletes."

Whether or not college athletes are actually being exploited shouldn't even be a question. The only question is how we can rectify this problem.

I looked to athlete-activist pioneer Oscar Robertson, an NBA legend and twelve-time all-star, to explore his role in changing the unfair system they were being subjected to in his day.

Interview with Oscar Robertson

Etan: My grandfather taught me about you at a very young age. I really credit you and Curt Flood for the entire free agency system that we have today. That all came about because of you challenging the system.

Oscar Robertson: The whole challenge started when I first entered the league. I was asked to get involved in the Players Association during my tenure in the NBA, and once I was in there, I saw so many things that were just wrong. Doctors not being in attendance; we didn't have a trainer. Say you played ten years and after the tenth year, you said, "Hey, I would like to go play for somebody else," they could keep you from playing. You had no legal way of getting back into playing and we felt that was wrong. So we went to court . . . And of course the NBA owners didn't like that at all. In fact, they railed at us and said how it was going to ruin basketball and all of these things, but of course it has not. Look at the players today, they are really small companies unto themselves . . . And of course the league is using them to the best of their ability, but the compensation and the piece of the pie that they are now receiving is definitely greater, as it should be.

Etan: Did you have any idea of the long-term effect that you would bring about?

Robertson: No, you can't anticipate that. We started this fight and we were just plodding away on a rowboat and we didn't know where we were headed or how this whole thing would end up . . . At first, it was hard getting players on board. They thought they were going to kick all of us out of the league, but that didn't happen. Now, we were definitely threatened along the way, and I didn't care about the threats because I felt that this was right and I was secure in my position in the league to be able to take that stance. Threats are interesting, and I have definitely been threatened throughout the years, but couldn't give into it . . . There are factions in the world that don't want certain things to change because they are making all of the money, so of course they don't want things to change.

Etan: So basically, it was like the league owned you—like you were property of theirs—and you couldn't do anything about it

Robertson: You had no say whatsoever. They held you without a contract forever . . . Up until then, everybody just went along with it because that's the system that was given to us. So we went to court, and it took a few years . . . It was something that I felt I had to do. The world is changing, it was changing then and the pendulums were starting to change . . . Like I said, I am happy when I see these young players making the money they are making and commanding the dollars they are commanding.

Etan: Curt Flood, who my grandfather also taught me about, really had to sacrifice a lot for challenging Major League Baseball.

Robertson: Yeah, I wouldn't call it sacrifice, because that's when you give up something and make concessions and things of that nature. Curt was *punished*. He was an all-star center fielder for the St. Louis Cardinals, played for like fifteen years through the fifties and the sixties . . . and what he did changed everything for baseball. He didn't accept a trade—and not only did he not accept the trade, he hired a lawyer and sued Major League Baseball . . .

He went all the way to the US Supreme Court with this, and he should have won that case hands down, but he didn't. He also didn't have hardly any teammates who supported him. He had Jackie Robinson and Hank Greenberg and that's it . . . They actually agreed that Curt Flood should have been able to be a free agent, but because of the antitrust laws that were in place, it could only be changed by an act of Congress. So they kicked him out of baseball, and he went overseas for some time, no longer allowed to play baseball. He eventually checked into a psychiatric hospital and recently passed away, so it was a really sad story . . . They went out of their way to prove to Curt Flood and the entire league that "we still have control of the situation and there will be a severe punishment for trying to go against us." You see how things are now, and don't get me wrong, they are far from perfect, but I was born in Tennessee, and I remember not being allowed to ride in the front of the bus.

I remember seeing *Whites Only* signs and *Colored* signs, couldn't go into any of the restaurants downtown, and when I came to Indianapolis, it was worse than Tennessee. When I lived in Tennessee with my grandparents for a while, the racism was there, but it paled in comparison to when I went to Indianapolis and I saw Ku Klux Klanners literally all over the place . . . Those were the times I grew up in. And we still have a long way to go, but we have progressed somewhat. Look at what sports has done for the world, and the Olympics, and how sports has been a bridge across the world. But what hasn't changed is that they still want athletes to just play on the court or the field . . . and just be thankful . . . But how could you, as a man, not say something about it if you have been blessed with the platform to be able to do so?

Etan: Do you feel that players are muted completely now?

Robertson: Definitely not. I was just reading where the players from the

New England Patriots have said that they are not going to the White House, and they are going to be criticized, but I always say, "If you can play, it doesn't matter." What is going on today, guys have been elevated from simply being college players or professional players to now rock stars, and for them to keep quiet . . . would be ridiculous.

Etan: So you see guys speaking out on different topics—what do you think? Do you feel proud?

Robertson: Definitely proud. I get a big smile on my face every time I see one of the current players using their voice. Like a proud dad watching his son playing ball and making the moves he used to make. I think back to Muhammad Ali, and when he didn't go into the army . . . they just didn't want him to influence other Black kids into not going into the army, because they knew the level of influence he had. Well, the same goes for today. They don't want these athletes to influence Black kids. They want you to be peaceful, sedated, grateful to them . . . But you look at societies of the world—when things are going bad, people have a right to demonstrate and have a right to voice their disapproval, and that includes athletes. I was so glad to see [Steph] Curry get upset when the Under Armour guy said he was a big Trump supporter. Well, good, and you know why? Because they need Curry, and this is why it's great to take advantage and know who you are.

Etan: So how would you encourage players, especially those who have the limelight—the LeBrons and Steph Currys and Carmelos—to use their power?

Robertson: I would repeat to them that they are speaking not just for themselves but for other people. Let's take the Affordable Care Act—or as they like to call it, Obamacare. That benefits so many people—how could you take that away from them? It's almost asinine, and you see these politicians who could care less about how many people would be affected by them taking it away, and you see other people fighting for it who may be able to afford their own health care but understand how much this benefits everyone. And that's what I would keep pointing out to the current athletes, and they seem to get it . . . Of course, you have some outliers, but this young generation, they look ready and willing.

Interview with Jimmy King & Ray Jackson

Could unionizing collegiate athletics be the answer? It worked for Oscar Robertson, but they were met with exactly the same arguments that we are hearing today as to the catastrophe unionizing would cause—for the sport, the country, and the entire world. Mark Emmert said that everything we hold dear in our hearts would be ruined. The treasured customs that are embedded in fans' traditions and in their souls would be ruined. The camaraderie, the tailgating, the atmosphere of a stadium packed with tens of thousands of fans, and the pride of cheering for a university team would somehow, I'm not sure exactly how, all go away in a cloud of smoke the moment we decide to allow college athletes to get a piece of the pie. So in Emmert's mind, he was in essence trying to do what was best for the American people as a whole.

It's almost laughable how ridiculous that is. But just as that doom-and-gloom scenario didn't occur when Oscar Robertson helped bring about the new system of free agency in the NBA, it wouldn't happen if NCAA athletes were paid. Hopefully, years from now, athletes will look back at the absurdity of this system the same way we look back at the backward system where a team owned your rights for the entire duration of your career and you had absolutely no say in where you would play.

Kevin Trahan of *SB Nation* reported that according to an ESPN.com survey of top football recruits, 60 percent of them would support unionizing and more than 86 percent are in favor of athletes receiving some sort of stipend.

Unionization would in fact change everything. Players would be able to challenge the NCAA to see the overall books, negotiate for a portion of the billion-dollar television deal behind March Madness, discuss BRI and FRI (basketball- and football-related income), and figure out how they should divide the money accordingly (just as they do now for coaches and everyone else working in the athletics program). They could add provisions so that universities could no longer do what Syracuse attempted to do to Nichole and take his or her scholarship away if they are injured and can no longer play. They could negotiate that all universities are required to cover medical expenses for former players if those expenses were a result of playing at the school. The opportunities are endless.

Despite an overwhelming number of people vehemently opposed to college athletes forming unions, the fact remains that a union would put pressure on the NCAA to change a lot of the things they have absolutely no intention or desire to change. Again, the system is working exactly how they designed it to work. And they do not want to relinquish their Scrooge McDuck hat. They have grown quite comfortable in their position.

In *Time* magazine Kareem Abdul-Jabbar has written:

Our relationship with college athletes is much clearer. We adore and revere them. They represent the fantasy of our children achieving success and being popular. Watching them play with such enthusiasm and energy for nothing more than school pride is the distillation of Hope for the Future. But strip away the rose-colored glasses and we're left with a subtle but insidious form of child abuse. Which raises the question: How will things change? When I was a young, handsome player at UCLA, with a full head of hair and a pocket full of nothing, I sometimes had a friend scalp my game tickets so I could have a little spending money. I couldn't afford a car, which scholarship students in other disciplines could because they were permitted to have jobs, so I couldn't go anywhere. I got bored just sitting around my dorm room and frustrated wandering through Westwood, passing shops in which I couldn't afford to buy anything.

To delve more deeply into this topic, I asked two members of the legendary Fab Five to share their experiences at Michigan and to further explain how the NCAA is not fair to its athletes. Jimmy King went on to play basketball in the NBA, while Ray Jackson—the only member of the Fab Five to never play in the NBA—was drafted into the Continental Basketball Association.

Etan: Talk to me about the education you received at Michigan on the economics of the NCAA.

Jimmy King: The things that we experienced firsthand as college freshmen being highly touted—we had no real idea about how the actual economics of college basketball worked. We understood some of the things, but it was a learning process . . . We came to the realization that if we did speak out about this, that it would have a tremendous impact on college basketball as a whole and our community as a whole. So we wanted to be advocates and not solely concerned with taking our piece.

Etan: So talk to me about what exactly y'all decided to do. Y'all stopped wearing the Michigan Wolverine warm-ups with the school logo on it.

Ray Jackson: That was something we decided to do as a team once we really began to discuss and pay attention to . . . the fact that we were being exploited. Sometimes you just have to take a stand. And to be honest, the entire process of the Fab Five was a protest. From the shorts to the socks to the demeanor, we wanted to get away from the norm. We wanted to enlighten people and we wanted to take everything to another level and represent the culture that we came from. And in the end, we wanted to reap the benefits from the foundation that we laid down . . . It wasn't just the Fab Five; it was other guys that had been at Michigan, the seniors and juniors who all saw the money that was changing hands but was skipping over the student-athlete. We were all on the exact same page as far as this was concerned . . . It's something we have to continue to educate the masses of college athletes on and express to them to not take this exploitation lying down.

Etan: When y'all see how high school football in Texas has become this incredible big-money sport, or when you watch the college football championship and you see these young men getting concussions and being permanently damaged in horrendous ways, and now the coaches are making six or seven million dollars per year, do you feel that in your heart—the gap between what is just, as far as compensation for the actual players?

King: Well, the numbers speak for themselves. I know that if you are comparing high school football to any other amateur athletics, it really isn't comparable because high school football, particularly in Texas, has always been big business . . .

Jackson: When you start looking at the numbers like we did when we were at Michigan, and you start counting attendance and how many behinds can sit in those seats, and how much they pay to sit in those seats . . . it's crazy. It's absolutely ridiculous. And the thing that has to change as far as I'm concerned, while we are talking about the dollars, is the education of our kids at a young age. Young athletes need to know and understand that by the time you reach high school, you are actually playing for dollars. You're just not seeing any of it, but it is definitely being made . . . The kids and the parents need to understand the process and the level of exploitation that is happening so that they fight for a percentage of the T-shirt money or concessions money, and things will change. We will be looking sometime in the future and discussing, "You remember how back in the day college athletes and high school athletes allowed themselves to be exploited to the tune of millions of dollars, and for some reason everybody was okay with it?" But it's going to take being educated to realize how you are being exploited before you can be pushed to do something about it.

Etan: Y'all were part of this historical experience twenty-five years ago. The Fab Five will be talked about for decades to come. Do either of you have any regrets?

King: Looking back, easily Ray and I know that had we gone to a different school, that our NBA careers and long-term careers may have been more monetarily rewarding, but the education that we have received both on and off the court during our time at the University of Michigan has really allowed us to be the people we are supposed to be . . . I tell my kids all the time, basketball is a microcosm of life. The things you learn just from being around this game are going to prepare you for life. And there was no better preparation for life than being involved in the Fab Five and the things that we saw. And that's what it's about, the fight, and being educated on where we have come from historically as Black people, and not allowing the structure to suck in more of our community and our kids. So I would add on, not only do we need to educate the kids, but we need to liberate them . . . We really need to be on that focus. We have enough resources now to do that. We don't need to look to Nike. If we pooled all of the athletes' money right now, we could start something special . . . We have to meet those challenges head-on and be willing to fight for what's right, fight for our education, fight for our brother, and fight for our survival in this society and in this day. And refuse to be silent and use our voice.

Interview with John Wall

In this new era of one-and-done athletes, I wanted to talk to John Wall about his willingness to speak out on various matters, including the exploitation of college athletes. John could easily avoid saying anything that might rock the boat and continue to soar in his fame and glory. But that's not the route he has chosen for himself. He is fearless, appreciative, he honors the players who came before him, and he has paid attention to the activism of his predecessors. He doesn't feel any restraints or fear any repercussions. This is the way it should be. I couldn't imagine having to walk on eggshells or bite my tongue in an organization that wasn't supportive of the fact that I was actually a human being who had opinions, thoughts, and beliefs outside of basketball.

Etan: I interviewed Ted Leonsis, the CEO of the Wizards, and I talked to him about how the Wizards are not one of those organizations that makes players feel that they can't speak out on certain things that are in their hearts, whether it's a murder at the hands of the police, actions taken by Donald Trump, or something going on in their city. Is that pretty accurate?

John Wall: Most definitely. Ted Leonsis is very observant just like we are. We see things that are going on in the community and throughout the world just like everyone else does. We also have opinions, just like everyone else does. And if we want to say something about it, he definitely gives us the leeway to speak our mind . . . When things happen in society, some things are bigger than basketball, and he understands that and we understand that.

Etan: That was my experience here as well. So, earlier this year, after the murders of Philando Castile and Alton Sterling, Bradley Beal made a statement about it, and he received a tremendous amount of backlash from fans. But he didn't retract his statement, and the Wizards didn't force him to issue an apology to the fans he may have offended.

Wall: *(Laughing)* That would've been messed up. Do other organizations do stuff like that?

Etan: Well, you would be surprised. But my point is, it seems like current athletes as a whole are just a lot more comfortable speaking their minds now, and nobody is afraid.

Wall: Definitely. You can go back to the ESPYs when LeBron and D Wade and Melo and Chris Paul went up there and spoke . . . I mean, they were on that big of a stage, talking about police brutality, talking about Black Lives Matter, telling the world that there was something wrong with the system, and then challenging everyone to do something about it. They had a call to action in front of the entire world. And they organized that themselves . . . That right there showed the whole world that not only do our top guys, the faces of our league, care, but they want to do something about it. Whether you are retired or you're still playing, or even about to get drafted, or in college, you have a lot of say so. People look at everything we do, and are definitely going to pay attention to everything we say.

Etan: You mention college athletes, and I want to ask you about the NCAA. Do you think it's a fair system?

Wall: I definitely think they should pay them, and no, that system is nowhere near fair . . . People keep saying that we . . . should be grateful for the opportunity of the college experience, and that's really a slap in the face. That's like, "Shut up and be grateful." Of course they should pay college athletes, but they won't do it unless somebody *makes* them do it. Everything is working the way they want it to work. They not gonna just all of a sudden start paying college athletes because they feel bad for exploiting us for all these decades, just like they are not going to lower the tuitions, which are astronomical, because they feel bad.

Etan: I feel you. And I will also add that I think it's incredibly selfish for fans to be upset when guys leave college early.

Wall: Man, I can talk about this all day . . . I do think that you have exceptions, of course, like LeBron and Kobe, but most guys, just from a development standpoint, need to go to college. And a lot of coaches out there were criticizing Coach [John] Calipari, saying that he doesn't care about their education [at the University of Kentucky] and is encouraging a "one-and-none" system. Well, your student did three years, and he didn't get a degree either . . . But here's the thing: you can always go back and get your degree, like I am doing. I take classes in the off-season, and I will get my degree. You have some guys . . . who are four-year guys, and they still don't get their degree . . . If it's not your focus, it's not going to happen no matter how long you physically stay there.

Etan: That's a good point.

Wall: But if you come back to school and . . . you get injured, you may have very well forfeited your chance of ever playing in the NBA. It's a gamble with your career. Anything can happen in that year of you being a "student-athlete." Millions of dollars are at stake. Would they risk millions of dollars for a degree that they can always go back and get? That's not even realistic. Nobody would do that. If you are in college, and say a Fortune 500 business wants to hire you at the end of your sophomore year and guarantees you a six-figure salary, and allows you to go back to get your degree, what would you do? What, not go because you need to stay in school for what reason?

You would take advantage of that opportunity . . . That's the advice Coach Cal gives his players and it's good advice. I promised my dad before he passed that I was going to go get my degree, and that's exactly what I'm going to do.

Etan: So what do you think it's going to take for this system to change?

Wall: Well, I think the NBA is going to have to get involved . . . You have to create a system where guys can develop and don't have to choose between being exploited or taking care of their families . . . If they create a system that will provide the players with, let's start off with a percentage of what their particular university is making off them, then maybe that will be enough incentive for them to stay and develop, and not be forced to leave early for financial reasons.

Etan: And of course the first argument is, "How are we going to pay *everyone?*" Well, if your sport is not generating any money, then you are not worried about leaving early. But even if you want to have all of the sports covered, there is enough to go around for everyone to get something. When you have college coaches all making millions, there is enough to go around for everyone.

Wall: Exactly. Everybody is getting paid but the athletes. You mean to tell me that you can't take some of that money that the coaches are making and divvy that up between the players?

13 *Education Matters*

***Coach Carter* is one of my favorite movies to show young athletes.** For those who haven't seen it, it's a riveting film inspired by the true story of a coach (played by Samuel L. Jackson) who takes over a struggling high school basketball team in Richmond, California. Coach Carter is cut from a different cloth and doesn't tolerate bad team chemistry or students not taking their education seriously. The school board rejects his methods and even fires him when he puts the entire team on academic ineligibility.

Like many schools, the school in the movie is only concerned with wins. The team is undefeated, and more wins usually translates into more money for the schools. But Coach Carter takes on the entire town, parents, community, and school board, who are all furious with him for shutting down the season until the players bring up their GPAs.

I showed this to some of Malcolm's teammates while we were on our way to a Wizards game; I wanted to use the movie as a teaching tool. And the message definitely resonated. I told the boys how I grew up with guys who didn't have a coach like this, someone who held them accountable, made sure they respected themselves enough to give their absolute best both on and off the court.

One character in the movie, Junior, can hardly even read. How can a student make it all the way through middle and high school, become a senior like Junior, and not be able to read? That's a catastrophe, but it happens. This is art depicting real life. And when you are finished playing, after school has used you all they possibly can, they may not return your phone calls because they don't need you anymore. They have moved on. Which is why it is so upsetting to see so many guys put all of their eggs in one basket. No preparation, no future planning, nothing to fall back on. There have been so many guys I grew up with who I know should have made it to the NBA before me, but they lacked the discipline that Coach Carter demanded from his players—the preparation, the focus—and made a lot of bad decisions that not only ruined their sports careers but essentially ruined their lives.

I told the boys that getting your college paid for is an accomplishment in itself. Using basketball to get a degree, where you don't have to spend the rest of your life in debt trying to pay off student loans and you can use that education to better yourself, is a huge achievement. Although so many people assume basketball is your only ticket out, in actuality it is much easier for you to become a doctor, lawyer, agent, businessperson, or entrepreneur than it is to become a professional athlete.

Chris, our center, was the first in the group with a question. He asked if most schools only care about what you can do on the court. I told him yes, unfortunately. I shared how my high school coach, Nate Harris, would give me the hardest time because I was just as focused on speech-and-debate as I was on basketball. He told me that I was wasting my time and needed to be focused on basketball and nothing else. I remembered telling him that I was really good, and winning in numerous categories—poetry, original oratory, standard oratory, and dramatic interpretation. His reply was simply that I needed to get my priorities straight. My response was to win a state championship in speech-and-debate *and* in basketball during my senior year. The boys all looked at me with eyes wide open, and I told them to never let anyone limit you academically, not even your coach.

I then asked them if they noticed the part in the film where Samuel L. Jackson talks about the school's statistics. Tra Quan, one of our point guards, said he remembered Jackson's character explaining that only half of the students are expected to graduate, and out of that, a large percentage of them are girls. Josh, one of our other centers, remembered that among young Black males who drop out of school, a large percentage of them will end up dead or in jail. I said, "Exactly." Then I asked if they saw what ended up happening to all of the guys on the team. In unison, the boys said, "They all went to college and played ball." I said, "Exactly, but if Coach Carter wasn't there, they probably wouldn't have made it to college." I then went into a rather lengthy monologue about how the system is set up for them to fail, and that adults aren't being honest enough with them about this fact. I told them to read Michelle Alexander's *The New Jim Crow,* a book about the mass incarceration of Black Americans. And that when they pick what school they want to play for, they should pay attention to the coaches' philosophies—if they are activists like Coach Carter, fighting the system, standing up for their education, and leading them the right way; or if they are only concerned with their play on the court.

On another trip to a Wizards game, I showed the guys *Finding Forrester*. I absolutely love this movie because it mirrors so many of my experiences in school. I had teachers like Professor Crawford, the teacher of the main character, Jamal, who doesn't think the kid deserves to be in his classroom because he plays basketball. Professor Crawford also accuses Jamal of plagiarism because he doesn't think a kid from the Bronx could produce the quality of work that he produces.

I shared my experiences with the guys—how my sixth grade teacher, Ms. Stewart, accused me of cheating because she didn't think that I could do so well on a test. I also told them about how my ninth grade English teacher, Ms. Ennox, accused me of plagiarism because she didn't believe that I wrote a paper that I had handed in to her. Malcolm, who has heard all of these stories before, asked me to tell them about my elementary school teacher Ms. Scalet. I said, "Okay, sure, well, Ms. Scalet was my fifth grade teacher and she told my mother that I would never be able to write in complete paragraph form because my brain developed slowly and I had a problem focusing." Josh, another one of our centers, said, "That's really messed up." I said, "Yeah, it is, but I didn't let her low expectations stop me. And as I got older and started writing articles and books, my mother would always send them to her." They all started laughing, and Jaden, one of our guards, said, "Ooooooh, crack her face all over the pavement." I hadn't heard that expression before but I could put together what it meant.

I explained that people are going to have low academic expectations for them as athletes. I told them about the hardest class I have ever taken in my life, calculus. I was a business major and calculus was a required course. I was never someone who loved math, but I wanted to learn business, investing, and real estate. That way, if I did turn professional, I would know how to manage money. The first day of class, I walked into a big lecture hall filled with hundreds of people. As the professor was telling everyone to get seated, he looked right at me and said, "Hey, aren't you Etan Thomas?" I replied yes. He said, "The basketball player?" Again I replied yes, now with a bit of skepticism as to where exactly this was going. And the professor's next words are ones that I will tell my grandchildren about. He said, "What are you doing in my classroom? Shouldn't you be in 'Rocks for Jocks' or something?" I just stared at him in disbelief for a few seconds. I didn't know if it was a bad joke or if he was trying to put me down. Unfortunately, it turned out to be the latter. I took my seat, shell-shocked.

I paused the story and looked at the guys, and they were hanging on my every word. Roman, one of our power forwards, asked, "What happened next? Did you cuss him out, go off on him?" Red, one of our other guards, said, "I would've lost it." I told them that I didn't lose it. I just told myself that I wasn't going to let this cat defeat me and that I was going to prove him wrong and be successful in his class. Now, anyone who has taken calculus knows that it's a rather challenging class—ridiculously hard. There were many times it crossed my mind to quit. This class was really, really hard and taking up all of my time. I had no time for anything but calculus. I had a tutor and a study group that I met with two times a week. I remember all of the coaches coming to me at different times saying basically, "Why are you killing yourself with this hard class?" They didn't tell me to drop the class or take something easier per se, but they did stress that I needed to work on my game as much as I was studying. It was a subtle suggestion that I shouldn't forget why I was there.

I remember explaining to Coach Orr what had happened and that I couldn't let this cat win, that if I didn't study like this I would fail. Coach Orr understood completely and turned it into an entire lesson for me. He said, "Oh, you definitely can't quit now." He went off about how we are supposed to be student-athletes and not athlete-students. He told me to make sure I was successful in this class and that he would meet with me after my study group and do some extra drills. And that nobody would question my commitment ever again. I thanked him for having my back.

I ended up making it through the class, and of course the teacher never apologized to me, nor did I expect him to.

I told my players that they need to have the courage to never let anyone in life defeat them, and that I wanted all of them to grow up to be athlete-activists in their own right. See, I use AAU and coaching as a way to build young men. It's not about running a basketball factory. Now, don't get me wrong, we have talent, and although we are a church team, we have a list of elite teams that we are determined to beat. But we are teaching the players life lessons, which is why I take them to panel discussions and field trips to museums, plays, and lectures. Teaching young athletes about the types of people they should aspire to become is crucial, especially when you want to fully prepare the future generation to carry the torch of athlete activism.

Interview with Scoop Jackson

I wanted to conduct an experiment, so I asked my team if they believed that if they wore Steph Curry's shoes, they could shoot like him. Some of them said that they honestly thought it would help. I asked if they truly believed that if they wore an arm sleeve like Russell Westbrook, it would help them with their jump shots. A few of them said, "Well, yeah, probably." So I turned this into a lesson. I told them that they needed to watch what guys do off the court to see how they become successful after basketball is finished. Michel Jordan makes more money after basketball than he did while he was playing. Most people can't make that claim. LeBron James is setting himself up to be in the same boat as Jordan, but it takes proper planning, education, dedication, and discipline in order for that to happen.

Nobody will ever list Jordan with the great athlete-activists of the past. He's wasn't Muhammad Ali, he wasn't Bill Russell. He is typically regarded just as Bill Rhoden describes him in *Forty Million Dollar Slaves*:

> *Michael Jordan is one of the most intriguing athletes of the twentieth century, a sports icon like Babe Ruth but not a paragon of principal like Muhammad Ali. Jordan was a marketing maven who never capitalized on his potential to mobilize African American athletes. Had he said, "Jump," they would have jumped. Instead, he chose to remain publicly neutral in all matters political and racial. The essence of Jordan's legacy is what he accomplished; the tragedy is what he could have done.*

It is important to note that Jordan has evolved. Yes, he is alleged to have once defended his decision to not publicly support Black Democrat Harvey Gantt by saying, "Republicans buy sneakers too" (though Jordan denies having said this). That will probably haunt Jordan for the rest of his days.

Michael Jordan actively supported President Obama in both the '08 and '12 elections. I actually attended a huge fund-raising event that Jordan hosted called the "Obama Classic." Almost fifty different NBA and WNBA athletes joined him in this.

The fact that so many athletes wanted to be involved in President Obama's reelection campaign ran contrary to the popular image of professional basketball players. The reason for our stance? Many of us come from humble beginnings. And we have not forgotten where we come from. Personally, I don't need a tax break, and I think many of us share this view. Teachers, firemen, construction workers, receptionists, farmers, Joe the plumbers—those are the ones we need to help along. It's that mentality that caused all of these athletes to lend their names, time, and effort to help reelect President Obama—spearheaded by none other than Michael Jordan.

In the following interview, weekly columnist for ESPN and *ESPN the Magazine* Scoop Jackson offers a different perspective on Michael Jordan. It's one that is very rarely presented—that Jordan's form of Black Power has been a lot more revolutionary than many people think.

Etan: I want to go back to the article you wrote about me back in 2006 called "Etan Thomas' Voice Is One Worth Listening To," where you were calling on other athletes, especially the main top-tier athletes, to really be that voice. You brought up a lot of good points.

Scoop Jackson: I think that this article in particular still resonates today because it seems like things have changed and there is a lot more visibility in athletes taking stances, and I think that has come with the social climate that we are currently in . . . There are so many other players that had much more probably to lose than you did that were taking less of a stance than you were. And we are seeing a shift in that now, which is good . . . And I've always looked at you as being a symbol. But I still don't see athletes doing the work nonstop that I saw you doing while you were with the Wizards and that I see you still doing. There seems to be more visibility to the symbolic gestures, but I still don't see as much of the consistency that I would like to see.

Etan: But people like LeBron and Carmelo and D Wade and Chris Paul and Steph Curry have been doing a lot, and those are the top athletes of today.

Jackson: I'll put it this way—to me, you are a protest person and they are statement people. There is a difference to making a statement and a protest . . . I always looked at you as a protest athlete. What LeBron and D Wade and all of them were doing, I look at as statement athletes . . . Now, I don't want to start splitting hairs, but to me, Carmelo seems to be more of a protest athlete. He seems to be the athlete that is not afraid to get his hands dirty. He's out on Front Street in Baltimore in the rallies on the street with the people speaking with his mouth, marching with his feet, representing Muhammad Ali 24/7 and what he stood for . . . He leads the town hall meetings that go on after the ESPYs thing he did with D Wade and LeBron and Chris Paul. Then he has the courage to show up on the cover of *ESPN Magazine* dressed as a Black Panther. That's protest. So therein lies the difference. I see what everybody else is doing and they are making statements, which are great statements and very much needed in this day and age, especially with everything that is going on in present-day society . . . Now we just need some more protest athletes. And there is a place for everyone. There is a place for the Michael Jordans, who never gets mentioned in these conversations, but there is a definite value to the role that the Michael Jordans play as well.

Etan: Interesting, Jordan's name always comes up in these conversations. You wrote a piece for ESPN.com called "Michael Jordan's Contribution to Black Issues Greater Than Perceived," which you begin by quoting Roland Lazenby, the author of *Michael Jordan: The Life*: "I say that M.J.'s story is a black power story, not the black power of protest and politics, but the black power of economics." Talk to me more about Jordan's role in this discussion.

Jackson: I think that we become really monolithic in how we judge people who are involved in that. We look for the Jim Browns, the Muhammad Alis, the John Carloses and Tommie Smiths. We look for those athletes who were very vocal about their protests and about their views and ideologies . . . And I understand that, but we are doing ourselves a disservice when we adopt the philosophy that everybody needs to look the same or have the same method of fighting, because there are different fights . . . It's not strategic if you have too many of one and not enough or none of the other . . . Universal freedom for us in this country is us fighting to get freedom, justice, and equality in many fields, not just socially, not just politically, but also economically. America, if anything else, is rooted in and based in economics. We can break down the entire slavery movement and see that it's strictly about economics . . .

So while Jim Brown and Muhammad Ali and John Carlos and Tommie Smith were standing on the front lines screaming for our equality on one end, for us not to have anybody in the economic field trying to find us leverage isn't helping at all. Now, Jim Brown was in fact trying to do that in the entertainment business after he retired from football, and that was needed. And bringing it to the present . . . we are screaming on Michael Jordan to do the exact same thing when we really should be paying attention to the financial and business power moves he is making that we could tremendously benefit from.

Etan: That's a very good point and one that is often completely left out of this conversation, so talk to me about the particular financial power moves that you are referring to.

Jackson: Okay, but I don't want you to think that this means that there isn't room for criticism of Michael Jordan even in the business world. I have written about how I felt that the first thing that Michael Jordan should have done when he retired was divest from all his other business ventures and focus on buying out Jordan from Nike and take that company under his name . . . and have it be a self-containing business where he is the principle owner of it . . . I've always wanted him to do that. And I have always been critical of him for not doing it. But I didn't understand what his long-term goal and vision was. Nike would've looked at him as direct competition and they would've eventually folded Brand Jordan, because Nike was that powerful to do so at that time. He actually played it smarter and forecasted that he would benefit more if he did it this way . . . He has been able to turn that into a billion-dollar business. He now has Black people and executives who have been hired and put in place, and that still has not been matched by any corporation, any Fortune 500 company in America.

And then for him to become the only primary African American owner in America of a sports franchise . . . nobody across all the sports in America has an employment staff with as many Black people working for them in top management positions. From the janitors to the presidents of basketball operations of the Charlotte Hornets, it's like Chocolate City. These are two companies—Brand Jordan and the Charlotte Hornets—that Black folks have been put in power to be able to create gateways and leverage in this playing field. Nobody else is doing it.

Etan: Is the statement, "Republicans buy sneakers too," going to haunt him for the rest of his days, even though he denies saying it?

Jackson: No question. There will always be someone who brings it up whenever this discussion of athletes and activism takes place. A lot of individuals have shortsighted vision, and that's why I am glad you are including this . . . I've read a lot of good books about this topic; none of them have recognized this point. I'll give you a classic example . . . It's interesting to me how nobody brings up the name of Denzel Washington and how he has subtly, over the course of his career, been the most powerful Black person in Hollywood that we have ever had. If you look at what he's done and how he's done it . . . Everything he has done has been Black. Like Black Black. Real Black. And Denzel isn't out there talking about it, he is moving in silence. Do you know how many Black people have found places and gotten opportunities in Hollywood because he is the one who is in front of these films? . . . He is making things happen for us. And is quiet about it.

Etan: So now you have LeBron, and he has been one of the most high-profile "statement athletes," to use your phrase, who we have had in this generation. He didn't go the apolitical route, and he still leads just about all athletes in endorsements.

Jackson: Yeah, but let's see what happens when the ball stops bouncing. I do believe he comes up in a generation that has a little more freedom to be vocal without feeling the immediate repercussions financially, and I do think that LeBron has put himself in a position where it would be a natural transition for him to remain vocal once he stops playing basketball and he is able to solely concentrate on the economic power and opportunities he can create for Black folks. I love what he is doing on both sides, as the social activist and the economic activist, but I still hold reservations.

Etan: The moves that he's made off the court have kind of forced mainstream America to deal with him on a different level already.

Jackson: I hear exactly what you're saying. But I still say that from a perception standpoint, he's still looked at as a basketball player, and I'm saying once that is removed completely, it's going to be interesting to see . . . When he becomes bigger than just a basketball player and he is still making noise vocally, that's when I think we will be better equipped to answer that question.

Etan: Going back to M.J., right after the Alton Sterling murder and the Philando Castile murder and the policemen in Dallas were murdered, M.J. wrote a letter. Bemoaning both the deaths of the police officers and the injustice felt by Black people at the hands of law enforcement, he called for unity and problem-solving while also offering to donate one million dollars to both the Institute for Community-Police Relations and the NAACP Legal Defense Fund. Some people complained that it felt so carefully worded that they would rather he hadn't said anything at all. I didn't take that stance. I was happy that he even said anything. What was your response?

Jackson: Of course, the one that was given to the *Undefeated,* I know it very well . . . I'm just happy that he wasn't silent again. So I am exactly with you on this: at least he said something. And let me also point out, M.J. deliberately chose the *Undefeated* as the site that he put this letter out on. He didn't go to *ESPN* or *USA Today* or any other white publication that would have gladly put out his statement and even paid to put out his statement . . . but he purposely chose the *Undefeated.* Why? He picked the one who prides itself on being the premiere platform for examining race and sports and culture. He picked the only major news organization that has a Black editor in chief. He didn't have to say that's what he deliberately did, we gotta be able to put two and two together.

Etan: Is it encouraging to you to see the younger athletes beginning to use their voices?

Jackson: We definitely needed something, from a civil basis, from a unity basis, to counter what was going on . . . Seeing young people respond in the way that they have to Eric Garner, to Trayvon Martin, to Donald Trump, created a sense of hope. Especially for an old guy like me . . . And we have seen the impact that sports has had on us as Black people in this country in finding our liberation. Without it, I would question where we would be. People forget that it was Jackie Robinson and Don Newcombe who were the athletes that Dr. King thanked for giving him the strength to do what he did. He used their stances as the platform for him to even get involved. They were his heroes, and they were sports athletes . . . So I'm with you.

When I saw that, I immediately was overcome with a sense of hope, because these young individuals to a certain degree get it, and I am happy they will stand for something and use their sports platform. Let's go to the University of Missouri, with the football players who protested until things were changed, until the president was fired. And all of that happened through sports, and we cannot lose that sense of history, that sense of what sports means and the power that sports has.

Interview with Michael Bennett

I remember it clear as day: We were at AAU nationals and teams from all over the country—New York, Philly, LA, Detroit—were in a big hall receiving an inspirational message. I must have been in eighth grade at the time. I was just learning about Malcolm X and reading about my history and my culture, and I was on fire. I was ready to read everything I got my hands on. So the speaker picked me out of the crowd, looking to use me as an example for his lecture. He asked me for my name, and I told him my first name only. Then he asked me for my last name, and I said that I did not know it, and he walked away, saying he wasn't even going to waste his time on a fool like me. Then he went on to continuously reference me as a person who thought everything was a joke and wouldn't be successful in life.

After he had concluded his talk and he asked if there were any questions, my coach, Reverend Potter, raised his hand. He said that he would like me to explain why I said that I didn't know my last name. So all eyes—the entire auditorium—turned and looked at me. I took a deep breath and responded, "When my people were kidnapped from our native land and brought here in chains by your people, the first thing your ancestors did was take away our history, our heritage, and give us new names, which were many times their own last names. So what I have now is a slave name, and thanks to your people, I don't know my real last name."

At that point, Reverend Potter said to the speaker, "I think it was very presumptuous of you to attempt to embarrass him the way you did without knowing all of the facts." The guy's face turned red like a beet and he started sweating. When he walked off the stage, all of the players in the audience started clapping.

My AAU coach Rev Potter is the perfect example of the power of mentoring through sports. It wasn't all about winning trophies and ribbons—he taught us about life.

The man did find me later and offered his apologies and said that he was not at all prepared for anything that I had said. He told me and Coach Potter that he had been hired to conduct a motivational and educational speech, but he was the one who'd been taught the lesson. I talked to Reverend Potter for two straight hours that night. He said that I better be serious about my education if I was going to keep talking like that. He said that his prayer for me was that I would put myself in a position where nobody could harm me financially for saying the things that I wanted to say. He used Michael Jordan as an example. Jordan has created so much wealth, not just in what he received as paychecks in the NBA, and nobody can tell him nothing. He can say what he wants. Coach Potter told me that is the financial model I needed to pay attention to and follow. He pointed out that even Malcolm X had the Nation of Islam, which attempted to control what he said because they handled all of his financial affairs. The Black church tried to control Dr. Martin Luther King the same way. He stressed to me that it's so much easier to speak your mind when you have financial freedom.

Coach Potter also told me that I better always be serious about my education both in and out of school. He had no worries about me getting good grades but said my real education would take place outside of schoolwork. He gave me a list of about twenty books to read, and I actually got through the entire list. He told me to promise him that I would never fall into the trap of basketball complacency. I really didn't know what he was talking about until I got older, but I made the promise and he said that I had a special kind of fire that he hadn't really seen in a few decades. He said he would always have my back like he did that day, but that I better make sure I continued to go beyond what was taught in school. Some of the best advice I have ever been given.

That's exactly what happened with Seattle Seahawks defensive end Michael Bennett. Once he was educated beyond what he was taught in school, and his eyes were opened to broader realities, he had a whole new understanding of the world that changed the course of his life.

Etan: You have said that you view people like Muhammad Ali, John Carlos, and Angela Davis among your heroes, and that you see yourself as someone trying to build upon their history of both athlete activism and informed resistance.

Michael Bennett: It all started with my mother. She went to a historically Black university and I grew up being educated on my history . . . And as I got older, I wanted to follow in the footsteps of the people I grew up reading about. The system is made to not encourage people or athletes specifically to speak out, in my opinion. You get so much notoriety and fame because of what you can do, but if you speak out and someone disagrees with what you are saying, they come down on you. The criticism starts to pour in from every direction.

Etan: You and your brother have been very supportive of Kaepernick. You spoke out about your encounter with the Las Vegas police when they profiled you and had you on the ground with a gun to your head. You continue to sit during the national anthem and, in general, you and your brother have both really taken some strong stances. What has inspired all of this activity?

Bennett: Like I said, it all came from my mom. She was a teacher, and growing up I got a chance to be taught all of the things that I wasn't being taught in school. The past struggle, the history, what we had to overcome as a people, what so many people fought and died for and sacrificed for me to be in the situation I am in today. So I value the opportunity now to use all of the info my mom taught me, and the classes we did at Grambling University and the NAACP program, so I have the opportunity to be woke. I think a lot of times as athletes . . . we forget that we are still Black men living in this society and the struggle is real.

Etan: Right. You said, "I'll be done playing football someday, but I'll be Black forever."

Bennett: It's the truth. Society wants us not to get involved in these conversations, because at the end of the day, we aren't necessarily granted true equality and acceptance just because of the money or the fame that we receive from playing our particular sports . . . No matter what happens, no matter how much money I make or accolades I receive, or championship rings or whatever, at the end of the day, I am still a Black man.

Etan: You recently announced that you have chosen not to go to an NFL delegation to Israel. And you talked about how you didn't want to go if the Palestinians were going to be rendered invisible. The day before you decided to cancel, our mutual friend Dave Zirin published an open letter to all of the NFL players going on the trip. The letter was signed by the US Campaign for Palestinian Rights, Jewish Voice for Peace, Dr. John Carlos, Danny Glover, and many others, and it urged players cancel their plans, noting that they "now have an opportunity to speak out against the injustices facing Palestinians." How much did being educated on this subject affect your decision not to go to Israel?

Bennett: I wasn't aware before . . . But after being educated on everything and shown what was really going on, my entire perspective changed. I actually spoke to John Carlos and Angela Davis and was really educated even further on exactly what was going on. I was pointed in the right direction so that I can research for myself and make an informed decision. She shared with me her personal experiences of going through Palestine and how they were being treated, and their living conditions, and the history of everything and how their land was taken away from them, and how they are persecuted—so when I started doing my own research, what I found was horrifying. I related and identified and had empathy for how the Palestinians were being mistreated.

There's a lot of things that they don't show us here in America. Even if we watch the news, our news especially on this topic is completely skewed. We're dealing with Black Lives Matter and we're dealing with the police brutality here, and little do you know, around the world, people are dealing with the same issues and worse. So I feel connected to the Palestinians, and for me to go all the way to Israel, and intentionally not be shown their story, that's not something I could accept . . . I wasn't going to allow the NFL to use me in that way.

Etan: I was reading about how you checked out an article in the *Times of Israel* that described the real purpose of the trip as a highly organized government-designed trip that would pretty much isolate you from the Palestinian people. Why do you think they would intentionally *not* expose you to the full story?

Bennett: That's exactly the question I asked and what really baffled me. Why would they intentionally do that? I took a step back and shared with the world exactly what my thoughts were in an open letter, and you can print the letter in your book if you want.

Etan: Okay, we'll do that:

> *Dear World,*
>   *I was scheduled to make a visit to Israel with fellow NFL players. I*

was excited to see this remarkable and historic part of the world with my own eyes. I was not aware, until reading this article about the trip in the Times of Israel, that my itinerary was being constructed by the Israeli government for the purposes of making me, in the words of a government official, an "influencer and opinion-former" who would then be "an ambassador of good will." I will not be used in such a manner. When I do go to Israel—and I do plan to go—it will be to see not only Israel but also the West Bank and Gaza so I can see how the Palestinians, who have called this land home for thousands of years, live their lives.

One of my heroes has always been Muhammad Ali. I know that Ali always stood strongly with the Palestinian people, visiting refugee camps, going to rallies, and always willing to be a "voice for the voiceless." I want to be a "voice for the voiceless," and I cannot do that by going on this kind of trip to Israel.

I know that this will anger some people and inspire others. But please know that I did this not for you, but to be in accord with my own values and my own conscience. Like 1968 Olympian John Carlos always says, "There is no partial commitment to justice. You are either in or you're out." Well, I'm in.

Sincerely,
Michael Bennett

Etan: So, after this statement went viral, a lot of athletes retweeted it. You really started educating others after you received your own education. What was the response that you received from the letter?

Bennett: Of course there were a lot of people who didn't like what I said, but I got a lot of support, especially on social media, and that always is encouraging. I also have been invited to do a lot of speaking engagements now because of that letter. People want to hear more, which is good because I am willing to say more . . . For me, not being deterred by what people think is something that I try to live by.

Etan: And again, that all started with education.

Bennett: Education is everything. The lack of education or awareness can really keep someone completely in the dark and unaware of what is going on. We have to control the type of education we receive, even if we can't change what we are being taught in school. We have to teach our children what they need to know at home, so you get two different types of education.

Etan: Changing gears again, you had a very public debate with your teammate Richard Sherman after his statements during a press conference where he acknowledged police brutality and the impact it has on Black lives, but he also expressed that the more pressing issue was Black-on-Black inner-city gun violence. I actually wrote an open letter to him as well shortly after he made the comments, and both your debate and my open letter seemed to have been received very positively by Sherman. Talk about the importance of being able to educate someone on a respectful level.

Bennett: If you are not in tune to what is going on, and if you do not do your own research and rely solely on what the media presents to you, it is easy to become misguided and develop a not-complete understanding of what the full picture is, as I had with the NFL trip to Israel . . . I wanted him to realize that here is a problem with Black people killing Black people, white people killing white people, Mexican people killing Mexican people, but there is a system that is systematically putting this in place and having laws to create situations that we see in our communities, such as inadequate schools, lack or resources, lack of jobs, police violence, etc.

Black lives matter and *should* matter, just as much as everyone else's lives, and unfortunately, it doesn't look like society agrees with that . . . I feel that it is important for us to stand up and say that no matter how you are treating us, we are not going to accept it as okay . . . While I respect him and his opinion, I felt that I needed to give my perspective and my opinion so that two different sides are presented to the world. He understood where I was coming from and after our discussions he started to open up and see that maybe there is a bigger problem, and he was appreciative of the different perspectives that we both presented to him, and presented to the world, especially all of the young people who are watching. I tell the media all the time that as much as you guys love to glorify what we do on the field, glorify some of the work we are doing *off* the field as well.

Etan: What do you say to young people about the importance of educating themselves?

Bennett: To be honest, young people gotta get off their behinds and realize the power they have. They are the future. If you don't like the type of education you are receiving, it doesn't take much to research something yourself, especially with modern technology—you can look up anything you want . . . Young people gotta have a thirst for knowledge, they gotta want to know and want to be educated, and they can't wait for someone else to educate them, they gotta educate themselves.

Etan: But do you agree that there is a problem with what they are *not* being taught in school? I mean, when I was young, my mother taught me what I needed to know at home, and my grandmother and grandfather taught me about my culture and my heritage. As a community, we need to stop relying solely on the schools to educate our children, don't you think?

Bennett: Oh, 100 percent. Recently I had a problem with my kid's school. I went to them and I said, "Look, I'm paying all this money for my kids' schools, and you mean to tell me that they aren't learning any Black history at all, whatsoever?" So I connected with this historian . . . and we put together a program for Black History Month for the school.

Etan: Wow, that's great. We homeschool our kids so we are able to teach them a lot, but it's really interesting thinking about how when I was younger, I really wasn't taught Black history in school.

Bennett: It's crazy because I'm a grown man and even now I am researching and learning stuff that I didn't know and was never taught in school and should have been taught at some point.

Etan: Talk about the specific athletes you look up to and who have influenced you to be the athlete-activist that you are today.

Bennett: Obviously Muhammad Ali. I mean, he stood up to the American government in the sixties, at a time where we were being lynched and having water hoses turned on us and dogs attacking us, and he said, "I am not going to your war." That was just amazing. And of course John Carlos and Jim Brown, but I really loved reading about Malcolm X and Marcus Garvey as a kid and Charles Hamilton Houston and James Baldwin and Billie Holiday's "Strange Fruit." We have a long way to go, but I really feel that athletes possess the power for change . . . Imagine all the athletes who are sponsored by Nike saying, "We're not going to wear any more of your products unless you put ten million dollars into our inner-city schools that are all dilapidated and have old books and poor conditions." You think they wouldn't give in to that demand? . . . We have so much unrealized power and once we realize what we can really do, the sky's the limit.

Interview with Mahmoud Abdul-Rauf

Once you become educated everything changes, just as it did for Michael Bennett. I remember when my mother first introduced me to the story of John Carlos and Tommie Smith at the 1968 Olympics. I remember when I learned about how the third verse of the national anthem celebrates slavery. I also learned about the 1921 attack on Black residents and businesses in Tulsa known as the "Bombing of Black Wall Street." Needless to say, the more I learned, the more reasons I had to protest. I began doing the Black Power salute during our Pledge of Allegiance in school assemblies. I remember how two teachers in particular grew irate with me. One went off on me in the middle of class, saying that I was anti-American. That I didn't understand how privileged I was to live in the United States, and if I didn't like it so much, I should consider leaving. I remember telling her that my forefathers built this country and if anyone should leave, it certainly isn't their descendants. She looked at me with eyes that could kill.

One day my middle school principal, Ms. Bobbie Johnson, threatened to suspend me if I didn't stop doing the Black Power salute during our school assemblies. We had a big debate that started in the hallway and ended in her office. I remember citing the First Amendment and saying (with all due respect) that we didn't live in a dictatorship, and denying me freedom of speech would be not only a violation of my rights, but unconstitutional. Ms. Johnson couldn't come up with an argument against that one.

I remember watching NBA player Mahmoud Abdul-Rauf take his stance during the national anthem in 1996 when he was playing for the Denver Nuggets. I was amazed at how fearless he was. How strong he stood in the face of such hatred spewed in his direction. I was in high school at the time and I remember watching the backlash he received and how he stood firm in what he believed. Born Chris Jackson, the NBA point guard changed his name in 1993 after converting to Islam, a controversial decision that bothered many Americans.

It was such an honor to be able to sit down with Mahmoud Abdul-Rauf. He was Kaepernick *before* Kaepernick. His career wasn't cut short in 2001 due to injuries or diminishing basketball abilities; it was the result of the controversy he sparked for refusing to stand for the national anthem and calling the flag of the United States a symbol of oppression. The entire NBA, along with the rest of the country, immediately turned on him.

Abdul-Rauf was transformed into the symbol of an ungrateful American who didn't appreciate the riches and fame that the NBA had provided for him. He lost a great deal of money, but he proudly says he has no regrets. When I asked if I could interview him, he replied, "Whatever you want, brother," and said that he respects me for the stances I have taken throughout the years. That was an absolute honor to hear.

Etan: What gave you the strength and the courage to stage your protest in 1996?

Mahmoud Abdul-Rauf: First answer is my faith in God and my relying on Him. Growing up, you see things. And you know that these things are wrong . . . seeing people in my neighborhood have this dismissive, slave-like approach to dealing with issues. And I borrowed some of that, I received some of that. And so as I began to analyze my life. I said, "Man, I don't like the way this feels, this is not natural." I made a decision. I said, "I gotta get out of this. I don't want to live this way. I want to be able to speak regardless of the consequences." And I was introduced to Malcolm by Dale Brown; he gave me the autobiography when I was at LSU. And I'm starting to read about this brother and I'm looking at how courageous he was, and I said,

"This is what I'm aiming for." And it was at that point that I started on a journey . . .

Etan: What were some of the specific challenges you faced while you were in the NBA?

Abdul-Rauf: The name change for some people just disturbed them. When you change your name, for a person that understands it, that's huge because it's just not a name change. It's a change of ideology, it's a change of the way you see the world and the way you're thinking, and it frightens some people because some people want you to stay in that same place that you were before. This whole idea that because I am a Muslim, and Muslims are associated in some way with a negative radicalism and terror. Our life is in need of some radicalism sometimes, of going against the grain. That's what protesting is and we need that. I used to have challenges with the team in terms of praying, fasting, and all of those types of things . . . I was like, "Come on, man, do a little bit of reading, educate yourself a little more." I am big on dialogue. I don't care what your faith is or what your political persuasion is, I think we get a lot done from sitting at the table communicating. We may not agree, but at least we can come away from the discussion fully understanding each other, and that's missing a lot.

Etan: You lost a lot of money but you say that you would do it all again.

Abdul-Rauf: I definitely feel that way. When I make a decision, especially when I have thought it out, I stick to that decision. And anytime I can learn from it, I don't look at it as a moment to have regrets. There is a quote that I have come across: *Straight roads don't make skillful drivers.* In looking back at all of the decisions that I've made and looking back at my life now, I see the growth, I see the development, and I wouldn't trade that for anything.

Etan: Do you think Islamophobia has gotten worse since your time in the NBA?

Abdul-Rauf: No question. It reminds me of when I read about the history of communism. America usually has to identify an enemy to be able to jus-

304 ☆ WE MATTER

tify their exploitation globally. And then it was communism, everything was about communism. And now it's Islamic terrorism . . . Of course it's going to add to the condemnation that comes your way . . . Almost everything you see on television, and it's a huge influence, and mostly everything you read, you're seeing, *Islamic terrorism. Islamic fundamentalism, Islamic radicalism.* There is a tendency for the mind when you constantly hear this. It's like walking the streets and you see a brother with his pants sagging down and a hood over his head, it's like it's ingrained in us . . . to think, *Uh oh, he must be a gangster, he must be a thug.* Words are powerful. Images are powerful. But that brother could be a 4.0 student and got his college paid for. We're quick to judge based on what we hear and see every day.

Etan: When Colin Kaepernick refused to stand for the national anthem, you offered support right away. And we also saw other pioneers like Kareem Abdul-Jabbar and Jim Brown and John Carlos and Tommie Smith and Craig Hodges offer words of encouragement. Why did you feel the need to offer your immediate support?

Abdul-Rauf: I think he understands what's going on and he came to this conclusion on his own, because . . . he wanted to investigate before he made this move, and I thought it was extremely intelligent to do that . . . It's nice to know that there are people out there supporting you . . . that see things in a similar way that I see them. Which is why I wanted to come out and say, "Look, man, I'm for you 1,000 percent." Especially the reasons why he chose not to stand in terms of police brutality and oppression of Black folks, but I think he even extends further beyond that.

Etan: I definitely agree, and as I'm watching everything unfold, I see an interesting parallel between your situation and Kaepernick's. Correct me if I'm wrong, but not many of your teammates really had your back; they remained silent and didn't support your First Amendment rights. Were you at all surprised?

Abdul-Rauf: No, I wasn't surprised. We live in a society where we're taught in a sense to think of ourselves first and sometimes only. I understand it, but I don't agree with it. Because these are things that we talk about all the time

. . . yet when it comes to making a public declaration, we become silent because we are threatened with the loss of what we worked so hard to gain. And we're looking at it as a loss. We're looking at it with limited vision. We're not thinking about the future, how this can impact the future minds and decisions of others . . . When you look at history, if you look at almost all of the individuals who we admire today, who kind of like stood alone, they didn't have an overwhelming amount of support . . . We do what we do because the truth means more to me than the love of these things. I believe God is the best provider. So if it's something that is meant for me, then I'm going to have it . . . I'm on a path and a journey to live with a free conscience and a free soul, whether anybody likes it or not, and whatever the consequences are, at least I can go to sleep knowing I'm free.

Etan: A common criticism lobbed at Kaepernick is, "Who is he to speak about injustices when he has made so much money in the NFL?"

Abdul-Rauf: Who is he *not* to? We're human beings . . . We see the same things you see. We're affected by the same things that you're affected by. We're asked to vote every year, we pay taxes every year. If there's a war and prices go up, we're affected by those prices just like you. So to use money as an argument . . . is ridiculous as far as I'm concerned . . .

They can talk about the problems in America. But why can't *we*? And a lot of it is because we've been conditioned to view athletes and entertainers just as athletes and entertainers. And now when one comes out and speaks, it doesn't look normal. It's like, "Wait a minute, hold on, this is not how we want people to see athletes. We want to see you self-absorbed. We want to see you into your fame and into your materialism." It just bothers me that they bring up this stuff dealing with riches. Sometimes riches can be an instrument to purchase our silence, and when that is done, the fact that you have millions that you are trying to save makes you oppressed.

Kaepernick's ex–college coach had mentioned something about, "Oh, he is selfish if this is true," and I said, "No, I disagree, I think he is self*less* because he has more to lose. He has his career that he's worked most of his life for . . . His finances are going to be threatened. His life possibly. His family's life is threatened. So he has way more to lose." I'm not saying that we shouldn't think about our families or ourselves. That's human nature. Of course we should. But the society is more important than the individual. There is a saying in African philosophy, *I am because we are.* How can one be happy when the rest of us are sad? It takes those persons to come outside of themselves and to view an issue as bigger than themselves . . . And this is what I love about this brother with his stand.

Etan: That's what makes you so special. And that's why young athletes are going to be reading about you and learning from you and being inspired by you for decades to come. Much respect to you.

Abdul-Rauf: And much respect to you too, and all of the athletes who are fighting for change. We have so much power, and it's beautiful to see so many of the younger generation continue to use their voices. We can't afford not to.

Such an honor to shake hands with Mahmoud Abdul-Rauf, an athlete-activist legend. He was Kaepernick before Kaepernick.

Toys R Us Kid
BY MALCOLM THOMAS

I'm a Toys R Us Kid and uhhhhhhh,
I don't wanna grow up
I've seen what it does to folks.

Treat each other the way you want to be treated,
Be nice to others,
Use kind words,
Show respect,
Let us love one another.
We learn these rules in kindergarten
But they all get forgotten in the lives of grown-ups.

And that's why I don't wanna grow up,
See, I'm a Toys R Us Kid,
And I've seen grown-ups filled with hate, greed, dishonesty, racism, and evil, but still
    act like they're the people who kids are supposed to want to grow up to be.
They act like we can't see,
They want us to listen to their words but ignore their actions,
So don't do what we do but do what we teach,
Don't live how we live but follow what we preach,

And that's why I don't wanna grow up,
I'm a Toys R Us Kid,
And I'd rather play
Cops-and-robbers like Ralphie in that movie my daddy likes to watch every single
    Christmas,
Instead of being Tamir Rice shot down because his toy gun looked too realistic.
Black Lives Matter shouldn't have to be shouted at marches and rallies because it's
    something that should already be.
Freedom and equality for all is what y'all teach,
But Trayvon Martin, Mike Brown, Sandra Bland, Freddie Gray, Eric Garner, and way
    too many other names didn't have justice anywhere near their reach.

Don't try to teach me how the system works, I've already learned it.
Guess you gotta be one of Mike Vick's dogs if you wanna get a guilty verdict.

And they say I'll understand much better when I get older
How the hearts of grown-ups can't help but get colder,
But one thing that's easy for me now to understand
Is why Peter Pan wanted to stay in Never Never Land.

And that's why I don't wanna grow up,
I'm a Toys R Us Kid,
And I'd rather watch
Kung Fu Panda
And *Alvin and the Chipmunks,*
Rugrats
And *Avatar: The Last Airbender,*
Instead of bending the truth teaching things that never happened,
Telling made-up stories
Like Christopher Columbus discovering a place that was already here.
But how could that be if there were already ppl living here for many many years?
How can I discover your house
And say it's mine,
Push you out and make up Thanksgiving holidays to celebrate this crime
With turkey and cranberry sauce,
Teaching children that this was actually a happy and loving time?

See, grown-ups love to play happily-ever-after fantasies,

They act like the civil rights days and Dr. Martin Luther King and segregation were
    sooooo long ago,
That all that racism and hate is ancient history,

That the police now would never treat Black ppl like they did back in the sixties,
    but the police at the "Hands up, don't shoot!" protests in Ferguson looked just like
    the police in the Selma movie to me.

I get nervous every time we pass a police car, and no matter how many times my daddy
    tells me that there are good police and bad police, I see him tense up too,

I see him looking at me like he's afraid for me, but I wanna say, *I'm afraid for* you.

But they say I'll understand much better when I get older
How the hearts of grown-ups can't help but get colder,
But one thing that's easy for me now to understand
Is why Peter Pan wanted to stay in Never Never Land.

And that's why I don't wanna grow up,
I'm a Toys R Us Kid,
And I'd rather play Spider-Man,
The Incredible Hulk,
Teenage Mutant Ninja Turtles,
X-Men and Wolverine,

Instead of living in a world where I'm scared to eat the food that's sold to me.

But they act like it's all right.
My mommy taught me about the evil empire called Monsanto who wave their magic
    wands and give everyone poisonous apples like that witch did Snow White.

You can barely even eat fruit no more
Because it's all covered with pesticides,

It's like they're doing it on purpose,
And we wonder why we have so many diseases, right?

Grown-ups are bad
And that's why I don't wanna grow up,
I'm a Toys R Us Kid,
And I'd rather play hopscotch and Skip to My Lou
Instead of skipping from marriage to marriage like the grown-ups do.
I can't stand grown-ups.

The words "I do" become meaningless as people change wives like they change
    their shoes,
But y'all tell us to work out our problems and forgive and forget,
To play nice in the sandbox, not to be selfish, don't hold grudges, say you're sorry,
    and an apology is something you have to accept

But the rules change when you're the ones who feel you've been wronged,
And instead of Barney we get to enjoy singing the children-of-divorced-parents song:

I love you,
You love me,
But we're no longer a family,
And we can't work out our problems maturely.

Y'all tell us that wrong is wrong and right is right but y'all support ppl who do wrong
because they sing or dance or play ball how y'all like.

See, grown-ups change rules that aren't theirs to change and make things okay
because it's the type of Kool-Aid that they like,

But they say if I tell I'll be stepping out of line,
To stay in a child's place and go back to that children-should-be-seen-and-not-heard
time,

But just because it seems
That our eyes are only focused on our video game screens,
Don't think we can't see what's really going on.

Grown-ups,

I've heard my pastor say that we need to make sure we are living *in* the world but not
of it,
And that we need to cover ourselves with the whole armor of God because . . . when
it comes to evil, grown-ups seem to love it.

So even if you think we're too young,
our eyes are open
And we're ready to rise above it.

We don't have to be corrupted,

We have to know who *not* to listen to

And that we don't have to follow in the footsteps of grown-ups.
Peace.

Malcolm wearing his favorite jersey.

You Matter

BY ETAN THOMAS

For cats who weren't born with a form of silverware
But inner-city dental care,
Or dudes who pursue red, white, and blue promises from people who fail the
    acknowledgment that for some, life just ain't no crystal stare,
For constant letdowns from juries who fail to purge, punish, or hold those accountable
    who are sworn to protect and serve,
For those who keep hearing about all of these good cops but always encounter the
    bad,
And cats who are tired of seeing victims on trial for their own murder whenever the
    triggerman has a badge,
Who can't stand seeing these wack jurors come out after the fact with how they be-
    lieved the cop was guilty but for some reason couldn't convict them,
All I wanna do is take the chains off,
Tired of seeing killers suddenly become victims.

For every Emerald Snipes and Jahvaris Fulton, every Tiffany Crutcher and Allysza
    Castile, every Cameron Sterling and Erica Garner, and every other child who has
    lost their loved ones to trigger-happy cops who get paid leave and GoFundMes,
Don't you believe for a minute that your life doesn't matter.
No matter the chatter across non-indictments and not-guilty verdicts,
Don't ever let them insert inferiority no matter how much their injustice burns.
I know you're perplexed by the earth because it seems to get worse when it turns
And we're still yearning for respect
In a system that was built for us to fail,
Telling us tales of freedom and justice for all,
Gaming us like an arcade, spending our little quarters straight playing ourselves
Until our lives are over.
Trying to have us swinging and kicking in the air without the Wii controller,
Straight wasting our energy.
But this ain't no game,
They're letting monsters free,
Like Darren Wilson and Betty Shelby,

Daniel Pantaleo, George Zimmerman, Howie Lake II, and Blane Salamoni,
Cowards hiding behind badges
Like Rudolph Giuliani,
Stopping-and-frisking our reality,
Trying to destroy our souls, diminish our spirits, and subjugate our mentalities.

But they want to say it's about the flag,
Knowing we had a list of Kaepernick's grievances from the genesis of his taking his stance.

That's why they're taking a knee:
To protest political corruption, systematic racism, and police brutality.
They straight hijacked the message into disrespecting the country and the military.
It's like they gentrified the entire protest,
Put up a Starbucks, a dog park, and a tanning salon turning our statement into a
    watered-down All Lives Matter mess.
This is bigger than Donald Trump and his foolishness,
This is about justice.

They wanna see us
Fall like it's autumn,
Snakes in our garden, but with a scope we spotted them.

We remain targets that enter your optics,
Our objects appear bigger in your mirror but it's clearer to see
The fear in your eyes when you see
Us in your view.
Shoot first, ask questions last.
That's how too many of these so-called policemen act.

But we see you
Straight denying the truth,
Putting on a facade of protect-and-serve and a false equivalency to your red, white,
    and blue.

But the darkness will come to light
And our strength will surprise you
When your walls come tumbling down just like Confederate statues.

And no matter how many of our heroes you get to follow your nose like Toucan Sam,
Putting a camera in their face for them to condemn a people you can't stand,

Just to get pats on the top of their heads by pale hands,
You're not keeping us in your frying pan,
Purposely burning our idols,
Straight fricasseeing their minds,
While they're holding the mic,
So they can no longer see the difference between what's wrong and what's right.
Got them saying things potent as a lightning bolt when it strikes.
It's a pity,
Seeing them make statements that drown our energy.
How many millions
Did it take for them to break icons and get them to spit what they ain't feeling,
Embracing Satan while they're slithering with pythons?
But we won't let their steppin-and-fetchin create dissension within our midst,
We know Black Face ain't ever cease to exist,
Your created illusions ain't nothing but failed magic tricks.
Forget happiness,
Our pursuit is of justice, and we refuse to let go of the clutch
Until we force you to switch up your style like girls in double dutch.
We're weathering your storm
With the strength of our ancestors.

Before our courage is born,
The weight of your hate gives us contractions and births determination into
    existence.
You can't see these.
You see the fire we spit when we unleash the dragon, call us Khaleesi.

See, pressure can either bust pipes or produce diamonds,
And no matter how high the mountain, we keep climbing.

So that's why we stay blasting off like rockets,
And why no matter what you do your arms are STILL too short to box with . . .
We've got God rolled up in our pockets,
You can't stop us.
No matter how much your privatized prisons and mandatory sentencing you use to
    try to lock us,
We're taking your evil and teaching our youth
That y'all don't teach them in school cuz y'all don't want them to know the truth,
Like how society's out to get them,
How they flood the airwaves with music that will land them in the prison system,

About the school-to-prison pipeline and your plan to get them in them,
But how they're purposely not taught and it's not put in their curriculum.
See, we're assisting cats like Westbrook,
Setting them up for greatness,
We're telling them that ain't no such thing as halfway crooks
And y'all will go all out with how much y'all hate us.

You can't take our heart no matter how much you try to break us down.
That goes for every person, place, or thing that describes a noun.

Everyone in Gotham City wants to throw rocks at our dome,
We're like Bruce Wayne out the bat cave in his home,
King of the jungle, we're a bunch of Mufasas on the throne.

Can't none of y'all defeat us,
Like Muhammad Ali looking at the draft board sayin, *Even if you try to punish me,*
*   you still can't beat us,*

We come from brass feet and hair of lamb's wool,
The only thing that can bring us down is gravitational pull,
So keep lying to yourself thinking we'll ever give up on us.
We're still screaming, *Black Lives Matter,*
And we're going to keep pursuing justice.

Afterword
by Dave Zirin

We Matter **was conceived and executed by Etan Thomas** as this new athletic revolt was just finding its feet. The resistance started truly in 2012, as Etan writes, when the Miami Heat appeared in their hoodies calling for justice for Trayvon Martin. What makes this book dynamically important is that it lays out a road map for how we got to where we are today: a polarized and politicized sports world, with young athletes answering a generational call to resist police brutality and systemic racism. It also explains why President Trump's decision to demonize Black athletic protesters has had such explosive results. So far the Trump years have been defined by his desire to distract, deflect, and divide by targeting. Yet he has dramatically underestimated the athletes he targets, and even those he hasn't targeted.

The central politics of the new resistance were laid out with utter clarity by Colin Kaepernick when he said, "I am not going to stand up to show pride in a flag for a country that oppresses Black people and people of color. To me, this is bigger than football and it would be selfish on my part to look the other way. There are bodies in the street and people getting paid leave and getting away with murder."

As Etan has detailed in this book, several dozen NFL players subsequently took a knee or raised a fist in the wake of the "kneel heard 'round the world." Throughout the league, a remarkably invigorating and inspiring energy could be found, causing the locus of NFL power to shudder. This newfound activism also reached spheres of influence within other sports leagues, including NBA circles, where the best basketball player on the planet, LeBron James, as well as stars like Steph Curry, John Wall, and Draymond Green, and coaches like Steve Kerr and Gregg Popovich, pledged solidarity with Kaepernick.

Demolishing competition for the most "woke" league right now has to be the WNBA, led by former star Swin Cash and the New York Liberty, with their orchestrated media blackout in which they discussed only Black Lives Matter and police killings in postgame interviews. In September 2016, in her final game as a pro, Tamika Catchings and the entire Indiana Fever team took a knee during the national anthem before a playoff game. Black women have historically been a lynchpin of social movements, so it's no surprise that the WNBA, with its 69 percent Black majority, would lead the way on these critical issues. Etan's interview with Allysza Castile, the sister of Philando Castile (who was killed by police in July 2016), captures just how deep the real-life impact has been from the activism of the courageous women of the WNBA.

It's important to remember that so much of the athlete activism that Etan explores started as a response to police killings. Patrick Harmon, Philando Castile, Alton Sterling, Sandra Bland, Samuel DuBose, Brendon Glenn, Freddie Gray, Natasha McKenna, Terence Crutcher, Walter Scott, Christian Taylor, Michael Brown, Eric Garner, Akai Gurley, Laquan McDonald, Tamir Rice, Yvette Smith, seven-year-old Aiyana Mo'Nay Stanley-Jones, Rekia Boyd, Shereese Francis, Sean Bell, Amadou Diallo, Trayvon Martin . . . the list doesn't start or end here; these are just some of the victims who Black athletes have been mourning, remembering, honoring.

What Etan does so effectively is to reveal how police brutality invades the lives of not just poor Black people, but *all* Black people, including world-famous athletes and celebrities. And it is not simply Etan's love for his kids that has them playing a prominent role in this volume; concern for the safety of children undergirds the Black Lives Matter movement, despite all the obfuscation surrounding it.

One of the first battles waged by Trump upon assuming the presidency involved the now-infamous travel ban—a round of restrictions on admission into the United States from seven countries, all of which are predominantly Muslim, along with various limits on refugee travel—mere days after his inauguration. The policy was hardly surprising given Trump's blatant appeals to Islamophobia during the 2016 campaign, but what came next would almost certainly count as unforeseen. Thousands of people all over the country packed terminals and airport lobbies in cities like New York, Atlanta, and San Francisco to resist a president bent on demonizing Muslims. As airports became spaces of resistance in the wake of the travel ban, one of the most visible athletes at this new ground zero of protest was Seattle Storm star Breanna Stewart. Stewart, who had never been to a protest in her life at that point, did not think twice about heading to nearby Los Angeles International Airport, joining hundreds demonstrating against the new administration's vindictive policies. Talking to reporters about her decision to stand in solidarity with refugees and folks affected by the ban, Stewart said: "I play for Team USA. My dad wears an American flag tank top. I feel deeply patriotic, but I also recognize how privileged I have been, and this ban just goes against everything that makes me proud to be an American." At the same time, we must remember that Islamophobia is not a new phenomenon, as Mahmoud Abdul-Rauf reminds us in Etan's interview with him.

When World Cup soccer champion Megan Rapinoe followed Colin Kaepernick's lead and took a knee in a National Women's Soccer League (NWSL) game in September 2016, to say that her action was poorly received by the powers-that-be would be quite an understatement. In fact, days after Rapinoe courageously kneeled, NWSL opponent Washington Spirit decided to play the national anthem *before* the players took the field, denying Rapinoe and others the opportunity to make a political statement. "We decided to play the anthem in our stadium ahead of schedule rather than subject our fans and friends to the disrespect we feel such an act would represent," the Washington Spirit said in a statement. Months later, the US Soccer Federation would pass Policy 604-1, mandating that all players and staff stand for the anthem. Undeterred, Rapinoe has continued to speak out against inequality and oppression, calling the Fédération Internationale de Football Association (FIFA) "old, male, and stale"; she has also advocated on behalf of gay women of color, and she defied 604-1 when she joined teammates in staying in the locker room as the anthem was being played before a game in September 2017. And who can forget the across-the-pond solidarity from members of the Hertha Berlin men's soccer squad, who the following month all took a knee in solidarity with the NFL protests?

The search for white *male* symbols of solidarity can at times feel like seeking out Sasquatch, and yet there is a tradition of white men in the world of sports standing with their marginalized brothers away from the playing arena. Perhaps the best example of this in our current political moment is Philadelphia Eagles defensive end Chris Long. Long has been outspoken in his support of Colin Kaepernick, was a leading figure in standing against white supremacists in his native Charlottesville, Virginia, and refused to go to the Trump White House after the New England Patriots (his team at that time) won the Super Bowl.

Long's willingness to speak out on these issues echoes fellow white sports figures like Australian track star Peter Norman, who stood in solidarity with the famous 1968 Olympic podium protests led by John Carlos and Tommie Smith; 1960s NFLer Dave Meggyesy, a civil rights and antiwar activist; and football Hall of Famer Ron Mix, who chose to support a boycott of the 1965 AFL All-Star Game because of racism experienced by Black players in the host city of New Orleans. These were all white men who made the decision to sidestep their privilege in an effort to speak up for their brothers on the field. However, there is still plenty of work to be done here, as Long pointed out in August 2017: "I think it's a good time for people that look like me to be here for people that are fighting for equality."

If you want to see struggles for justice influenced by Kaepernick outside the pros, the high school and college ranks have provided a trove of resistance. There's Southern Methodist University's marching band in lockstep with students at the school, kneeling before their game against Texas Christian in September 2016. There were football players at the University of Michigan and Michigan State raising their fists in the air as the anthem played. There was the entire Evanston Township High School girls varsity and junior varsity volleyball teams that kneeled during the anthem before their game in September 2017. There's also the members of the Bethesda Academy School soccer team becoming activated and protesting outside the Department of Homeland Security headquarters in Washington, DC, when their fellow teammate was detained by Immigrations and Customs Enforcement, which has been given carte blanche to do whatever the hell it wants under our current president. Not to mention the cheerleaders at Howard University also taking a knee before a football game in October 2017.

And who can forget the Beaumont Bulls, a football team comprising eleven- and twelve-year-olds down in Texas that saw fourteen of its twenty-two members take a knee à la Kaepernick in the fall of 2016. After all this, Coach Rah-Rah Barber, who supported the protest, was fired for creating a "hostile mood" at a team meeting, and a supportive parent was banned from practices and games. The Bulls would go on to have their season *canceled* for their act of resistance, but NFL players Anquan Boldin, Malcolm Jenkins, Torrey Smith, and Devin McCourty then stepped up and donated twenty thousand dollars to a spin-off team, the Southeast Texas Oilers, and Rah-Rah Barber was named coach. The new team made the bold decision to not play "The Star-Spangled Banner" before home games. According to Coach Barber: "It's not a song that we will be playing . . . We might play 'God Bless America' [or] 'America the Beautiful.' As an organization, as a board, we all agreed it's not an appropriate song. It's a degrading song."

This is new territory: professional sports is now officially a contested space, a site of resistance. Where this goes from here is a great unknown, but the distance it has traveled during these dark days is more than inspiring—it's revolutionary. And who better to shine a light on this phenomenon than Etan Thomas, himself a revolutionary NBA star who was in fact the first American professional athlete to publicly oppose George W. Bush's 2003 invasion of Iraq? While Etan humbly highlights the voices and great work of these other role models included in this volume, he himself has often been leading the charge, risking his career and his reputation, for a very long time.

Dave Zirin is the sports editor for the Nation *magazine, host of SiriusXM Radio's popular weekly show* Edge of Sports Radio, *and curator of the Edge of Sports imprint of Akashic Books. He also cohosts the radio program* The Collision: Where Sports and Politics Collide, *alongside Etan Thomas. Zirin is the author of eight books on the politics of sports and is the recipient of a 2015 New York Press Club Award for Journalism in sportswriting.*